"At last! A book for and about adults with attention deficit disorders that neither panders to nor patronizes its readers. . . . A must-read for both clinicians and the newly diagnosed adult with ADD!"

> —WADE F. HORN, PH.D.,
> Director, The National Fatherhood Initiative

"A great addition to the growing collection of books on adult ADD . . . Kevin Murphy brings his warmth, his clinical experience, and his pragmatism together in this very helpful book for adults with ADD."

> —KATHLEEN G. NADEAU, PH.D.,
> Editor, A *Comprehensive Guide to Attention Deficit Disorder in Adults*

"A readable, real-world discussion of ADD in its various guises. It provides a wealth of suggestions as to how those who have ADD can teach themselves to cope."

> —PAUL JAFFE,
> Editor, *ADDendum* newsletter

"A wonderful guide for living well with ADD, offering a vast array of understandable, practical and constructive approaches to the many problems that challenge adults who have ADD."

> —PATRICIA HORAN LATHAM,
> coauthor of *Succeeding in the Workplace*, and Director, National Center for Law and Learning Disabilities

"Murphy and LeVert have written a book that readers with ADD will want to finish, from cover to cover, without getting distracted."

> —HARVEY C. PARKER, PH.D.,
> Director, Counseling Care Center

"There is much to recommend. This book presents a wealth

of scientifically sound and practical advice on this commonly misunderstood disorder."
> —MARK A. STEIN, PH.D., Director, Hyperactivity, Attention, and Learning Problems Clinic, The University of Chicago

"An ideal book for both adults who feel they may have the disorder and who are looking for help, as well as professionals, such as family physicians, who want to learn how to diagnose and treat ADD."
> —GABRIELLE WEISS, M.D., F.R.C.P.(C), Clinical Professor of Psychiatry, The University of British Columbia

"A valuable addition to the literature on adult ADD. It is concise and easy to read but manages to cover all of the major areas that one needs to truly understand adults with ADD. . . . An extremely useful guide to coping with the symptoms of this disorder."
> —HOWARD SCHUBINER, M.D., Director, Wayne State University Adult ADD Center

"Although written for the individual with ADD, this book is a valuable resource for parents, professionals, siblings, and employers. Any person affected by individuals with ADD should read this book."
> —C. WILSON ANDERSON, JR., MAT, education consultant, and technical support person for the Kansas ADD Training Grant

"A superb book which really sets the standard for all other books on adult ADD."
> —STAN MOULD, Chairman, L.A.D.D.ER UK

OUT
OF THE
FOG

OUT OF THE FOG

OF THE

TREATMENT OPTIONS AND
COPING STRATEGIES FOR
**ADULT ATTENTION
DEFICIT DISORDER**

Kevin Murphy, Ph.D.
and Suzanne LeVert

HYPERION

A Skylight Press Book • New York

Library of Congress Cataloging-in-Publication Data

Murphy, Kevin R., 1957–
    Out of the fog : treatment options and coping strategies for adult attention deficit disorder / Kevin Murphy and Suzanne LeVert.—1st ed.
      p. cm.
    "A Skylight Press book."
    Includes bibliographical references and index.
    ISBN 0-7868-8087-2
    1. Attention-deficit disorder in adults—Popular works.
I. LeVert, Suzanne. II. Title.
RC394.A85M87 1995
616.85'89—dc20   94–46261
                                             CIP

Design: Carla Weise/Levavi & Levavi

FIRST EDITION

10 9 8 7 6 5 4 3 2

Research about Attention Deficit Disorder is ongoing and subject to interpretation. Although every effort has been made to include the most up-to-date and accurate information, there can be no guarantee that medical opinions expressed in this book will not change over time. The reader should bear in mind that this book should not be used for self-diagnosis or self treatment. The reader is encouraged to consult with appropriate medical professionals regarding Attention Deficit Disorder and all health issues.

In order to protect the privacy rights of persons interviewed in connection with this book, all names have been changed.

ACKNOWLEDGMENTS

Many were supportive and helpful in the creation of this book and deserve my thanks. First, I must thank the patients who gave so much of themselves in an effort to help others. Their willingness and desire to get their hopeful message out was the driving force behind this book. I will always be grateful for how much I have learned and continue to learn from them. My sincere thanks is extended to my good friend and colleague Mary Richard for her especially valuable contributions: her poignant and personal Introduction, and her intense dedication to making a difference in the lives of those who struggle with ADHD. My special thanks is extended to Suzanne LeVert for her extraordinary effort and skill at communicating the message of this book; to Russell Barkley, Paul Barreira, and Arthur Anastopoulos for their helpful comments; and especially to my wife, Bonnie, for her constant support and love.

KEVIN R. MURPHY, PH.D.

I would like to thank my editor, Laurie Abkemeier, for her unflagging good humor and professional guidance; Kevin Murphy, for his wisdom, patience, and generous spirit; and the men and women with ADD who so openly shared their stories with me. Most of all, I am indebted to my parents, Bill and Rita LeVert, who have supported me in every way throughout my career and, in particular, during the writing of this book. I couldn't have done it without them.

SUZANNE LEVERT

CONTENTS

INTRODUCTION

What have you heard or read about ADD lately? As this book is being written, the disability called Attention Deficit Disorder has been receiving a great deal of notice in the print and broadcast media. Recently, the focus of this coverage has expanded from its original emphasis on children and adolescents to include features about adults. Although the diagnosis of ADD can help adults understand their related difficulties and lead more satisfying and productive lives, a few magazines, newspapers, and network news programs sidestep these facts in favor of more sensational reporting. As a hidden disability, ADD is vulnerable to this kind of distortion and serves as a perfect target for criticism from those who do not accept the existence of conditions they cannot readily observe. Others characterize ADD as a "trendy affliction" or offer invalid stereotypical descriptions of the "ADD personality." Finally, some view ADD not as the result of a neurobiological disorder, but rather as stemming from cultural dysfunction and the decline of American character. What is a reader to think?

Out of this fog of misinformation Dr. Kevin Murphy and Suzanne LeVert have written a book based on sound information that reflects years of research and practice. In these pages, the authors share their keen expertise related to ADD and their genuine compassion and positive regard for adults experiencing this disability. You will hear the voices of adults who share their personal experiences with the disorder. You will find a powerful correspondence between Dr. Murphy's clinical understanding of ADD and adults' ways of knowing about it from their life experiences. I believe this book will ring true for anyone who has been or knows someone who has been diagnosed with this disability.

Reading through the text took me back a number of years ago to the time when my young sons were diagnosed with ADD by their pediatrician and a child psychologist. As I learned more about the disability, I had an "Aha!" experience. A light came on in my head and within a few months, I was also diagnosed with ADD and started multimodal treatment along with my sons. By multimodal I am speaking of a treatment approach that utilizes the resources of counseling, education, and medicine to address the patient's needs. For our family, this was the first step toward more satisfying and productive lives.

Those who have doubts about the existence of hidden disabilities should know more about what it is like to grow up with undiagnosed, untreated ADD. Until now, I have shared my story with very few people. However, I feel so strongly about the value and honesty of Dr. Murphy's book that it seems appropriate to do so here. I do so for two reasons: First, children with this disability are seldom able to articulate this experience, and thus it seems incumbent on adults like me who have found their voices to speak up; second, I believe it is important to reach out to the large population of adults who have undiagnosed ADD. Not only does this disability have the potential to hinder the ability of adults to live as successfully as they might otherwise, but some have fallen into serious trouble and most are experiencing pain. I consider myself to be among the fortunate few who have been buffered against substantial injury, and, out of gratitude for those who have assisted and believed in me, I hope to extend encouragement to others.

I started to sense that I was "different" in elementary school. In spite of what I believe were my best efforts (and those of my parents), as a young child I either daydreamed or talked too much in class—and felt unhappy most of the time. Comments about me included: *"Overtalkative, can't keep her hands and feet still, absent-minded professor, interrupts others, clumsy— can't jump rope, can't remember math facts, could do more if she would apply herself, very disorganized, forgetful with band instrument, messy handwriting, chews her nails, desk is still messy after she cleans it out, inconsistent performance, doesn't finish her work."* No one knew what was underlying these behaviors or what to do about them. However, my love of books and the guidance and encouragement of my parents nurtured my interest in learning and life, shielding me from an overfocus on my "performance deficits." I also received great support from my other family members, music and church school teachers, and several of my parents' friends who displayed their value and unconditional friendship for me.

I eventually became less restless and more successful in school. In spite of this and my comfortable home and high cognitive ability, I was so exhausted from the struggle to pass for normal, that I became depressed. I believe I became an overachiever in an attempt to outrun the constant fog and confusion in my life. Nothing was available at that time to help me understand or manage the unknown neurobiological source of my symptoms that included difficulty maintaining concentration, restlessness, and disorganization. On many occasions I shared my frustrations with my friend, Abby, who assured me that I did not have to be perfect in order for us to be "best buddies." Her friendship taught me the importance of genuineness and loyalty in relationships, and gave me confidence that friendship can surpass the boundaries of differences. I have carried this lesson into teaching and counseling as well as into the many friendships I have developed over the years.

While I was successful in college, able to function as an

adult, and loved teaching regular and special education students at the elementary and secondary levels in the Iowa City Community Schools, these symptoms continued. I had difficulty with managing both my time and my checkbook and felt constantly overwhelmed. Very few people could have been aware of my difficulty, for I had become a very good actress, concealing my problems from almost everyone but myself. My husband's love and my deep interest in my students gave me a sense of anchoring. Time after time I have appreciated my great fortune in having these wonderful people in my life. I want to emphasize the difference their unconditional love has made. It is very striking to me that even without understanding what "made me tick," my husband and family have always been loyal and encouraging. They have consistently supported my strong areas without dwelling on the weaker ones.

Unlike the relatively predictable babies our friends had produced, when our children were born it appeared that I had given birth to the creatures in Dr. Seuss's story, *The Cat in the Hat*—Thing One and Thing Two! They were beautiful, wakeful, howling, climbing, hyperactive children. They were the bane of the church nursery and two preschools. We loved them anyway, but began to realize that the persistence and intensity of their behaviors far exceeded normal. At the ages when diagnosis could be established, our pediatrician initiated discussions with us about multimodal treatment for the boys.

While discussing ADD with a family might have been a routine event for our doctor, it was a life-changing event for our family. After my children and I started multimodal treatment, our family began to thrive like never before. Since ADD cannot be cured, life is a perpetual challenge. But I cannot say enough about the improvements that treatment has brought to our lives. We have all benefited enormously from Ritalin and have not found our spontaneity and individuality to be diminished in the least. The diagnosis and treatment of this hidden disability has empowered each of us to get a hold on our lives, exercise responsibility, learn, and achieve. I am certain that the level of personal and professional success I have attained can be partly attributed to these interventions that began years ago. Life is good!

For the last five years, I have provided education and services to students who have learning and attentional disorders through the office of Student Disability Services. I believe the high rates of retention and graduation of these students attest to the effectiveness of the role our office plays in multimodal treatment. Related to this, here is a recent incident involving one of my students who was diagnosed with ADD during her sophomore year of college.

Nichole had referred herself because she was having great difficulties in a required foreign language class. During our first interview, she described herself as having been "the most hyperactive girl in her elementary and secondary schools." Her other grades were quite good (especially for a person who couldn't sit for long), she had fine personal character, was warm and outgoing, and could hold forth on at least ten subjects in twenty minutes. It was not a difficult decision for me as her student disability services counselor to refer her to a local clinical psychologist for assessment for ADD, which he diagnosed in short order. Today, Nichole is an honors student in psychology and has completed her foreign language requirements by taking foreign civilization and culture classes. She has gained a new control over her life through multimodal treatment including counseling, medication, and educational adjustments. She is not only working up to her academic potential, but has become a fine advocate for students with disabilities. She is preparing to start graduate school to train for work and research with students who have ADD.

But that's not all. Recently, while waiting to pick up a friend at the airport, Nichole crossed paths with Senator Tom Harkin who was flying to the University of Iowa to address the first state conference in the nation on the Proactive Implementation of the Americans with Disabilities Act in Higher Education. Knowing of his interest in people with disabilities, Nichole told him her story. Clearly he was moved, for the next day he related his visit with her to the conference attendees and praised her success from the podium. Hearing Nichole recognized in this manner was an unforgettable experience for me.

Out of my concern for children with ADD, a number of years ago I founded a support group for their parents which later affiliated with CH.A.D.D. (Children and Adults with Attention Deficit Disorders). CH.A.D.D. is a national organization that has grown, in seven short years, to over six hundred local chapters across the United States. It was through CH.A.D.D. that I met Dr. Murphy. As a member of CH.A.D.D.'s national board of directors, I was asked to introduce his colleague, Dr. Russell Barkley, with whom he was copresenting a preconference institute for professionals on the topic of assessing and treating adults with ADD. Dr. Barkley was well known to me both as an eminent researcher and clinician in the field, and as a strong supporter of CH.A.D.D. through his activities as a member of its national professional advisory board. Dr. Barkley introduced Dr. Murphy, who proceeded to engage the room in as fine a professional development session about ADD in adults as I will ever hear. I had another "Aha!" experience: this expert and thoughtful psychologist would be able to provide the insight and guidance that was needed by CH.A.D.D.'s newly established standing committee on adult issues, which I chaired. Dr. Murphy has never let me or CH.A.D.D. down. He has been extremely supportive, hardworking, and faithful to our work to improve the lives of people with ADD.

Out of the Fog is written by and for people I care about. It is an honest book that does not mislead the reader regarding matters of research, science, or practice. It contains realistic advice and suggestions that respond to a clear need. Most adults grew up at a time when very little was known about ADD, and even less about its diagnosis or treatment. As a result, those who are living with the condition, especially those who are undiagnosed and untreated, may be experiencing a number of problems, some of which stem directly from the disorder and others that are the result of associated adjustment patterns. However, these adults are not necessarily easily identified. Contrary to some of the misinformation, no two people with ADD are alike and there is no one ADD personality profile. Some adults with ADD are outgoing; others are withdrawn. Some can concentrate if they are interested or excited, while others have difficulty concentrating under any circumstances. Some enjoy risky pursuits and high levels of stimulation, while others crave solitude and quiet. Some have poor social skills; others are ardent people-pleasers. They may have ADD alone, or in combination with other psychological conditions that often coexist with ADD.

Dr. Murphy and Ms. LeVert's good news is that in spite of these individual variations, scientists and mental health professionals are coming closer every day to developing standards by which adults can be accurately diagnosed. What's more, appropriate management of your educational, personal, and social development can improve your chances for leading a more satisfying life.

For those like Nichole and me, who were identified as late as adulthood, this book is a guide through the diagnostic and treatment process. Part I: Demystifying Adult ADD is designed to help sort through your personal history and current symptoms to evaluate how ADD might be affecting your daily living. You'll learn about the symptoms of ADD and their emotional side-effects, as well as current diagnostic procedures. Part II: Treatment and Strategies That Work will guide you through the medical treatments, psychological counseling, and lifestyle changes that might be helpful in treating the symptoms of ADD. This section outlines drug therapy available to treat the disorder and explores the need many adults with ADD have for psychological counseling in order to work through feelings of low self-esteem, anger, and frustration that have developed over the years. Finally, this section explains how making simple changes in your daily routine—such as improving eating and exercising habits and learning to relax—might help alleviate your ADD symptoms. Part III: Outmaneuvering ADD is really the heart of this book. It contains my favorite piece of advice for the college students with whom I work: "Procrastinate wisely by planning ahead." Many other suggestions in these four chapters are dedicated to helping you live and thrive with the disorder. Adults with ADD discuss how they've learned to cope with their disability and share hundreds of strategies for better managing daily living, working, and personal relationships.

The future for adults with ADD looks brighter today than ever before. Adults who are correctly diagnosed with the disorder can benefit by working with trained therapists and following the strategies in this book. The authors offer nothing less than a realistic message of hope: with treatment, adults with ADD will be able to gain a new sense of control over their lives and a positive sense of their prospects for a better future.

—MARY MCDONALD RICHARD
DECEMBER 19, 1994

Richard is a counselor at Student Disability Services at The University of Iowa, where she assists students who have attention, learning, and psychological disorders. She has served the CH.A.D.D. National Board of Directors as the executive editor of the CH.A.D.D.ER Box; National Secretary, Chair of the Adult Issues Committee; and member of the Professional Education Committee. She will serve as national president of CH.A.D.D. for one year, beginning in September 1995.

DEMYSTIFYING ADULT ADD

Chapter One

ADD: IT'S NOT JUST FOR KIDS ANYMORE

- Marion is an advertising executive who thrives on courting prominent clients, brainstorming with her creative team, and flying in the face of impossible deadlines. Her colleagues consider her messy desk and tendency to forget important meetings as evidence of the creative mind at work.
- Photographer Sam covers sporting events around the world for major national magazines. His steady customers now know enough to make scheduling arrangements and follow up on all assignments with his assistant, Simon. Sam's wife handles the family finances.
- Bonnie, an engineer, knows dozens of people and is invited to many social events. Her acquaintances believe she turns down their invitations or misses dinner parties because she has made other plans; they assume that she does not have a steady man in her life because she's "too picky."

By all appearances, Marion, Sam, and Bonnie are successful, motivated people with everything going for them. Beneath the surface, however, they all are suffering terribly from something they cannot define and which has been a part of their lives for as long as they can remember. "All my life," Marion admits, "I've felt like a cat chasing its tail." She knows that her inability to maintain a schedule, follow up on important tasks, and establish priorities has held her back from what she considers true success. And she feels a cringing sense of shame when she thinks of the opportunities for advancement she may have blown.

Sam shares the same sense of frustration. "During any thought process, there is what I can only call a 'mental storm in my head,' like fireworks," explains Sam. "Whatever I'm attempting to do is competing for attention with as many as ten other subjects, ideas, and thoughts. It makes long-range planning impossible." To compensate, he hired an assistant who runs virtually every aspect of the business except the actual snapping of the pictures. Because he needs so much help to do his job, Sam feels in his heart of hearts that he is unworthy of his accomplishments.

As for Bonnie, it is true that her social calendar (if she kept one) could have many entries. Her quick wit and vivacious personality make her attractive to a wide range of people. But her close friends are few, she often misses important events, and she hasn't had a steady boyfriend in years. "I've always felt different and out of place. It's never been easy for me to make friends. Or, rather, to *keep* friends. I've always been a little hyper, and a little rude, I guess, blurting things out without thinking about what I'm saying," she recounts with a sigh. "And worst of all, I seem to have a pretty short attention span when it comes to men, and the instant I find a reason not to be in a relationship, I chop it right off. Despite the fact that I seem like such a busy person, I'm pretty lonely most of the time."

Marion, Sam, and Bonnie are not alone in their sense of personal failure and frustration. Their difficulties are shared by an estimated four to ten million other American adults who live with Attention Deficit Disorder (ADD). A neurobiological condition that primarily affects an individual's ability to concentrate and to control or regulate motor and speech impulses,

ADD can place an enormous burden on those who suffer with it, a burden that may have an impact on every aspect of life.

If you're reading this book, chances are that you believe that you or someone you love may have ADD. Perhaps you recognize in yourself Marion's inability to organize her work life, Sam's difficulties with planning ahead, and/or Bonnie's problems with sustaining relationships. If you can trace these feelings and behaviors back through the years of your life, back into your childhood and adolescence, you may be one of the millions of adults with this serious, disruptive disorder.

Indeed, ADD does not develop overnight. By definition adults with the disorder have been suffering from its symptoms since early childhood. Some were diagnosed and treated for the condition then known simply as "hyperactivity" until they reached adolescence, at which time professionals believed the disorder resolved itself. Many others had symptoms that went undetected altogether, and were able to compensate for the effects of its symptoms until the pressures of adult responsibilities or goals intruded. Among both groups, an estimated 50 to 70 percent—from four to ten million men and women—now experience symptoms that significantly impair their ability to live full and satisfying lives.

Many adults with ADD, like the three people described above, function quite well and even thrive in a variety of careers, lifestyles, and relationships, largely because they have learned over the years how to manage their lives fairly well, despite still suffering with the effects of the disorder. Others, however, do not fare as well. For a variety of reasons, their attempts at coping have failed and the disorder has interfered with their careers, personal relationships, and goals for the future:

• Ben, a thirty-four-year-old man with above-average intelligence and exceptional ambition, now works two jobs: selling tickets at a bus station at night and delivering newspapers in the morning. When asked to recount how many jobs he has had since leaving college, he wrote, "Couldn't even begin to count." He explains his difficulties at work by saying, "Can't settle on one task for too long; boredom sets in, and I have to be *constantly challenged*. I was accused of trying to do too many things, and as a result, really didn't have the time to achieve any *one* of them to full capacity." In response to another question, this one about his social life, he honestly admits to avoiding romantic relationships altogether. "It's hard for me (sometimes) to feel 'liked' by someone else." At thirty-four years of age, he still lives with his parents.

• Mark has had more jobs than he can count in the years since he graduated from high school. The main reason for his remarkable employment record? His inability to follow rules or control his temper. "I can't tell you how many bosses I've told off just because they ordered me to do my job like I'm supposed to. Or I'd get bored or frustrated, and that would set me off," says Mark. "Any excuse to let off some steam by walking out the door." Although of superior intelligence, Mark took nearly fourteen years to obtain his college degree. "I now know part of the reason was because of my ADD," he admits, "but some of it was because I didn't believe I could do it. The voices of grade school and high school teachers telling me that I was stupid and lazy echoed in my head. After a while, I was believing it, too."

• Ken's twenty-year history of severe ADD has sent him down some dark paths, including drug and alcohol abuse and one attempt at suicide. Floating from job to job without direction or hope for his own success, Ken fought against overwhelming feelings of anger and frustration, and often lost the battle. After arguing with one of his superiors, Ken jerked a telephone from its jack and threw it across the room, almost hitting a colleague with it. Following his prompt dismissal, Ken went on a three-day drinking binge.

Until recently, Ken did not realize that adults could suffer from the same symptoms with which he struggled on a daily basis, nor that these symptoms were attached to a condition with a name. Diagnosed with hyperactivity and medicated as a young adolescent, Ken knew the relative peace of mind that comes with proper treatment for a few short years. "So many times I think about what my life would have been like if I'd stayed on the medication. Where would I be?" The knowledge that the troubling syndrome of disturbing symptoms and negative behaviors has a biological basis that can be treated has given him great comfort, as has the support he receives at the group ADD meetings he attends on a regular basis. Ken now feels as if he is on a positive journey forward, a journey of self-exploration.

Traveling with Ken are millions of men and women who can now put a name—and a set of solutions—to a problem that has plagued them for many years. In many ways, it is a journey also shared by the medical profession itself, for the study of ADD in adults remains in its infancy. There is still much we do not understand about its causes, its many manifestations, and the most effective ways to diagnose and treat it.

WHAT IS ADD?

Attention Deficit Disorder seems almost tailor-made for the late-twentieth-century industrialized world, a place where the demands of daily living are heavy and unceasing. The infamous "information superhighway" has begun to intrude into nearly every aspect of our lives, pushing us to keep up an ever faster pace of information-gathering and communication. Television, a medium where quick visual imagery has triumphed over thoughtful exploration, dominates the average American's landscape—the constant click of remote control buttons flicking our brains from one subject to the next in fast and furious measure. The ubiquitous fax machine and cellular telephone challenge the very concepts of solitude, reflection, and relaxation. "So much stimuli, so little time" might just be the perfect motto for our age.

In fact, there may be no one alive today who has not experienced at least some of the symptoms related to Attention Deficit Disorder: most people feel distracted, disorganized, and impulsive at times. Many have difficulty keeping to deadlines and chafe against the rules and regulations imposed by superiors at work or by society at large. For the vast majority, such feelings and behaviors are triggered by external circumstances over which they presume to have some degree of control. They are able to sort and prioritize the stimuli that enter their world on a minute-by-minute basis. Those with ADD, on the other hand, are driven by a faulty *internal* mechanism that prevents them from appropriately assimilating or responding to external and internal messages. This faulty mechanism has been present for many years, perhaps even since birth, precipitating a myriad of symptoms and side effects.

Exactly what that internal mechanism is and what causes it to misfunction is still under investigation. At this point, there remains no concise definition or standard method of diagnosis for ADD in adults, nor is there a definitive set of symptoms that applies to everyone with the disorder. Instead, ADD must be seen as a complex syndrome of symptoms, ranging in severity and expression from person to person.

For many people, Sam's description of a "mental storm" is a remarkably accurate characterization of what it feels like to have ADD. Other people nod in recognition when Bonnie speaks of being "driven by some kind of inner force or energy." Still others explain ADD as the feeling of being "fed a constant stream of equally important facts, thoughts, and emotions." Although these descriptions are inexact—and you, no doubt, have a favorite metaphor that relates to your own distinctive set of symptoms—they remain an important piece of the diagnostic puzzle called ADD. They have, in fact, allowed the medical profession to put a reasonably accurate name to a condition that has been known by various other terms since it was first recognized in 1902 by British pediatrician Frederick Still.

Over the years, many labels have been given to the disorder now known as ADD, including hyperkinesis (excessive movement), minimal brain damage, minimal brain dysfunction, and hyperkinetic reaction of childhood. Most of us over the age of about twenty-five probably know it best simply as "hyperactivity," since that's the way it was broadly diagnosed until the 1970s. In the past decade or so, extensive research and interviews with patients have allowed for a more realistic and comprehensive picture of ADD to emerge, and thus a more accurate name for it to be adopted.

According to the latest version of the official diagnostic manual of the American Psychiatric Association, called the *Diagnostic and Statistical Manual of Mental Disorders IV (DSM IV)*, published in 1994, the official name and acronym for the condition suffered by the six individuals just discussed is Attention Deficit Hyperactivity Disorder, or ADHD. Reflecting the diverse forms the disorder can take, three major types of ADD are recognized and described in the *DSM IV*:

1. ADD that has inattentiveness as its primary symptom
2. ADD with hyperactivity and impulsivity as primary symptoms
3. ADD in which hyperactivity, inattentiveness, and impulsive behavior are combined

In the interest of simplicity, we will use the term ADD to refer to all three types of the disorder. (Please see Table 1 below.)

TABLE 1 **Attention-Deficit/Hyperactivity Disorder Diagnostic Criteria According to the DSM-IV of the American Psychiatric Association**

A. Either (1) or (2):

1) Six (or more) of the following symptoms of **inattention** have persisted for at least 6 months to a degree that is maladaptive and inconsistent with developmental level:

Inattention
a) often fails to give close attention to details or makes careless mistakes in schoolwork, work, or other activities
b) often has difficulty sustaining attention in tasks or play activities
c) often does not seem to listen when spoken to directly

     d) often does not follow through on instructions and fails to finish schoolwork, chores, or duties in the workplace (not due to oppositional behavior or failure to understand instructions)

     e) often has difficulty organizing tasks and activities

     f) often avoids, dislikes, or is reluctant to engage in tasks that require sustained mental effort (such as schoolwork or homework)

     g) often loses things necessary for tasks or activities (e.g., toys, school assignments, pencils, books, or tools)

     h) is often easily distracted by extraneous stimuli

     i) is often forgetful in daily activities

2) Six (or more) of the following symptoms of **hyperactivity-impulsivity** have persisted for at least 6 months to a degree that is maladaptive and inconsistent with developmental level:

Hyperactivity

     a) often fidgets with hands or feet or squirms in seat

     b) often leaves seat in classroom or other situations in which remaining seated is expected

     c) often runs about or climbs excessively in situations in which it is inappropriate (in adolescents or adults, may be limited to subjective feelings of restlessness)

     d) often has difficulty playing or engaging in leisure activities quietly

     e) is often "on the go" or often acts as if "driven by a motor"

     f) often talks excessively

Impulsivity

     g) often blurts out answers before questions have been completed

     h) often has difficulty awaiting turn

     i) often interrupts or intrudes on others (e.g., butts into conversations or games)

B. **Some hyperactive-impulsive or inattentive symptoms that caused impairment were present before age 7 years.**

C. Some impairment from the symptoms is present in two or more settings (e.g., at school [or work] and at home).

D. There must be clear evidence of clinically significant impairment in social, academic, or occupational functioning.

E. The symptoms do not occur exclusively during the course of a Pervasive Developmental Disorder, Schizophrenia, or other Psychotic Disorder, and are not better accounted for by another mental disorder (e.g., Mood Disorder, Anxiety Disorder, Dissociative Disorder, or a Personality Disorder).

Attention-Deficit/Hyperactivity Disorder, Combined Type: if both criteria A 1 and criteria A 2 are met for the past 6 months.

Attention-Deficit/Hyperactivity Disorder, Predominantly Inattentive Type: If criterion A 1 is met but criterion A 2 is not met for the past 6 months

Attention-Deficit/Hyperactivity Disorder, Predominantly Hyperactive-Impulsive Type: If criterion A 2 is met but criterion A 1 is not met for the past 6 months

Attention-Deficit/Hyperactivity Disorder Not Otherwise Specified: This category is for disorders with prominent symptoms of inattention or hyperactivity-impulsivity that do not meet criteria for Attention-Deficit/Hyperactivity Disorder.

PRIMARY SIGNS AND SYMPTOMS OF ADD

If you believe that you or someone you know may have ADD, the first step in coming to terms with the disorder involves gaining an understanding of three symptoms—inattentiveness, hyperactivity, and impulsivity—and how they are expressed and experienced by the adult man or woman with ADD. Keeping in mind that every individual experiences ADD's symptoms in different ways, see if you recognize yourself in the descriptions below:

Inattentiveness

Although the lack of an "attention span" is what many people think of first when ADD is mentioned, it is more accurate to describe inattentiveness in adults as "distractibility." It is not that the adult with ADD cannot focus on a given topic or task, it is that he or she is unable to do so *consistently over a sustained period of time.* Many individuals with ADD admit to becoming quickly bored with repetitive tasks (such as paying a stack of monthly bills or folding laundry) and are easily diverted by any new stimulus. This inattentiveness may manifest itself in a number of different ways. Sam, for instance, tends to procrastinate, primarily because he cannot choose an activity or thought process from among the many stimuli to which he is exposed. "On any given morning, I wake up thinking of about ten things I'm supposed to do," he admits. "Because I can't figure out what to do first, I don't start even one thing. Before I know it, the morning is over."

Others appear as workaholics to the outside world, often because they are unable to successfully shift their focus from one task to another without becoming distracted and thus must work extra hours to get the whole job done. "I can't tell you how many nights and weekends I've worked—just to keep up," says Marion. "Before I hired my assistant, I'd find myself in the office on a Sunday afternoon trying to file my correspondence or write a few follow-up letters because they never seemed to get done during the week. At those moments, I hated my job. I hated myself, too, truth be told."

Do you suffer from inattentiveness?
- Do you find that you frequently make careless mistakes such as misfiling letters, leaving out ingredients in a recipe, misdialing phone numbers?
- Are you intimidated or frustrated by the thought of performing a task that requires sustained effort, such as reading a long novel, preparing a complicated report, or participating in a lengthy discussion?

- Do you often lose track of what someone else is saying during conversations?
- Do you have difficulty completing tasks or following directions?
- Are you constantly distracted away from an important activity by extraneous sounds or thoughts?

Hyperactivity

"I can't think of the last time I sat through a movie without having to get up and walk around at least twice," recalls Mark. "It's like I'm fine for about a half hour, then I start to literally feel itchy. By about the sixty-minute point, I'm ready to jump out of my skin. When it happens at work, it looks really bad." The hallmark symptom of ADD in childhood (as we'll discuss in more depth in Chapter Two), hyperactivity most often manifests itself in adults with ADD as restlessness—fidgeting, pacing, tapping a pencil, etc. These feelings of being on edge often prevent people from sitting for long periods of time at work or even at a movie or a concert.

Another frequent manifestation of hyperactivity in adults is excessive talking—some people with ADD speak rapidly and in run-on sentences, making it difficult for listeners to follow the thoughts being expressed or, indeed, to get their own words in edgewise. "I know that part of my problem in dealing with other people," Bonnie admits, "is that I have the fastest mouth on the East Coast. At first, I guess some people find it kind of charming that I'm so hyper, but it ends up wearing everyone out, including me."

Are you hyperactive?
- Do you often feel restless or fidgety?
- Are you constantly tapping your fingers or feet or otherwise keeping your body moving while performing sedentary activities?
- Does relaxing with a good book, watching a movie, or

simply doing nothing seem to you like a profound waste of time, even when you're not under pressure?

Impulsive Behavior

Many people with ADD respond to stimuli with astonishing speed and with little thought about the consequences that might result from their actions. Perhaps the most dangerous of the adult symptoms of ADD, impulsivity can cause someone to blurt out confidential information, frequently spend money he or she cannot spare, mouth off to the boss (the way Mark often did), and/or to launch new, expensive, sometimes time-consuming projects without thinking them through. At the same time, it should be said, thinking and acting impulsively may be an asset in many aspects of someone's life and personality: Marion's ability to brainstorm with her creative team might be seen in a positive light, as might Bonnie's quick wit and sparkle.

"Although ADD has made me pretty miserable and held me back in so many ways," Ben explains, "there's a part of it that I really like and don't ever want to lose. It's what makes me different from some of the other people I've known, the people who are stuck in a rut, who can't be spontaneous. So far, I'm glad to say that the medication has helped me concentrate more intensely but hasn't left me dull!"

Are you overly impulsive?
- Do you find yourself constantly interrupting others during conversation?
- Are you restless waiting in lines at the market or movie theater?
- Have you blurted out inappropriate remarks without meaning to?
- Do you frequently find yourself doing or saying things that you end up regretting?
- Do you often spend money on things you cannot afford?

SECONDARY SYMPTOMS OF ADD

In addition to the major symptoms of inattentiveness, hyperactivity, and impulsivity, ADD may involve a host of related characteristic behaviors that often go along with the disorder. These behaviors include, among many others:

Disorganization: In what amounts to an often ugly vicious cycle, many adults with ADD are unable to begin to organize the tasks of daily life that, once established, might lead to a less chaotic existence. "Someone once gave me one of those appointment books with all the compartments and sections to help me get organized," Marion recalls. "Just opening it up made me crazy. Instead of helping, it completely intimidated me." Missed appointments, chronic lateness, and failure to meet deadlines are frequently the result of such disorganization.

Lack of follow-through: Either because they become distracted in the middle of an activity or because they impulsively take on a series of projects they can't possibly be expected to finish, many people with ADD are accused of being lazy or of lacking perseverance. In fact, they are often simply unable to focus on one goal long enough to reach it.

Thrill-seeking: People with ADD often express the need for constant stimulation from the outside world, some kind of activity that is novel enough to divert them from the "mental storm" raging inside their heads. In many ways, thrill-seeking can be seen as a positive compensatory skill that allows those with ADD to work out their frustrations and keep them focused. "I find after indulging in my favorite hobby, which is white-water rafting, I'm much more relaxed and ready to buckle down," Sam claims. "And that feeling can last for a few weeks, too."

On the other hand, the need for such high-intensity stimulation can lead to unhealthy behavior: Ken's experimentation with—and then addiction to—drugs and alcohol is a good example of the negative side of thrill-seeking. High-risk sexual activity is another dangerous and ultimately self-destructive activity reported by some adults with ADD.

Impatience: Many adults with ADD display an especially low tolerance of frustration. There are two ways that this impatience might manifest itself: frequently interrupting others during conversations and failing to finish tasks, either because the tasks are complicated or because they are perceived as being boring or tedious.

As discussed at the beginning of this chapter, these symptoms and related behavior patterns of ADD do not develop overnight. Instead, most people with ADD can trace the onset of symptoms and side effects to about six or seven years of age—just about the time they started school. In Chapter Two, we'll explore in more depth how ADD manifests itself in each stage of life. In the meantime, here's a brief overview of ADD in childhood, adolescence, and adulthood.

THE NATURAL HISTORY OF ADD

Infancy and Toddlerhood

"My mother has told me that even as a baby I was hyper," Mark recounts. "I cried more than my brother, and, as a toddler, I was always getting into something I shouldn't have. My mom tells me she couldn't turn around for a second or I'd be running for the stairs, or the stove, or even out the door." Many adults have been told similar stories about their childhood experiences by parents and siblings. Indeed, in more than half of all cases of ADD, the patient showed signs of the disorder prior to age four. Usually, however, these signs go unrecognized until children begin school.

Elementary-School Age

Although children have been diagnosed as young as age four and as old as age seventeen, most children with ADD are recognized when they enter their first years of school and are evaluated by teachers and other professionals. At this time, children start comparing themselves—and are compared by others—with their peers. Because of their symptoms, they may withdraw from social situations (often being labeled "shy" by teachers, friends, and family) or become class clowns and troublemakers. Most develop what could well become a lifelong feeling of being "different" or "weird."

No one knows exactly why, but ADD seems to affect more males than females. Some have suggested that females have been under-identified because they are more likely to have the inattentive type of ADD without the disruptive behavior, which tends to go unnoticed more by parents and teachers. This may be partially true, but most professionals agree that ADD still remains a predominantly male disorder.

In any case, children with ADD begin to fall behind their peers almost from the beginning of their education: "Fails to live up to potential" is one of the most common comments found on grade-school report cards of adult ADD patients.

Adolescence

Until recently, children diagnosed and treated for ADD were mistakenly believed to "grow out" of the disorder once they reached the age of twelve or thirteen, and hence were taken off of medication. Medical professionals now know that many adolescents with ADD, left to cope with the symptoms on their own, experience increased feelings of low self-esteem, frustration, and failure. They tend to act out more aggressively and experiment more with drugs and alcohol than their peers without ADD. To make matters worse, the tendency to seek out high-stimulation activities, such as speeding, petty crime, and skipping school, further contributes to the difficulties experienced by adolescents with ADD.

Another common problem seen in adolescents with ADD is a condition known as Oppositional Defiant Disorder (ODD). According to some studies, ODD coexists in about 40 to 60 percent of adolescents with ADD. Marked by a pattern of hostile, negativistic, and defiant behavior, as well as an inability and unwillingness to follow rules and regulations, ODD significantly adds to the difficulties young ADD patients have when trying to make friends and to learn in the classroom.

Young Adulthood

By the time the person with ADD graduates from high school, he or she has learned certain compensatory skills, some positive and some negative. Those with relatively mild cases of ADD often learn to thrive and flourish despite their handicap and, in fact, use the symptoms to their advantage. For instance, Bonnie decided to join the theater troupe in high school, where her creativity and impulsive thinking were seen as assets.

Other young adults with ADD are not as lucky. They have learned to avoid tasks, activities, and relationships at which they feel unable to succeed. They drift from job to job, or find themselves stuck in positions they know are beneath their abilities and ambitions. The frustration they feel at having the raw material to succeed (e.g., intelligence, drive, energy, creativity) steadily mounts as they continue to lack the ability to translate these assets into positive outcomes. And self-esteem continues to plummet.

Adulthood

By the time a person with undiagnosed and untreated ADD reaches his or her mid-twenties, certain patterns of behavior and thought have been established, and the struggle to adapt to the mysterious inner turmoil takes a further toll. It is not hard to imagine that, after years of struggling to cope with one or more of these symptoms and related behaviors—and attempting to control the effects those behaviors have on daily life and relationships—an adult with ADD might also develop a serious coexisting psychological condition such as depression, anxiety disorder, or drug or alcohol addiction. In fact, such psychological problems are common to most forms of chronic illness, in which no end appears to the disturbing symptoms and their effects on one's life.

Perhaps the most common mood disorder to coexist with ADD is *depression*. Approximately 35 to 40 percent of the adult patients at the ADHD Clinic at the University of Massachusetts Medical Center have met criteria for either major depression or dysthymia (chronic low-grade depression) at some time in their lives. Some of these adults have become so demoralized over their past failures, and over being misunderstood and mistreated by others, that they may require additional treatment for the depression that results.

Others with ADD may suffer from severe *anxiety*, particularly when attempting to cope with situations that have been unsuccessful or troublesome in the past. "I know it sounds silly," Marion acknowledges, "but I become extremely tense and nervous whenever I have to go to the grocery store. Sometimes I become so overwhelmed at the thought of all the steps involved—making the grocery list, clipping the coupons, searching up and down the aisles for the right products—that I give up altogether, not a very good solution and one that my therapist calls *avoidance*."

For those adults with ADD who have had difficulty making and keeping friends, social situations are particularly apt to provoke extreme anxiety. Due in part to their impulsivity, interrupting or intruding on others, forgetfulness, hyperactivity, or mood swings, ADD adults are frequently seen by others as being rude, insensitive, or irresponsible. Over time, such reactions from others lead some people with ADD to associate social interaction with embarrassment, disappointment, or criticism. When confronted with future opportunities to make friends or involve themselves in a group activity, these ADD adults may become so anxious that annoying symptoms—such as inter-rupting or talking too fast—are exacerbated. If this occurs often enough, some people decide to avoid the experience altogether by staying at home. In either case, a sense of social isolation and, often, profound loneliness results.

For anyone suffering from depression, loneliness, and/or constant frustration, the temptation to self-medicate with alco-hol or other drugs is great. And, in fact, a significant minority of ADD adults gravitate toward *alcohol and drug abuse*, possibly as a way of relaxing or calming the mental restlessness they often experience. Approximately 35 percent of the people we see at our clinic have met criteria for substance abuse or dependence either presently or in the past. Many of these individuals appear to be self-medicating in an attempt to quell the manifestations of their underlying ADD symptoms. Most report using alcohol and/or marijuana as their primary drug of choice. As Ken recalls, "For years, marijuana was the only thing that allowed me to calm down and relax. It helped me to focus, too, or at least I thought it did. But then it started to slow me down too much."

Approximately 85 percent of the adults I've treated at the clinic have admitted to having *low self-esteem*. Many are plagued with a chronic inner sense of underachievement and intense frustration. Moreover, many have repeatedly heard negative messages about themselves either directly or indirectly from teachers, parents, spouses, friends, or employers, highlighting their weaknesses and shortcomings. The cumulative effect of such a history can sometimes lead to permanent internalization of these messages, leaving adults with ADD believing that they are indeed "lazy," "stupid" underachievers.

It is only when they are able to put a name to their symptoms that men and women with ADD can start to put their feelings and experiences into perspective. To find out, finally, that there is a medical reason to explain some of their frustration, a biologi-cal factor involved in their set-backs, and a community of mental health professionals ready to help, is the first step on the road to more fulfilling, satisfying lives.

THE CAUSES OF ADD

Most scientists now believe that a brain dysfunction or abnormality in brain chemistry could be to blame for the symptoms of, and behaviors related to, Attention Deficit Disorder. A landmark 1990 study by Alan Zametkin, M.D., published in the *New England Journal of Medicine*, demonstrated that adults with ADD may have low levels of activity in areas of the brain responsible for controlling attention, movement, and getting back on track when distracted.

An extraordinarily intricate structure, the human brain contains millions of complex electrical and chemical actions taking place every second. Everything we are, what we think about, the foods we like, how fast we run, who we love—all of these qualities and activities are stimulated by the brain and its network of nerve cells located within the brain itself and distributed throughout the entire body.

A Biological Source

The frontal lobes of the brain are thought to be most responsible for the regulation of behavior and attention. They receive information from the lower brain, which regulates arousal and screens incoming messages from within and outside of the body. The limbic system, a group of related nervous system structures located in the midbrain and linked to emotions and feelings, also sends messages to the frontal lobes. Finally, the frontal lobes are suspected to be the site of working memory, the place where information about the immediate environment—the activities and sensations of the moment—is considered for memory storage, planning, and future-directed behavior.

Scientists now believe that activity in the frontal lobes is depressed in people with ADD, although exactly how and why is still unknown. The study by Dr. Zametkin showed a decrease in the ability of the ADD brain to use glucose, the body's main source of energy, leading to slower and less efficient activity. Other studies have shown a decrease in blood flow to the frontal lobes. Another related theory focuses on the lack of certain substances known as neurotransmitters in the brains of those with ADD. These neurotransmitters are essential to the way messages are sent and received in the brain and throughout the body.

Just as a car requires oil to allow its gears to shift properly, nerve cells need certain chemicals, called *neurotransmitters*, in order to function properly. Neurotransmitters provide the connection between one nerve cell and another. In essence, neurotransmitters allow electrical impulses to pass across synapses from one neuron to another. It is now suspected that people with ADD have a chemical imbalance of a class of neurotransmitters called *catecholamines*. Dopamine, one such neurotransmitter, helps to form a pathway between the motor center of the midbrain and the frontal lobes, as well as a pathway between the limbic system and the frontal lobes. Without enough dopamine and/or related catecholamines, such as serotonin and norepinephrine, the frontal lobes are understimulated and thus unable to perform their complex functions efficiently.

A Possible Genetic Link

Whether it is a structural abnormality, a chemical imbalance, or a combination of the two that lies at the heart of the ADD puzzle, it is clear that there is a strong genetic component to the disorder. In fact, studies show that between 20 and 30 percent of all hyperactive children have at least one parent with ADD. Furthermore, studies performed on twins of children and adults with ADD reveal that in 50 to 90 percent of identical twin sets both twins had ADD; among fraternal twins (who are not genetically identical) only 33 percent shared the ADD diagnosis.

That ADD might "run in families" comes as no surprise to Sam, who is convinced that his father also suffered with ADD;

nor to Bonnie, whose mother's erratic behavior and tendency to forget important appointments was always laughed off as mere "eccentricity." As we'll see in Chapter Nine, however, the multigenerational nature of ADD often has a profound impact on every member of the family in many different ways.

Potential Environmental Influences

It should be noted that not all cases of ADD may be genetically linked. Some studies suggest that in a small percentage of cases smoking, drinking alcohol, and using drugs during pregnancy may be related to ADD, as may birth traumas such as lack of oxygen during delivery. Exposure to toxins, such as lead, may also play some role in altering brain chemistry and function. And some believe that in a tiny percentage of cases, allergies to foods and substances such as preservatives and dyes may aggravate the disorder, again by triggering a malfunction in the part of the brain devoted to attention and concentration. We'll discuss the importance of maintaining a healthy lifestyle further in Chapter Six.

HOPE FOR THE FUTURE: DIAGNOSIS AND TREATMENT

The good news about ADD is that it is a highly treatable condition once it is accurately diagnosed. Simply being able to put a name to the confusing and frustrating manifestations of this disorder often results in immediate benefits to someone who has sought help for his or her ADD symptoms. "I cannot tell you what it meant to me to know that there was really and truly something *wrong* with me," Marion admits. "I thought I was crazy, I thought I was the only one, I thought I was doomed to die this way. When I heard that there was a reason for at least some of my problems, I suddenly felt whole again."

Once Marion started to take medication, she began to see

her life slowly improve. "It didn't happen all at once or anything, but eventually my days weren't so erratic, I was able to follow through on things without having to be constantly reminded. And, slowly, I started to feel a bit more confident about myself."

Sam was also pleasantly surprised at how quickly and effectively the drug Ritalin worked for him. "Medication allows the fireworks in my head to fade off into the distance. You can't imagine how this makes me feel," he recounts. "Doors that have been forever closed to me have suddenly been flung open."

For Marion and Mark, and millions of other adults with ADD, medication is just the first step on the path to health. Psychological counseling to help mend the psychic wounds inflicted by the disorder over the years and behavior modification therapy to teach new ways to function more productively are common adjuncts to drug therapy. "Before anything else," Ken confesses, "I had to deal with how low my self-esteem had gotten. I didn't even realize how depressed and hopeless I really felt until my doctor and I discussed it. Now I'm seeing a therapist and going to ADD support group meetings every week to get a grip on all that."

Just as every person with ADD experiences different symptoms and related behaviors, so too will each person respond to medication and psychotherapy in a different way. In Part II of this book, you'll learn about some of the principles and techniques that have been helpful to others with ADD. In the meantime, read Chapter Two carefully. It will help you put your childhood experiences into perspective, allowing you to evaluate the symptoms and side effects of ADD and their impact on your childhood, on your experiences today, and on your future.

IMPORTANT QUESTIONS AND ANSWERS ABOUT CHAPTER ONE

Q Many of the symptoms of ADD, such as low self-esteem or restlessness, seem to be pretty common. How many do you have to have before you'll be diagnosed with ADD?

A It's true that some of the symptoms related to ADD are seen quite frequently in the population at large. In fact, symptoms exist on a continuum; everyone experiences them to one degree or another at some point in his or her life. However, there are some relatively strict criteria that must be evaluated and met before a health professional can make an accurate diagnosis. We'll discuss those criteria in more depth in Chapter Three.

Q Is ADD a new disorder? It seems like I've heard about it only just recently.

A In fact, the disorder now known as ADD has probably existed for as long as human beings have had the capacity to concentrate and focus. It was first identified in children around the turn of the century, but has been identified in adults only in recent decades. We do know that ADD knows no cultural, ethnic, or class boundaries and exists in almost every population around the world.

Chapter Two

HAVE YOU
BEEN LIVING
WITH ADD?

As this book is being written, Attention Deficit Disorder in adults continues to garner a great deal of media attention. The subject of recent talk shows, magazine cover stories, and newspaper head-lines, ADD appears to be the latest in a long series of "diseases of the week." Because its symptoms are so varied and its causes still largely unknown, ADD is a perfect target for those who claim that such conditions exist "only in your head."

For the millions of people who suffer with the disorder, however, ADD is far more than a trendy affliction that can be adopted or discarded at will. It is a troubling syndrome of symptoms and side effects with which they have struggled through-out their lives. Perhaps you yourself have wondered if your feelings of restlessness, distractedness, and/or low self-esteem are related to ADD or if you've been "duped" by the media hype that surrounds the disorder. If so, this chapter will help you evaluate your symptoms in an objective and thoughtful way.

"What really annoys me is how many people think that ADD is just the 'excuse of the moment,'" admits Rich, a forty-eight-year-old journalist and father of three who was recently diagnosed with ADD. "Some of the people I work with figure that I'm using ADD to avoid responsibility for being late on a deadline or missing an editorial meeting. What I want to make clear is that having ADD, for me at least, has meant fighting against an enemy I didn't even know I had. In other words, it's not just that I haven't been able to concentrate or follow through on things very well, I've also had to really work to compensate for those symptoms. For better *and* worse, ADD has shaped my sense of self more than any other single thing in my life."

It is true that ADD seems tailor-made for this day and age, when information comes at us from all directions and there never seems to be enough time or energy to complete daily tasks or meet long-range goals. And, in truth, at one time or another we've all displayed some or even most of the symptoms of ADD listed in Table 1 on page 9. Nevertheless, ADD is a very real and potentially devastating disorder affecting as many as four to ten million American adults. It is also a disorder that can be accurately diagnosed by trained professionals, then effectively treated and managed once the diagnosis is made.

Since you're reading this book, it is likely that you have either been diagnosed with ADD or suspect that your difficulties with concentration, hyperactivity, and impulsivity may be due to the disorder. This chapter is designed to help you put the symptoms you have today, and those you may have experienced during your childhood and adolescence, into perspective. In addition, we'll pay attention here to the damage ADD may have caused to your self-esteem and self-confidence over the years. The legacy of frustration, confusion, and futility left by a lifetime with ADD often requires as much investigation and understanding as do current symptoms and side effects of the disorder.

LOOKING BACK

"Just filling out the diagnostic questionnaires has been a learning experience for me," says Rich. "For the first time, I can see that there is a pattern to my chaos, a pattern that has kept repeating itself year after year. I'm reminded of a quote by Edna St. Vincent Millay, which stated, 'It's not true that life is one damn thing after another—it's one damn thing over and over.' Looking back on my life, that sure rings true."

Like photographer Sam, whom you met in the first chapter, Rich now has a successful career in a fast-paced, creative field. Working as a newspaper reporter allows Rich a great deal of flexibility and activity. In fact, his job demands constant shifts in attention and requires him to leave the office for interviews and research. For more than fifteen years, he's been able to use the traits—which had once been hindrances at work—as assets.

"But it hasn't always been like this. I've had some jobs that were completely unsuitable, like being a research assistant for a college professor that meant spending hours poring over technical documents. I thought I'd jump out of my skin," Rich recounts. "I lost that job in three months. Even my job as a book editor, which I really enjoyed and had for two years, was too constricting. I just couldn't seem to concentrate long enough to edit a whole manuscript or to keep track of production schedules. At the time, it felt like I got bored with it, but now I know it was more than that."

When asked during his evaluation for ADD to look into his past, Rich saw that he had experienced the same kind of trouble with focus and concentration as early as his elementary school and junior high years. Looking at a few old report cards, Rich found that he had excelled in classes that involved more active than passive participation—science lab rather than history class, for instance. He also discovered, much to his surprise, that his problems had once been recognized by a school guidance counselor.

"What I had forgotten until recently was that my mother had taken me to a doctor when I was seven years old, and I'd been given medication—Ritalin, I think—for about three years," Rich recalls. "I don't remember anything specific about taking the drug, but I know I started going downhill in eighth grade after they assumed I'd outgrown hyperactivity and took away the medicine."

By the end of his sophomore year in high school, Rich's grades and perceived lack of effort prompted a new guidance counselor to recommend that Rich pursue vocational school rather than college and put his dreams of writing aside. "And I almost did," Rich admits. "But I'm stubborn as well as hyper, so I just kept pushing until I found a way that worked for me."

For Amy, a thirty-five-year-old woman struggling to hold her third marriage together, searching for ADD-related patterns of behavior in her life has been a particularly painful—but ultimately helpful—process. Amy first sought help at a local mental health center for the sense of depression and despair that had weighed her down for more than a decade. After examining Amy, her psychologist confirmed that she was in fact suffering from a clinical depression. But upon further evaluation, the doctor felt an underlying factor at the root of this depression may have been Attention Deficit Disorder.

As a young girl, Amy, like many of her female ADD peers, appeared to be distracted and "spacey" rather than hyperactive. Her teachers, therefore, tended to overlook her problems and simply labeled her a "shy underachiever." This label stuck to her throughout her adolescence and young adulthood, leaving her feeling depressed and unworthy.

"The diagnosis came as a complete surprise to me at first," says Amy. "I never thought I had problems with concentration or hyperactivity, exactly. In fact, it's more that I've had trouble shifting focus from one activity or topic to another; I get lost if too much is going on at once. In high school, I could happily spend hours on, say, my math homework, but then I'd get completely confused if I had to shift my attention to another subject. Typically, I'd get an A in one subject, maybe two, and get D's in the rest."

Even more problematic for Amy was the impact that ADD had upon her ability to make friends. As a toddler, her aggressive behavior with other children caused her to be labeled "difficult" by her play-school teachers; in elementary school, her tendency to interrupt teachers and students alike made her the object of peer ridicule. "It was really a vicious cycle," she explains. "The more socially and academically frustrated I felt, the more withdrawn I became. By the time I was in fourth grade, I was ostracized by classmates. Most of the time I had just one or two friends, usually girls that were younger than me by a year or two."

As Amy grew up, her social and communication skills continued to falter. Her inability to shift focus made it difficult for her to follow conversations or participate in group activities. "I was called 'space shot' and 'weirdo' because I'd just zone out of conversations when I couldn't follow them," Amy remembers. "As I got older, people thought I just wasn't paying attention to them, that I didn't care what they thought. I began to believe them, to think of myself as an outcast, as unworthy of having good friends. I think my first marriage ended mainly because we got married too young. But I know that my second husband, who was an intensely verbal and social person, finally got tired of my tendency to withdraw and isolate myself. And I've been so very afraid that the same thing was happening in my third marriage. Now, after being diagnosed with ADD, I think maybe we can start to resolve things."

Looking at the Past through a New Lens

Being diagnosed with ADD has meant more to Rich and Amy than simply getting practical help for their current personal and professional difficulties. It has also allowed them to look at the past through a new, more accurate lens. Instead of seeing themselves as lazy, unmotivated, or just plain stupid, adults with ADD are finally able to recognize many of their past failures and frustrations for what they truly were: the side effects and consequences of a neurobiological condition over which they had little or no control.

"It surprised me how much getting the diagnosis changed the way I looked at my life," Rich confesses. "A lot of the anger and frustration I'd turned in on myself dissipated. I redirected some of it at teachers who should have known better than to make a child feel so lousy about his shortcomings, whatever the cause. And some of it I redirected at the simple unfairness of the world. I realized that although I'd failed at some things in the past, I wasn't a failure. Instead of my enemy, my past became my friend."

Rich's experience is shared by many adults who undergo testing and treatment for ADD. Unlike diagnostic procedures for physical ailments, like hypertension or kidney disease, or even those for other psychiatric disorders, those designed to evaluate a patient for ADD require a thorough investigation of the past in order to identify symptoms of ADD and its emotional and social side effects. Indeed, far more than the sum of its cardinal symptoms of hyperactivity, inattentiveness, and impulsivity, ADD involves cycles and patterns of behavior and emotion that can be traced, like dropped stitches in a knitted sweater, through the years of one's life. (See Table 2, next page). It is a process that many people find inspiring, enlightening, sometimes painful, and a little intimidating.

ESTABLISHING A PARTNERSHIP WITH THE PAST

"One of the nicest things about going through the diagnostic process," reflects Amy, "was that it gave me and my mom a chance to reminisce together. I can't think of the last time we sat and talked for so long, and there were so many things we didn't know about each other or about certain events." On the advice of her doctor, Amy visited her hometown for a weekend during which she and her mother pored through old report cards, yearbooks, family picture albums, and shoe boxes filled with letters and other documents. "It was painful, in a way, to relive some of those difficult times, to feel that sense of shame and confusion all over again. But I'm glad I did it."

TABLE 2 Tracing the Onset of Symptoms and Side Effects

Many adults with ADD can trace the onset of symptoms and their side effects all the way back to infancy. Here's a time line of behaviors and reactions that may indicate ADD in different stages of life. Check off those that may apply to you and bring it with you to your first appointment with a psychologist (or treatment provider):

Infancy and Early Childhood
_____ Excessive crying or fussing
_____ Resistance to being comforted or calmed
_____ Difficulty in maintaining eating or sleeping schedules
_____ Excessive running, jumping, playing
_____ Overly aggressive or withdrawn behavior in social situations
_____ Poor sibling relationships

Elementary School Years
_____ Inconsistent or poor grades
_____ Fidgeting
_____ Inability to pay attention in class
_____ Interrupting or blurting out answers inappropriately
_____ Poor emotional regulation (becoming emotional easily)
_____ Noncompliance with rules and regulations
_____ Delayed social skills
_____ Retention in grade

Adolescence
_____ Poor or inconsistent grades
_____ Chronic low self-esteem
_____ Difficulty with authority figures, including teachers and parents
_____ Excessive risk taking
_____ Early drug and alcohol use/abuse
_____ Continued peer relationship difficulties
_____ Poorly organized
_____ Low productivity in school

Rich, too, was asked by his doctor to examine his past in order to see if his current problems with concentration had their roots in his childhood. Unfortunately his search for information was hindered by the death of his parents a few years before and the subsequent sale of the family home. Although some family documents were kept, including a few report cards and yearbooks, most had been discarded.

Rich was forced to rely on his own admittedly sketchy memory and the memory of his older sister, Beth. "Partly because I haven't been the easiest person to know and partly because we just don't have that much in common, Beth and I have barely spoken for several years. It was tough to call her up and ask her for help. I was glad my doctor had given me a list of questions. It made it easier."

What to Look For

Chances are, you too have been (or soon will be) asked by a physician to examine your own past. What you'll be looking for are any indications that you suffered from problems with hyperactivity, impulsivity, and/or inattention during your childhood and adolescence. Often the signs of ADD are striking— chronic poor grades from elementary through high school despite evident intelligence, overly aggressive behavior, and/or a previous clinical diagnosis of hyperactivity. In other cases, the evidence is less clear and requires more investigation and interpretation on the parts of both the patient and the diagnosing physician.

What counts most, of course, are your own feelings about your symptoms and the impact they have had on your life. In the end, only you can describe the way you think and how your thought processes may have caused you to behave. After reading this chapter, you should be able to help your doctor make certain judgments based on what you remember, and what you can find out, about your past. In assessing the evidence, keep in mind that for ADD to be assumed, your problems with attention, hyperactivity, or impulsivity cannot have been transient or fleeting. Instead, these problems must have been *chronic* (more than sporadic periods of poor grades or bad behavior, for instance) and *pervasive* (carrying over from school to home to social situations). In addition, most cases have had an *early onset* (evident at least from the age of seven or eight), although especially bright children are sometimes able to compensate for their difficulties until later in their childhood, adolescence, or even adulthood.

Start at the Beginning

Where should you start your search? If your parents are alive, talk to them first. Although colored by time and their own perceptions, your parents' memories of your emotional and educational development remain an invaluable diagnostic tool. If possible, retrieve such documents as report cards, teacher evaluations, and the results of any physical or psychological testing. Report cards are especially useful in assessing symptoms of ADD in the classroom, where such difficulties are often noticed for the first time. A third source of information about your past are siblings and/or peers who may well remember things about your behavior and personality that you may have forgotten or of which you were unaware.

In the pages that follow, you'll find a series of questions that will help you focus on the kinds of behaviors that might indicate the presence of ADD in each stage of development. Answer as many as you are able, obtaining help from parents, grandparents, siblings, teachers, and friends as discussed above. Again, it is important to keep in mind that all memories—including your own—are malleable and certainly altered by the vagaries of time, experience, and hindsight. And, in some cases, your parents' perceptions of symptoms may differ significantly from your own reality. That's why it's so important to find supporting evidence in the form of report cards and other documentation whenever possible.

REMEMBERING INFANCY AND EARLY CHILDHOOD

- Does your mother remember your being "overactive" in the womb, i.e., excessively kicking or turning in the womb?   _____

- Did you have any developmental delays in walking, talking, or sitting up?   _____

- Did you have difficulty establishing or sticking to an eating and sleeping pattern?   _____

- Were you particularly colicky, moody, or difficult as a baby or toddler?   _____

- Did you have any problems getting along with your peers as a toddler?   _____

- Did you fight frequently with your siblings?   _____

- In nursery or preschool, did your teachers complain that you were noisy or disruptive?   _____

The Difficult Child

"I was told that I was trouble even before I was born," Rich relates. "Apparently, I kicked and turned all the time in the womb, screamed like a banshee through most of my infancy, and then couldn't stop talking once I got started. I was every parent's nightmare, and I haven't slowed down since."

In Rich's case, a difficult infancy was in fact an accurate predictor of ADD in his future. It should be noted at the outset, however, that most cranky and demanding babies do not have, nor will they develop, a neurobiological deficit like ADD; they are simply louder and more active than other babies. Nevertheless, anecdotal evidence appears to support the idea that a difficult infant may be slightly more at risk of having attention and hyperactivity problems as he or she matures than his or her more placid peers.

Many parents of children later diagnosed with ADD remember their babies' first years as an endless series of exhausting, confusing struggles: to create order and structure, to foster positive relationships between constantly clashing siblings, to provide love and comfort to a child who appeared to reject them.

"Ben was my third child, and I loved him from the moment he was conceived," says Ben's mother, Natalie. "But I was completely unprepared for what life would be like for him and for us as a family." According to Natalie, Ben (the thirty-four-year-old bus ticket salesperson you met in Chapter One) was fussy and difficult from the moment he was born, refusing to take a bottle, crying constantly, and wriggling so much that his older brothers called him "piggly wiggly."

For Ben, and for many other babies later found to have ADD, the greatest difficulty lay in regulating sleeping and eating patterns. Many mothers of these infants claim that the transition from wake to sleep appeared to cause the most disruption. "Ben would fight sleep with everything he had until he passed out from the struggle," Natalie remembers. "Then, when he woke up, it was as if he were furious at the world for still being here. And he never seemed to be just quiet and alert like his older brothers had been. He couldn't be amused by a mobile over his bed or by looking at the world around him. It sounds strange to describe a baby like this, but he just seemed *nervous* all the time."

A Parent's Dilemma

Like many mothers of difficult babies, Natalie felt helpless, guilty, and, eventually, resentful. Such feelings are particularly evident among first-time parents, whose expectations of parenthood are dashed by the behavior of their difficult children. "Rich was my first child," says his mother, Joanna. "It's difficult for me to admit even now, but as frustrated and tired as I got trying to comfort him, I was also so very disappointed. I'd always dreamed of cuddling with my baby, of making him giggle and coo. With Rich, those moments were few and far between, and of course I thought it was because I was a bad mother."

Unfortunately, many parents receive little help from either their peers or their pediatricians in learning to cope with a difficult infant. From other parents, they collect a bit of sympathy if they're lucky and countless offerings of folk wisdom— Joanna was told by her sister that Rich's sleeping problems were caused by a draft from an open window in his bedroom. From pediatricians, they often encounter a "good news–bad news" scenario. The good news is that their babies appear to be healthy, normal children; the bad news is that there is nothing they can do to help them through their difficulties.

"I was lucky," Ben's mother, Natalie, admits. "Ben's pediatrician came right out and told me that something was wrong with Ben's behavior. It simply wasn't normal for Ben to scream for hours, refuse to eat, or, as he got older, to run around the room knocking over everything in sight. That's not to say that the doctor cured the problem or anything. But he reassured me that I wasn't crazy or completely inept as a mother, and that was a great comfort."

The Preschool Years

As stated earlier, most difficult babies grow out of their early crankiness and develop into well-adjusted children. Those with ADD, however, may continue to be restless and hyperactive as they enter their preschool years and beyond. Coming into contact with peers for the first time can be particularly disturbing, especially for youngsters whose communication and socialization skills have been disrupted by a disorder such as ADD.

Amy's father, Bob, recalls that he first realized something might be wrong with his daughter when he placed her in nursery school. "Amy was a fidgety baby, but my wife and I were first-time parents and just dealt with it. We became concerned when Amy's nursery school teacher told us she was withdrawn from the other children most of the time, but then would lash out physically and verbally when she got frustrated. From that time on, we noticed that Amy had trouble making, and keeping, friends."

Frequent temper tantrums, displays of aggressive behavior, or hyperactivity, are all warning signs (but not conclusive proof) that a toddler or preschooler may have ADD. Other signs include difficulty in following directions, and general immaturity. In addition to setting the stage for later educational problems, such symptoms also affect a child's ability to develop proper socialization skills. Once ostracized by peers or adults, a cycle of poor behavior followed by social isolation may ensue.

Again, it is important to stress that a diagnosis of ADD, *at any age*, is a rather subjective task. Before a child enters school and can thus be compared more objectively on an educational and developmental level with his or her peers, it is often very difficult to draw the line between ordinary rambunctiousness and hyperactivity, shyness and social isolation, curiosity and inattention.

No matter what the reason for these problems, however, all difficult infants and toddlers are at risk of developing emotional and/or social problems if they do not receive love, acceptance, and nurturing during their first years of life. "As hard as we tried," Ben's mother, Natalie, says, "I know that we treated Ben a little differently than we did the other children. And he needed so much more attention from us, I'm sure that the other kids suffered—and the two older boys actively resented it. Ben was constantly teased by them, and by the other neighborhood kids. I think he still feels that sense of shame today. I know that he and his brothers still don't get along."

Problems at Home

When Rich talked to his sister, Beth, he too found out that many of their current difficulties stemmed from their relationship as children. "I thought all little brothers bothered their sisters," Rich relates. "But Beth tells me now that I was more like a plague than a pest. I created complete chaos in the household, and I was the subject of more than one argument between my parents. In fact, my parents split up for the first time when I was about four and divorced several years later. Beth has blamed me for that all these years, and I guess I've blamed myself as well."

In Chapter Nine, we'll discuss the impact that ADD often has on family relationships in more depth. For now, it is important that you understand that the patterns of behavior you feel are disrupting your life as an adult may have been a part of your life since your earliest moments.

REMEMBERING THE ELEMENTARY SCHOOL YEARS

- Were you accused of "daydreaming" a lot in grammar school?   _____

- Did teachers claim you were not "living up to your potential"?   _____

- Were you often sent to the office for talking out of turn or creating a disturbance in class?   _____

- Do you remember having trouble fitting in with your peers or making friends?   _____

- Did you ever visit a physician or psychologist for an evaluation for learning or behavior problems?   _____

The First Diagnosis

As previously discussed, ADD is often first diagnosed when a child with the disorder enters elementary school. For the first time, the child is forced to focus his or her attention over relatively long periods of time, follow directions and rules, and interact with peers in large groups—just the kinds of skills and behaviors with which ADD most interferes.

"Amy's father and I tried to deny that Amy was different, even after she'd had some problems in nursery school," her mother, Miriam, recalls. "We figured she'd grow out of it. Although she became less aggressive and less hyper as she got older, she always had trouble paying attention and staying on task. Her grades in most subjects were barely average, and they stayed that way through much of her academic career."

When Amy and Miriam went through old school records, they were surprised at how consistent her problems at school tended to be. Her first-grade teacher wrote: "Amy is a bright child, but she tends to daydream in class. When she gets lost, she interrupts the class or asks questions about a topic that is already past." From third grade: "Amy is having problems in social studies. Her homework is good, but she often forgets to bring it in. She also has trouble staying in her seat and waiting her turn." From fifth grade: "Amy is easily distracted. She needs to work harder during class time, she often wastes time daydreaming." And from sixth grade: "Amy often has to play catch-up, finishing her homework in class while the rest of us are going on with the day's work. She also needs to get to class on time; she was tardy fourteen times this term." Her guidance counselor added this comment: "Amy seems to have trouble making friends and spends her free periods alone."

Miriam remembers discussing some of these problems with Amy's teachers. Almost without exception, they reassured Miriam that her daughter was intelligent and generally good-natured. It appeared, however, that Amy had difficulty retaining information: What she seemed to learn on Monday would be forgotten by Tuesday. The reason for this, her teachers assumed, was that Amy simply refused to pay attention. She was thus labeled an "underachiever," like so many of her ADD peers.

"I think if I was accused one more time of 'not living up to my potential' I would have killed myself," Amy admits. "To this day, I don't know what that means. How could they even know what my potential was at the age of seven or eight or nine? And if they knew, why didn't they tell me something more specific? I always thought it meant I just wasn't good enough."

The Class Clown

Rich found the same kind of comments on the few report cards he retrieved from his sister's archives that Amy had found on hers. Until about fourth grade, when he thinks he began taking Ritalin, Rich apparently struggled just to keep up. His first-grade teacher wrote: "Rich is not working to the best of his ability. He is constantly disrupting the classroom." His third grade teacher penned this criticism: "Rich is frequently unprepared for class and lacks initiative. Although bright and funny, he interrupts others often and talks too much in class." And during the first term of fourth grade, his teacher felt compelled to let his parents know that his progress had slipped enough to warrant extra help: "Rich's work is inconsistent. I believe he should come in for remedial work on a regular basis, and I have sent my comments to the school guidance counselor."

Like many hyperactive children, Rich remembers spending more time in the hallway or the principal's office than in the classroom. Unable to control his verbal or physical impulses, Rich frequently blurted answers out of turn, wandered from his seat at inappropriate times, and disrupted the classroom with practical jokes. It was this kind of behavior that sent him to the guidance counselor and, finally, to a diagnosis of ADD by a school psychologist.

"I now know I was one of the lucky ones, at least for the three years or so that I took medication," says Rich. "I'm forever in debt to the guidance counselor who first sent me to the psychologist for a diagnosis. For the first time in my life, somebody understood what it felt like to be inside my head, somebody who knew I didn't want to disrupt the class or forget to do my homework. And then the Ritalin helped so much, too. I suddenly knew how all my friends managed to get stuff done. It had always been a mystery to me."

Falling Further Behind Every Day

Although as adults Rich and Amy were diagnosed with two different subtypes of ADD—Amy appears to have ADD with inattentiveness as its primary symptom while Rich's problems appear to involve hyperactivity and impulsivity rather than inattention—they both spent most of their academic lives struggling, and often failing, to keep up with their peers. And they both shared the same sense of defeat and despair at their lack of accomplishment.

Again, the problems faced by children with ADD are twofold. First, because they are unable to focus their attention on a sustained and consistent basis, they may not learn basic skills as quickly or as well as their peers. In many cases—upward of 30 percent of cases, according to current research—ADD is accompanied by learning disorders such as dyslexia or math disability. If these learning problems are not recognized and dealt with, children with ADD may fall further and further behind their peers. Because Amy's attention problems kept her from learning the basic rules of spelling and grammar, for instance, reading has always been difficult for her.

"My parents were both avid readers and there were always books around the house," Amy recalls. "Even as a toddler, they tried to teach me to love books. And you know what? Even though I never read a book from cover to cover until I was in high school, I went through all of the motions—taking out books from the library, carrying them around with me—just to please my folks. Even at six and seven, I had already learned to cover up my disabilities and insecurities. Because I got so good at it, I never got the extra help I needed. I always felt ashamed, though, because I knew I was a fake."

The Early Onset of Low Self-Esteem

Indeed, the second set of problems faced by children with ADD involve the threats the disorder poses to their sense of self-esteem. Ordered over and over again to "pay attention" when their brains prevent them from doing so on a consistent basis, reprimanded for fidgeting when their bodies demand activity, told repeatedly that they can do better when they are trying as hard as they can, children with ADD often simply give up on themselves and on the people around them. From a very young age, they feel misunderstood and alienated from their parents and siblings as well as from their peers and other adults. These feelings only intensify as they enter adolescence and the more challenging and competitive world of high school.

REMEMBERING THE ADOLESCENT YEARS

- Were your grades inconsistent? _____

- Were you disorganized to the point where it interfered in productivity at school or home? _____

- Did you often fail to complete homework? _____

- Were you ever suspended or expelled from school because of bad behavior, getting into fights, breaking rules, or inappropriate behavior? _____

- Did you have poor study habits? _____

- Did you finish high school on schedule? _____

- Did you stay back in a grade? _____

- Were your friends generally of a younger age than you? _____

- Were you involved in numerous car accidents and/or traffic violations? _____

• Did you experiment excessively with drugs
and/or alcohol?   _____

The Challenge of Adolescence

"Although I managed to get average grades as a freshman
in high school, I felt completely out of control," says Bonnie,
the engineer introduced in Chapter One. "I became extremely
belligerent toward anyone, including parents and teachers, who
presumed to tell me what to do. I was suspended or put on
probation countless times for breaking the rules (smoking, vio-
lating dress codes, etc.), skipping school, or mouthing off to
teachers. I finally dropped out and didn't get my GED until
four years afterward."

Bonnie's story is shared by hundreds of thousands of Americans whose educational and behavioral problems during adolescence were later related to Attention Deficit Disorder. According
to the most current research, approximately one-third to one-
half of all children with ADD do not, in fact, grow out of the
disorder, but end up struggling to learn and thrive despite—
and often without being aware of—its symptoms.

Even without having to contend with a disorder like ADD,
adolescence is a particularly stressful and challenging time. The
adolescent body grows at a more rapid rate than at any other
time of life except infancy, with weight almost doubling and
height increasing by approximately 25 percent. At the same
time, the hormones that control sexual development are produced, awakening what are often exciting and confusing sexual
feelings.

Intellectual and academic growth occur at a rapid rate during the high school years as well. Students are encouraged to
discover and develop their own special interests and skills, while
at the same time competing with their peers for grades, teacher
recommendations, and peer status.

Adolescence also signals an acceleration of another process:

that of attaining independence from one's parents by defining one's own identity. Teenagers make choices about everything from the clothes they wear, to the friends they make, to how late they stay out. These choices often involve breaking rules and regulations set up by parents and other figures of authority. Despite the inherent danger, experimentation with alcohol, drugs, and sexual behavior are also common—although certainly not universal—to the teenage years. The desire to fit in intensifies during this period and may contribute to a teenager's decision-making process more than any other factor.

For the teenager with ADD, the difficulty of making these intellectual, emotional, sexual, and social transitions is often made worse by the symptoms and side effects of the disorder. Academic studies, for instance, pose even greater challenges for young people with ADD-related concentration problems, especially since they may have failed to learn basic skills during elementary and junior high school.

Furthermore, the requirement of most high schools that students change classrooms and teachers often during the day may be particularly upsetting and confusing to those with ADD. Amy, for instance, recalled that it took her twenty minutes after a new class started to "calm down and be able to focus." With classes lasting just forty-five minutes, Amy typically "lost" nearly half of every class.

The Consequences of Growing Up with ADD

Most teenagers with ADD—especially those with undiagnosed and untreated ADD—carry an extra heavy burden of negative self-esteem acquired during childhood. Although most of their peers also struggle with questions of identity, popularity, and achievement, these young people are doubly challenged by effects of the disorder, especially young people with poor communication and socialization skills. Some become loners unable to make and keep friends; others find themselves befriending younger people whose social maturity levels are closer to their own; still others begin what is often a lifelong pattern of self-medication with drugs or alcohol in order both to concentrate better and to feel more comfortable among their peers.

"You know how they say that pot is the gateway drug, that it leads to other, more dangerous drugs?" asks Ken. "For me, it was caffeine. Really. Starting in junior high, I found out that drinking lots of coffee made me feel better, so every morning I'd drink four or five cups. Then, in my sophomore year in high school, I found speed. And boy, did that ever help. For a while, even my schoolwork got better and I made friends with my drug buddies. But then things started to fall apart when I needed something to slow me down, so I turned to pot or to Valium to cut the edge. My life was pretty much a fog after that."

In addition to having a high rate of drug or alcohol abuse, a significant minority of teenagers with ADD tend to have special trouble dealing with authority figures and the rules and regulations set up by society. The symptom of impulsivity—acting or speaking without regard to the consequences—causes some teenagers with ADD to engage in all kinds of high-risk behavior, from substance abuse, to petty crime, to promiscuous sexual activity.

When It's Not Just ADD

To add to the problem, approximately 30 to 50 percent of children and teenagers with ADD may in fact suffer from a concurrent behavioral problem such as Conduct Disorder or Oppositional Defiant Disorder. As discussed in Chapter One, these young people get into frequent fights, disrupt and abuse others, mouth off to teachers and parents, use excessive profanity, and even break the law. Vandalism and delinquency are frequent cohorts. Finally, these adolescents with ADD are often seen by their peers as being spiteful and vindictive people who blame others for their own mistakes.

Mark, the young man from Chapter One who had more

jobs than he could count after leaving high school, remembers swearing at a teacher who reprimanded him in front of the class for doing poorly on an exam. "I stood up from my desk, knocking my chair over in the process, and swore at him heartily. I then told him what I honestly believed: 'If you were a better teacher, I could learn this stuff.' And then I walked out. I was suspended for two weeks."

It should be noted that not all teenagers with ADD fail to thrive in the high school environment. Some teenagers compensate for the symptoms of ADD by finding study methods and communication techniques that work for them. "In elementary school and junior high, the only place we had to study was in the classroom or at communal desks in the library," Bonnie remembers. "I was constantly distracted. But in high school, the library had soundproofed study rooms, which had stark white walls, one desk, one chair. I could finally concentrate. To this day, I need that kind of quiet to work."

Finding Oneself Through ADD

Some teens with ADD come into their own during high school by discovering special skills and talents they never knew they had. The sports arena becomes a haven for many ADD adolescents who can channel their excess energy into an activity that may also score social points from their peers. For those with open and energetic personalities, like Bonnie's, community theater or student government can be a rewarding opportunity for self-expression and self-definition.

"Hard to believe, now that I'm a stodgy engineer," Bonnie laughs, "but I was part of the so-called artsy clique in high school. We hung around the art room, drawing, painting, doing pottery. We also created some pretty neat sets for the student theater. That's not to say that we didn't also skip school and get into trouble. We were all pretty wild. But for the first time, I felt like I belonged somewhere."

Even among teenagers who have learned to compensate in healthy ways for the symptoms of ADD, however, planning for the future may seem overwhelming. Having faced academic and social difficulties throughout their childhood, many of these young people look with some trepidation at making their way through college, finding and sustaining a career, and starting a family.

ENTERING ADULTHOOD WITH ADD

- Did you forgo college because you didn't think you'd measure up? _____
- Do you frequently feel upset about lost opportunities you have squandered in the past? _____
- Do you sometimes feel ashamed about lies or half truths you've told in the past? _____
- Have you had difficulty making and keeping friends? _____
- Is your employment record marked by frequent job changes and inconsistent performance, including firings and impulsive quits? _____

Learning to Live with ADD

"I scored a whopping 1050 on my SATs," Rich recalls, "and the lion's share of that score was in Verbal; my math skills were, and still are, deplorable. I decided to go to the local community college and, though it took me six years instead of four, I graduated with an English degree. Now that I've met so many other adults with ADD who never made it through college, or had an even harder time than me, I know what an achievement that was."

Indeed, by the time a young person with ADD comes of age, he or she has struggled with its symptoms for a decade or more. Depending on luck and body chemistry, some experience fewer symptoms and to a lesser degree than others. By learning compensatory skills and/or by choosing careers that use their thought patterns and energy levels to best advantage, they become well-adjusted, productive adults. They may pass through periods in which concentration becomes a problem, or when their self-esteem plummets, but by and large they make a successful transition into responsible adulthood.

The Daily Struggle

Many others, however, are not so lucky. Despite their best efforts to fight against their invisible enemy, these young people enter their adult years undereducated, undersocialized, and often plagued with a chronic inner sense of failure and frustration. The negative messages about themselves that they have heard either directly or indirectly from teachers, parents, spouses, friends, or employers play over and over again inside their heads. The primary symptoms of hyperactivity, impulsivity, and inattention and their side effects continue to disrupt their lives, economically, socially, and emotionally.

"What disturbed me most was the amount of lying it took to keep going," admits Mark. "You start lying to your boss about what you can do on the job, to your parents, friends and girlfriends about everything, and then you can't stop. Once people catch on—and they always do—you end up alienating them, then you get angry at them and at yourself. It gets worse and worse until you don't want to feel anything anymore."

Amy agrees. "I'm not sure where ADD ends and my emotional problems begin, and vice versa," she remarks when asked about her lingering depression. "Sometimes I feel that my confusion actually works for me by keeping me so distracted that I can't recognize or release my real feelings—of loneliness, of anger, of disappointment over my own lack of accomplishments. This distraction also keeps me from getting practical things accomplished or making any lasting personal or professional commitments, which ends up adding to the vicious cycle."

In future chapters, we'll discuss further the impact that

ADD may have on the lives of men and women—and their friends and families—as they grow older. We'll also show you healthy, effective ways both to cope with current symptoms and to begin to heal any emotional wounds that may remain. In the meantime, it is important for you to take the time to gather the information requested in this chapter, and to reflect upon what that information may mean to your life today.

Did you answer yes to most of the questions at the beginning of each section? Did you relate to many of the experiences related in this chapter? Do you feel that you still have problems with attention and/or impulsivity? Even if you answer yes to all of these questions, you should not assume you have ADD unless you've been diagnosed by a trained professional. Chapter Three introduces you to the diagnostic process, showing you some of the guidelines used by qualified physicians and psychologists to evaluate a patient suspected of having ADD.

IMPORTANT QUESTIONS AND ANSWERS ABOUT CHAPTER TWO

Q I didn't seem to have any trouble with attention or hyperactivity all through grammar school, and it wasn't until I was in eighth grade that I started to have trouble at school. Yet I was diagnosed with ADD. I thought you had to have symptoms from a very young age. Isn't that true?

A It is likely that you did indeed first begin experiencing symptoms when you were very young. However, perhaps because you were particularly intelligent or your environment was particularly supportive, you learned to compensate for your difficulties without ever realizing you had them. Sometimes people are able to successfully compensate for their symptoms when the demands for sustained attention are not particularly difficult. When organizational and structural challenges became increasingly complex, in junior high, high school, or sometime later in life, the impairment may then become more problematic.

Q I bought this book because my sister was recently diagnosed with ADD. But I certainly can identify times in my life when all of these symptoms applied to me. Does that mean I have ADD, too?

A Not necessarily. It's impossible to say without examining you. However, as discussed here and elsewhere in this book, symptoms such as restlessness, inattention, and distractibility can certainly occur under many other circumstances and as a result of many other physical and emotional conditions. Think back on the times when you felt those symptoms: Were you under particular stress or were you suffering from another illness? If you are concerned about this issue, talk to your doctor about it.

Q I've been practicing law for about five years—pretty successfully, I might add. But I've always felt behind somehow, and I always had to work so hard to make it through my classes and keep track of where I'm supposed to be and what I'm supposed to be doing. On the outside, though, it seems like I'm doing great. Is it possible that I have ADD?

A Many adults with ADD are high achievers with particular qualities that have allowed them to compensate for their symptoms. Some are highly verbal, able to talk their way through their difficulties; others have high I.Q.'s or are particularly talented. What they all have in common with you, however, is a sense of not quite living up to their own potential, of having to struggle to stay even with the rest of the world. If you are concerned that you might have ADD, talk to your doctor—it truly doesn't matter how your life looks from the outside, it's what's happening on the inside that counts.

Chapter Three

FINALLY,
A DIAGNOSIS

So far in this book, you've met eight men and women who have struggled with symptoms and side effects of ADD in their adult lives and during their childhood. By reading their stories—and thinking about your own life—you've perhaps come to better understand what a truly *personal* disorder ADD is. ADD affects each individual differently, shaping his or her personality and intellectual capabilities in unique ways and with varying degrees of severity.

Because of the wide variability in symptoms and side effects, and since so much is still unknown about its cause, making an accurate diagnosis of ADD remains a tricky and rather subjective task. As discussed, much of the diagnostic process involves tracing patterns of behavior through childhood and adolescence, a task you began by reading Chapter Two and responding to its questions. Armed with that information, your doctor will be able to make a more accurate and informed assessment of your condition.

Equally important to the diagnostic procedure is a complete

and accurate evaluation of your current emotional, social, and intellectual problems—in short, a thorough evaluation of the symptoms that induced you to seek professional help in the first place. Some people first knock at a psychologist's door because their marriages are falling apart, for instance, or because they've had difficulty holding down a job. Others are depressed or anxious. Many are suffering from general malaise, feeling restless yet empty and unmotivated. Very few are aware that ADD might be contributing to their difficulties.

It is important to keep in mind that the majority of people who seek help for psychological and/or psychosocial problems do not, in fact, suffer from ADD. Remember, ADD is a relatively uncommon and quite specific neurobiological disorder that probably is present in only about 2 to 5 percent of the adult population. On the other hand, because ADD is often masked by such conditions as mood disorders (e.g., depression and anxiety), substance abuse, and antisocial behavior, many psychologists and health professionals will mistakenly overlook ADD as a possible contributing factor for current difficulties. This chapter is designed to help you move quickly to an accurate diagnosis.

Unfortunately, many adult patients with ADD have found the road to diagnosis to be a long and circuitous one. Mark, for example, saw two medical doctors, one psychiatrist, and three psychologists before he found someone who identified ADD as the root cause of his educational failures and employment problems. Marion, the advertising executive introduced in Chapter One, took part in weekly therapy sessions for over two years with a psychologist who failed to see that she suffered from the disorder. And the list of people with similar stories goes on.

Why is it so difficult for ADD to be diagnosed in adults? The reasons are varied, and include the fact that it is only in recent years that adult ADD was recognized as a distinct syndrome. Another stumbling block is the lack of a single test— medical or psychological—that will confirm the presence of ADD in an individual. Furthermore, the tests that do exist were originally designed to assess symptoms in children, and researchers are still working to create scoring keys and rating scales that are as accurate for adults as they are for younger age groups. As it stands today, however, diagnosing ADD in adults primarily involves observation, evaluation, and, above all, good judgment on the part of a trained health professional.

Later in this chapter, you'll find information on:

• choosing an appropriate health care professional
• understanding the diagnostic procedure
• establishing a partnership with your doctor
• coping with a diagnosis of ADD

In the meantime, the following test in designed to measure the degree to which you currently experience the symptoms and side effects of ADD. Like the questions you were asked to consider in Chapter Two, this test will prove to be an invaluable asset: The doctor you choose to evaluate you will be grateful for the information it provides, and you yourself should gain a deeper understanding of the disorder and its effects on your daily life by completing it. Please note that this exercise is not a substitute for a thorough examination by an expert, but rather is meant as tool for self-exploration and professional evaluation. If you suspect you have ADD, visit a physician or psychologist as soon as possible.

TABLE 3 Your Adult ADD Self-Exploration Exercise

After reading the description of the symptom, estimate on a scale of 0 to 3 how severely it affects you on a day-to-day basis:

0 = symptom does not affect you
1 = symptom is rarely a problem
2 = you're often affected by the symptom
3 = symptom is a significant, constant problem in your life

In the next column, check off all those symptoms that affected you during your *childhood*. This part of the test will help you to remember that what is important in assessing ADD is the presence of a *pattern* of behavioral, social, and cognitive problems. When you finish the test, tally the results and show them to the psychologist who is evaluating you for ADD. The information it provides will be of enormous help during the diagnostic process.

Section A
Section A is designed to evaluate the presence and impact of *inattentiveness*. This symptom may be defined as the inability to concentrate on any given subject or task over a sustained period of time.

SYMPTOM/BEHAVIOR	SEVERITY (0–3)	CHILDHOOD (✓)
1. Failing to give close attention to details	____	____
2. Difficulty in sustaining attention to tasks	____	____
3. Not seeming to listen when spoken to directly	____	____
4. Difficulty following through on instructions or failing to finish tasks	____	____
5. Difficulty organizing tasks or activities	____	____
6. Avoiding or disliking tasks which require sustained attention	____	____
7. Misplacing or losing things frequently	____	____
8. Easily distracted from task at hand	____	____
9. Forgetful	____	____
Totals:	____ (POINTS)	____ (CHECKS)
Highest possible:	27	9

Section B

Section B is designed to evaluate the symptoms of *hyperactivity* and *impulsivity*. Hyperactivity in adults usually manifests itself as chronic restlessness, causing someone who has it to fidget, pace, tap his or her feet, and/or talk excessively. Impulsivity involves responding to stimuli quickly and with little thought about the consequences of that response.

SYMPTOM/BEHAVIOR	SEVERITY (0–3)	CHILDHOOD (✓)
1. Fidget excessively	＿＿	＿＿
2. Difficulty remaining seated for periods of time	＿＿	＿＿
3. Excessive feelings of physical restlessness	＿＿	＿＿
4. Difficulty in engaging in peaceful or quiet leisure activities	＿＿	＿＿
5. Always on the go as if driven by a motor	＿＿	＿＿
6. Excessive talking	＿＿	＿＿
7. Often blurting out answers before questions are completed	＿＿	＿＿
8. Often impatient; cannot wait in line or for one's turn	＿＿	＿＿
9. Often interrupting or intruding on others	＿＿	＿＿
Totals:	＿＿ (POINTS)	＿＿ (CHECKS)
Highest possible:	27	9

Section C
Section C is designed to measure the possible impact of ADD on various aspects of your daily life. Many adults with ADD experience very minor symptoms of ADD and/or have learned healthy and efficient ways of coping with the disorder, while others are nearly paralyzed by the disruption ADD causes in their lives. A treatment plan will be created by you and your physician depending upon where your problems fall on this wide spectrum.

SYMPTOM/BEHAVIOR	SEVERITY (0–3)	CHILDHOOD (✓)
1. Always starting, but rarely finishing, tasks or hobbies	_____	_____
2. Make decisions or act too quickly or without considering consequences	_____	_____
3. Inconsistent work performance	_____	_____
4. Low self-esteem	_____	_____
5. Daydream a lot	_____	_____
6. Procrastinate often	_____	_____
7. Few close friends or intimates	_____	_____
8. Often have trouble with authority figures	_____	_____
9. Bored often	_____	_____
10. Work best under pressure	_____	_____
11. Consider yourself lazy	_____	_____
12. Difficulty managing checkbook and finances	_____	_____
13. Difficulty managing paperwork on the job	_____	_____

14. Chronic pattern of
    underachievement   _____   _____

15. Pattern of traffic or
    speeding violations   _____   _____

	Totals:	_____	_____
		(POINTS)	(CHECKS)
	Highest possible:	45	15

OBTAINING A DIAGNOSIS

Ruben, a thirty-three-year-old actor and waiter, first became aware of adult ADD through a television news program. He later told his doctor that just hearing about adult ADD seemed like a miracle to him. "Until I read that an adult could have this disorder," Ruben remarks, "I just suffered in silence. Well, not exactly in silence, since my mood swings and irritability annoyed everyone around me. But I never knew that what I was feeling even had a name."

After learning that one of the centers for adult ADD research and treatment was located in a nearby city, Ruben made an appointment to see a therapist for an evaluation. "Now that I've had a chance to talk to other people with ADD," Ruben explains, "I realize how lucky I've been. I went to the right person first instead of last."

As discussed, diagnosing ADD in adults remains a difficult and subjective task that can only be performed accurately by an individual trained and experienced in dealing with adult ADD. Fortunately, finding such an individual is no longer as difficult or unpredictable a process as it once was. Psychologists are becoming increasingly aware of adult ADD, learning to recognize its symptoms in their patients, and are receiving training in diagnosing and treating adult ADD.

If you suspect you have ADD, discuss the matter with your

medical doctor or, if you are currently undergoing psychological therapy, with your psychiatrist or psychologist. Although your current therapist may know something about ADD in adults, it is more likely that he or she will refer you to someone with greater expertise in the diagnostic procedure. When Bonnie asked her psychiatrist about ADD, for instance, she was referred to a colleague at a mental health center in another city.

Finding a Doctor to Diagnose You

If you are not currently under the care of a physician or psychologist, the best way to find a reputable practitioner trained in diagnosing adult ADD is to contact one of the service organizations listed in the Appendix. Associations such as your local chapters of CH.A.D.D. (Children and Adults with Attention Deficit Disorder) and A.D.D.A. (Attention Deficit Disorder Association) may be able to help you find an experienced psychologist located in a city close to where you live. Unfortunately, you may have to travel a bit if you live in a particularly rural or isolated part of the country or otherwise have limited access to medical care.

Chances are, you'll visit a *psychologist* for your evaluation. A psychologist is a health care professional trained in the study of human behavior. He or she provides counseling and testing in areas related to mental health, but is not a medical doctor and cannot prescribe medication. A *psychiatrist* is a medical doctor able to prescribe and monitor medication. Although some psychiatrists have expertise in testing, the diagnostic evaluation is usually done by a psychologist. Another specialist who might be involved in your case is a *neurologist*, a medical doctor who diagnoses and treats nervous system disorders. A neurologist may be consulted in order to rule out neurological conditions, such as seizure disorders or Tourette's Syndrome, that may be causing your symptoms.

Later in this chapter, we'll discuss the importance of establishing a close working relationship with the doctor who will be your primary ADD caregiver. In the meantime, here are a few questions to ask the doctor before you make an appointment for the initial evaluation:

• *Do you specialize in adult ADD? About how many patients have you evaluated for the disorder?* As discussed, diagnosing ADD is a fairly subjective task that depends a great deal on the ability to accurately observe and interpret symptoms. The more patients a doctor has seen within this context, the more likely it is that he or she will be able to reach a reliable conclusion.

• *What do you charge for the diagnostic evaluation and will it be covered by my insurance?* You should feel free to discuss finances openly and honestly with your doctor *before* you make a commitment to see him or her. The costs of an evaluation of ADD will vary widely, depending on where you live, what medical, neurological, and/or psychological tests are deemed necessary, and how long the psychologist spends with you.

To find out what services are covered by your health insurance, call your insurance carrier before your appointment so that any delays in filing claims or receiving reimbursement can be minimized. If your doctor is affiliated with a hospital, and most are, ask him or her to recommend the services of the hospital social services department. A hospital social worker is trained to help individuals through the bureaucratic maze of health insurance and compensation and, under most circumstances, will be glad to answer your questions.

• *What kind of medical records and other documents should I bring with me?* Much time and energy can be saved if you arrive at the first appointment armed with as much relevant information as possible. In our ADD clinic at the University of Massachusetts Medical Center, we send new patients a questionnaire containing questions similar to those you've answered in Chapter Two and in the ADD Self-Exploration Exercise. We request that patients bring the results of any recent psychological tests with them as well. Particularly crucial to a thorough evaluation is any objective evidence of ADD symptoms in the past or present, including test scores from grade school and high school, report cards, employee evaluations, etc.

• *What can I expect to happen during the first appointment?* The length and substance of your first appointment will depend to a large degree on what the doctor discovers during the course of the meeting. Nevertheless, the doctor or nurse with whom you make the appointment should be able to explain to you the general procedure and how long it usually takes. Some doctors divide the diagnostic procedure into several parts, discussing medical, family, and psychological history in the first appointment, then scheduling one or more additional sessions for further testing. Others may choose to perform the entire evaluation in the course of one long appointment.

Once you've received, and are satisfied with, the answers to these questions, make an appointment for an evaluation. The good news is that although it may be a bit time-consuming, you're bound to find it stimulating and thought-provoking. It is likely that you will learn things about your past and present of which you were quite unaware. And, if you do receive a diagnosis of ADD, you will finally be able to put a name, and a set of solutions, to many of your current difficulties.

The Diagnostic Procedure

As discussed, evaluating adults with ADD remains a relatively new endeavor for most health care practitioners, and it is likely that every doctor will perform the evaluation in a slightly different way. Your psychologist, for instance, may depend more upon your past history than on current symptoms to make a diagnosis, while another doctor might spend more time evaluating the impact of symptoms on your present day-to-day activities. Both categories of information are important.

No matter what questions are asked or tests performed, your doctor should attempt to prove the following four criteria before diagnosing you with ADD:

1. You have had ADD since childhood and the symptoms have been relatively persistent over time.

2. You continue to experience symptoms of ADD to a significant degree.
3. The symptoms of ADD currently produce serious impairment in one or more areas of your life (on the job, in social situations, within the family, and/or in your daily activities).
4. Your symptoms cannot be better explained by any other psychological or medical condition.

In order to determine if the signs and symptoms you present meet the above criteria for ADD, a doctor must, in essence, don the apparel of another professional—the private investigator. Indeed, like a detective, the psychologist must delve into your private life more than you might expect in order to identify the underlying cause or causes of your symptoms and related behaviors. To do so, the doctor will attempt to gather as much evidence as possible from all aspects of your life—medical, psychological, educational, and social—through interviews, documentary evidence, and his or her own powers of observation.

Determining Criterion #1

The first step in that process is the taking of the *symptom history*. By asking you questions similar to those outlined here and in Chapter Two, the doctor will determine whether or not Criterion #1 has been met, that is, whether or not you suffered from symptoms of ADD during your childhood. In addition, your doctor may attempt to corroborate your testimony by taking evidence from your parents and siblings, from documents like report cards and teacher evaluations, and from any past psychological assessments.

Determining Criteria #2 and #3

Using the same general methods of interview and review of past documentation, your doctor will try to ascertain if Criteria #2 and #3 can be met: Do you still struggle with symptoms of ADD and do those symptoms have a significant—and negative—impact on your life today? The questions in the ADD Self-Exploration Exercise are among those often used by psychologists during this part of the evaluation. Testimony from spouses, children, and even co-workers may be quite helpful in assessing current symptoms and side effects of adult ADD.

Determining Criterion #4

Attempting to meet Criterion #4—that no other condition is causing your symptoms—is an integral and often complicated part of any evaluation for ADD. Because the symptoms of ADD are common to a number of other medical and psychological problems, the doctor has to rule out these other suspects before identifying ADD as the culprit. He or she will start this process by taking a thorough *medical history*. Past injuries, illnesses, and surgeries will be considered, with particular attention being paid to head injuries and allergies, which can cause the confusion and distractibility common to ADD. Your doctor will also weigh the possibility that a neurological problem, such as epilepsy or another seizure disorder, is at the root of your current difficulties.

Another medical condition with symptoms that may be confused with those of ADD is thyroid dysfunction. A bow-tie-shaped gland located at the base of the neck, the thyroid secretes hormones that work to set the rate at which your body functions. An overactive thyroid (causing a condition called *hyperthyroidism*) may cause ADD-like symptoms, including nervousness and confusion. Therefore, the possibility of hyperthyroidism should be considered, especially if you have a family history of the disorder or if you've experienced other symptoms of hyperthyroidism such as weight loss, high blood pressure, and swelling at the base of the neck.

Because certain medications have the potential to cause side effects that may resemble symptoms of ADD, you'll also be asked to recount your history with prescription medicine.

Even medicines used to treat common ailments, such as allergies and high blood pressure, have been known to cause a patient to become confused, agitated, and distracted. Ruling out such drugs as the cause of your symptoms is important to an ADD evaluation.

Finally, many adults with ADD are found to have had a long history of self-medication—a history of using alcohol or other drugs to alleviate the symptoms of ADD. Overuse of drugs or alcohol can also result in several related problems—such as difficulty holding a job, decreased ability to sustain relationships, mood swings, and depression—that are often related to ADD as well. By tracing patterns of substance abuse, the doctor is following an important clue in his or her investigation. It is often one of the first avenues explored during the *psychological history* portion of the ADD evaluation.

Along with evaluating your history—or lack of a history—of substance abuse, your psychologist will attempt to make what is called a "differential diagnosis." As discussed, many psychological disorders, including antisocial personality disorder, anxiety, and depression, have symptoms similar to those experienced by adults with ADD. Furthermore, many adult ADD patients suffer from one or more of these conditions at the same time.

In order to discover whether or not ADD is the culprit in your case, and/or if you have another concurrent condition that may require treatment, a psychologist may ask you to take one or more standardized personality and psychological adjustment tests. The results of these tests will help your doctor determine the best and most effective course of treatment for your particular constellation of symptoms.

Finally, your doctor may suggest that you take a standardized intelligence test and some screening tests of basic areas of academic achievement (reading, spelling, and math). The results of these tests will help to further pinpoint the diagnosis, as well as uncover any hidden learning disabilities that may be contributing to your difficulties.

Determining a Diagnosis

With the information your doctor has unearthed about your past and present difficulties, medical history, and current psychological makeup, he or she should have enough information to conclude whether or not your condition meets the four criteria listed at the beginning of this section. If so, it is likely that you'll receive a diagnosis of Attention Deficit Disorder. Depending on your symptoms, your diagnosis may be further categorized as ADD, inattentive type; ADD, hyperactive/impulsive type; or ADD, combined type. At this time, you may also receive a coexisting diagnosis, such as depression, substance abuse, or learning disability, which often go along with ADD.

Later in this chapter, we'll discuss in some depth what receiving such a diagnosis may mean to you—emotionally and medically. In the meantime, it is important that you take the first step toward coming to terms with your diagnosis by finding a doctor to help you through the process.

Choosing a Doctor to Treat You

Since diagnosing adult ADD remains a relatively specialized activity, the doctor you choose to visit for an initial evaluation may or may not be the person who will treat you on an ongoing basis. Marion, for instance, continued to see her original therapist who, once apprised of Marion's underlying disorder, worked with the diagnosing psychologist on an appropriate treatment plan. Ruben, on the other hand, chose to become a patient of the psychologist who originally diagnosed him with ADD. Bonnie was diagnosed at a clinic in another part of the country, then was referred to someone closer to home for ongoing treatment.

Because ADD is a chronic condition likely to require ongoing treatment, you're going to need to find a doctor with whom you feel comfortable forming a long-term and close working relationship. As we'll discuss further in Chapter Five, "The Benefits of Therapy," the relationship you'll be forming is one of partnership, a partnership between you, your family, and your doctor. You must feel confident that the doctor understands the complex symptoms and side effects of ADD, has compassion and empathy for you and your particular difficulties, and, above all, is willing to help you meet your personal goals.

After obtaining referrals from the diagnosing doctor, your family physician, and/or a service organization like CH.A.D.D., make an appointment to discuss a treatment plan with the potential caregiver. During this first appointment, ask the doctor these important questions:

• *Do you keep up-to-date on current therapies and research advances?* The field of adult ADD research is beginning to expand, and new and more effective drugs and therapeutic strategies are being developed in laboratories and clinics across the country. If your doctor is a member of CH.A.D.D., A.D.D.A., or another ADD-related service organization, or is involved with a mental health clinic devoted to studying adult ADD, it is likely that he or she will stay as current as possible with any new developments.

• *How much time do you estimate it will take to treat my symptoms?* The right answer to this question is probably "I don't know." How long your treatment will take, and how often you should be seen, is highly variable and depends a great deal upon your symptoms, your response to medication, and whether or not you have any concurrent medical or psychological problems. Any practitioner who promises dramatic improvements in a very short time is probably not very experienced in the complexities of ADD. ADD is a chronic condition, and most adult patients benefit from some continued therapy in order to obtain or maintain significant results. At the same time, a doctor who insists on seeing you several times a week probably isn't the right doctor for you, either.

• *What do you charge for your services?* As discussed previously, this is a fair question to ask a health care practitioner before you begin treatment. A doctor should respond openly and honestly to your request for information about his or her rates and keep you posted on any changes.

Even more important than receiving satisfactory answers to the above questions is finding out if you're personally compatible with your doctor. That may sound odd, but because of the very personal and complex nature of ADD, you will have to work particularly closely with your doctor. During your first couple of appointments ask yourself the following questions:

Does your doctor:

... **seem warm and concerned about you and your situation?** Although you should never expect to become friends with your doctor—he or she must keep a certain professional distance in order to provide the best care—you will be sharing with him or her intimate details about your life. It is essential, then, that your doctor listen to you with an open mind and a kind heart, and that he or she take your concerns seriously. Take your feelings about the chemistry between the two of you seriously; it is an important element in the therapeutic process.

... **communicate in plain, easy-to-understand language?** There is perhaps nothing more frustrating—or more unnecessary—than feeling as if you and your doctor are speaking two different languages. You should feel at all times like a full partner within the doctor-patient relationship and hence free to ask questions when something doesn't make sense or when terms are used that you don't understand.

... **welcome family involvement in the course of treatment?** Without doubt, ADD is a family affair. Because the effects of the disorder touch upon everyone in an ADD patient's life, family therapy is frequently necessary to mend past wounds and create a more stable environment in the present. Your doctor should respond enthusiastically if and when family members seek to become involved in your treatment, and he or she should offer to refer them to a family therapist should they so desire.

If you are dissatisfied with your doctor's approach to any of the issues raised by the above questions, you should consider finding a new health care practitioner, one with whom you feel more comfortable. Keep in mind that deciding to change doctors should not be done lightly, especially if your doctor is particularly well qualified in the treatment of ADD and/or has been treating you for some time. On the other hand, it is unlikely that you'll make much progress in overcoming the complex and personal challenges posed by ADD if you are unhappy with the quality of your care. The road ahead is a long one, and it is important that you have confidence in your partner on your journey forward, a journey that begins the moment you hear the diagnosis.

COPING WITH AN ADD DIAGNOSIS: THE SIX STAGES

Relief and Optimism

"I just broke down and cried with relief."

"My first feeling was one of euphoria."

"I felt hopeful for the first time in years."

As these comments so aptly illustrate, the first reaction of most adults who receive a diagnosis of ADD is usually one of exquisite relief. After years of struggling with an unidentified enemy, they can finally put a name to the source of their frustration, anger, and confusion. They are not hypochondriacs, they are not suffering from a mental illness, they are not just plain stupid. There is a name and, most important, a set of solutions for the problems they've been experiencing throughout their lives.

When the diagnosis is provided by an experienced, well-informed doctor, this stage can be extended and enhanced. Ruben recalls his experience: "My doctor had it all laid out for me. He had pamphlets and Xeroxes of journal articles about ADD that I could take with me. He told me about Ritalin and about the behavior therapy that could help me gain control of my life. We created a treatment plan that I could afford. By the time I left his office, I was really motivated."

Unfortunately, these feelings of relief and optimism often give way to other emotions as the reality of ADD begins to sink in: There is no cure for ADD, no magic bullet that will once and forever solve the problems it creates, and you will be coping with its symptoms and side effects to one degree or another for the rest of your life. As Ken put it, "It is one thing to find out you have ADD and another thing to come to terms with the fact that this will be a lifelong struggle."

Although each individual will find his or her own way through the maze of emotions that accompany the diagnosis of a chronic illness, there are some general paths through the process. In fact, many psychologists see similarities between the emotional responses to a chronic illness and those described by Elisabeth Kübler-Ross related to death and dying. We tend not to respond all at once, but rather we process the information and its effects on our lives in stages.

Denial

After the initial feelings of relief and optimism, you may enter into a period of *denial*. "After a while, I decided that there was simply no such thing as ADD," says Rich. "And if there was, I certainly didn't have it. My problems were all because I lacked discipline. If I just buckled down, I wouldn't have to take medication, or go to therapy. I'd be 'normal.' "

If you're like Rich and many other of your ADD peers, you too might decide that your symptoms are caused by stress or exist only in your imagination or will simply go away with time. Not only is it often necessary to pass through this stage in order to accept the help you need to cope with ADD, denial also acts as an important coping mechanism. It allows you and your family to avoid being overwhelmed by ADD's many challenges—and opportunities—and come to grips with your diagnosis slowly over time.

Anger and Resentment

After the denial stage has initially passed, many people with ADD will experience *anger*, anger at the unfairness of the world, at the medical profession for taking so long to make a diagnosis, at all the wasted years spent in frustration. "My anger kind of crept up on me," admits Mark. "Then I just seethed. I'd been told for so long that I was just not trying hard enough or didn't care enough to succeed and then, to find out that it wasn't all my fault . . . like that was supposed to solve everything. I just wanted to go back and shove the diagnosis in the faces of everyone who had held me back in the past."

If you pass through a difficult stage of anger and resentment, keep in mind that such feelings are both natural and healthy. When directed at the appropriate enemy—ADD itself—anger can be motivating. Once you accept that no one is to blame for your condition—not you, not your doctor, not your grade-school teachers, not your parents—you can use the energy that often comes with anger to start moving forward by gathering information, involving yourself in therapy, and helping your family and friends to understand.

Grief

For many people, anger soon turns to sadness and *grief*. Some mourn the loss of time spent in frustration before the diagnosis of ADD was made. Others describe feeling depressed at the thought of having a chronic condition requiring lifelong attention. Still others grieve the loss of their former "ADD selves," even if those former selves were troubled.

"Believe it or not, I felt sorry for myself because now there was an explanation for all that had gone on," Ken says. "For most of my life, I blamed myself, I blamed my parents, I blamed society for my failures and my addictions. Finding out I had

ADD took away those old enemies, and strangely enough, I kind of missed them."

Mobilization

If you become a little sad and depressed as you come to grips with ADD, it is important that you allow yourself to experience these emotions fully, then release them and go on. Talk to your therapist about your feelings; he or she can help prevent you from falling into a full-fledged depression and steer you toward the next coping stage: *mobilization*.

Indeed, this will be the time when your original euphoria will return. You'll be eager to learn how to better manage your condition and repair the damage that has been done in the past. Marion remembers how she felt when the energy returned. "It took me about six months after I was given the diagnosis before I really dug in and decided to help myself," Marion remembers. "At the beginning, I was excited. But then I got kind of down. I still did what I was told—took medication and went to therapy—but I was just going through the motions. Suddenly, though, I just snapped awake. I realized this was my *life*, and I had to start contributing to it."

The key to keeping this feeling of optimism and strength alive is to get the help and support you need. Fortunately, there are myriad resources available to you, including doctors, nurses, hospital social workers, and fellow adult ADD patients, all of whom have invaluable information that will help you and your whole family better understand and cope with the challenges that ADD often poses.

Accommodation

There is a final stage in the coping process called *accommodation*. Accommodation, defined as the act of adjustment and acceptance, occurs when you admit that the symptoms of ADD will in all likelihood place certain limitations on your life. If ADD symptoms prevent you from sitting at a desk and concentrating on paperwork, for instance, it is unlikely that working as a legal secretary will ever be a wise career choice, even after you receive drug and/or behavioral therapy. On the other hand, if you love the law and are willing to work hard, your natural energy and creativity may allow you to become an exceptional attorney—as long as you have a meticulously organized legal secretary of your own to handle the details.

Accommodation is never an easy process. Chances are, you'll reenter one or more of the other coping stages even after you've come to accept that ADD will always be a part of your life. For that reason, most psychologists who treat adults with ADD suggest that their patients join an ADD support group. Support groups, organized by service organizations like CH.A.D.D. or through a mental health clinic, meet on a regular basis. Their members discuss common problems, form friendships, and learn coping strategies from both professional guest speakers and fellow patients. Marion, for instance, learned several techniques about organizing her office for maximum efficiency from another support group member. Bonnie strategized her way through a cocktail party with an ADD "partner" who shared her difficulties with communicating in large groups. In Chapter Five, we'll discuss the role that support groups play in the treatment process in further depth.

Now that you have received a diagnosis and are on the road to acceptance and accommodation, it's time for you to take control of the practical aspects of treatment. As we've discussed many times throughout this book, ADD is highly personal: It affects each and every person a little differently. The same can be said for treatment. Each person with ADD will require a unique treatment plan based on his or her symptoms, lifestyle, and goals for the future. In the vast majority of cases, however, a treatment plan for ADD will include the use of certain medication—either stimulants such as Ritalin or antidepressants such as Prozac—whose effects and side effects will be discussed in Chapter Four.

IMPORTANT QUESTIONS AND ANSWERS
ABOUT CHAPTER THREE

Q I've read about research involving the use of PET scans to diagnose ADD. Should my doctor give me a PET scan during my evaluation?

A The use of PET (positron emission tomography) in diagnosing ADD is still experimental. A PET scan is a sophisticated form of X ray used to evaluate brain tissue activity. The studies using the test conducted by Dr. Alan Zametkin at the National Institute of Mental Health have shown some correlation between low glucose metabolism and symptoms of ADD, but more research must be completed before this test can be considered reliable and diagnostic.

Q I was recently diagnosed with ADD by a doctor who spent just about a half hour with me. He asked me just a few questions about my current symptoms and looked at my previous medical records, but he didn't delve into my childhood at all. Is it possible that he's wrong and I don't have ADD?

A It's impossible either to assess your case without examining you and talking with you further, or to make a judgment about another doctor's methods without more information. However, it seems unlikely that an accurate diagnosis of a subtle condition such as ADD—a disorder with symptoms that are common to a number of other neurological, physical, and psychological conditions—could be made reliably in such a short time. If you feel uncomfortable about it, get a second opinion before continuing with treatment.

Q I've been told that educating the people around me about ADD will help me as I try to manage my symptoms. But I work for a very strict, by-the-numbers accounting firm and I'm not sure how my boss would take the news. I think he'd just figure I was making excuses and find a reason to fire me. What should I do?

A You're right to be concerned. There is still much that is misunderstood about ADD, its symptoms, and its treatment especially with respect to employers. Although legally your boss cannot fire you just because you have a condition like ADD, he or she may make judgments about your performance and capabilities based on faulty assumptions about how ADD is affecting you. In short, whether or not to tell your boss or your colleagues is a decision only you can make based on your knowledge of their open-mindedness and compassion and weighing the possible pros and cons. If you do decide to discuss it with them, be sure to bring along some pamphlets that explain ADD clearly and concisely. That way, they can learn about the disorder from an objective source, and know where to go for more information.

PART TWO

TREATMENT
AND
STRATEGIES
THAT WORK

Chapter Four

THE ROLE OF MEDICATION

It's only been three weeks since I started taking Ritalin, and already I feel like a whole new woman.

Medication has allowed me to concentrate on paperwork for the first time in years, perhaps for the first time in my life.

Thanks to Ritalin, I can carry on a coherent conversation with someone at a party or in a restaurant. I finally feel in control of my mouth.

All the noise, all the confusion, all of the anxiety has been muted. I can hear and see everything with so much more clarity and order. All the static is gone.

These four comments were made by patients who were recently diagnosed with ADD and were prescribed medication to help alleviate their symptoms. And they are not alone. Approximately 70 percent of adults with ADD find that their symptoms significantly and sometimes dramatically improve after they take medication prescribed by their doctors. Often for the first time in their lives, these patients claim, they are able to concentrate on difficult and time-consuming tasks, curb impulsive behavior, and/or tame the restless twitches that have plagued them in the past. And most are able to derive these benefits without experiencing any serious side effects.

Nevertheless, it is important to point out at the outset of this chapter that, as effective as medication for ADD may be, it is not a panacea or a miracle cure. First, there exists a significant minority of people—about 20 to 30 percent of all adults—for whom drug therapy appears to have little effect. Second, even those who derive significant benefits from medication find that some of the psychological and behavioral problems caused by ADD are not solved by medication alone, but require further therapy or training to resolve.

"Don't get me wrong, I'm much better with Ritalin than without it," says Ken, "but I had some serious problems—my drug and alcohol addictions, my lack of job skills—that no medication could possibly solve for me. It's going to take a bit of therapy to get past those issues, and I know I've still got a long way to go."

That said, it is time to explore what is certainly the first line of treatment among most health practitioners experienced in the field of adult ADD—medication.

ADD MEDICATION: THE RHYME AND REASON

Despite an earlier reluctance to prescribe medication to adults with ADD, researchers have come to discover that medication can be extremely effective for a majority of adult patients. In most people with ADD, problematic symptoms are improved very quickly after drug therapy is initiated. And, after two decades of extensively monitoring children's reactions, recent studies have found that the drugs used to treat ADD tend to provide enormous benefits with very few (and relatively mild) side effects in adults as well. Hence drug therapy has become the cornerstone of adult ADD treatment among most health professionals who specialize in the disorder.

Exactly how and why these medications work, however, is still the subject of much research and a fair amount of speculation. As discussed in Chapter One, the intricate workings of the human brain remain largely a mystery, even to medical scientists. Brain chemistry—the production and function of chemicals called neurotransmitters—is particularly complex, and it is only in the last few decades that researchers have learned enough about it to design drugs to treat disorders like Parkinson's disease, which involves the loss of the neurotransmitter called dopamine, and ADD, which is believed to be caused by an imbalance of several different chemicals.

Two types of drugs—each of which works to fine-tune the balance of neurotransmitters—have been found to be most effective in treating ADD. *Stimulants* are drugs that, as their name implies, stimulate or activate brain activity. Although the exact mechanism is unknown, it is believed that they work by increasing the amount of dopamine either produced in the brain or used by the frontal lobes of the brain. There are several different stimulants that may work to alleviate the symptoms of ADD, including methylphenidate (Ritalin), dextroamphetamine (Dexedrine), and pemoline (Cylert).

Although stimulants are by far the most effective medications in the treatment of ADD, some patients respond well to *antidepressants*. Antidepressants also stimulate brain activity in the frontal lobes, but they affect the production and/or use of other chemicals, usually norepinephrine and serotonin. The antidepressants considered most useful for ADD include imipramine (Tofranil), desipramine (Norpramin), bupropion (Wellbutrin), and fluoxetine hydrochloride (Prozac). Later in this chapter, we'll describe the benefits and side effects of each of these drugs in further depth.

In the end, however, all of the drugs used to treat ADD have the same goal: to provide the brain with the raw materials it needs to concentrate over a sustained period of time, control impulses, and regulate motor activity. Which drug or combination of drugs will work best for any given individual depends largely upon his or her own particular brain chemistry and constellation of symptoms. As we'll discuss below, the process of finding the right drug can be a tricky one requiring more than a little finesse and fine-tuning on the part of both physician and patient. To date, physicians are not able to accurately predict how any one individual will respond to various doses or types of ADD medication. Doctors may have to adjust their patients' medications several times.

A Treatment, Not a Cure

It should be stressed here that medication for ADD only alleviates symptoms. There is no cure for ADD: No drug that exists today attacks the underlying cause of the disorder or permanently restores the chemical balance. Once a patient stops taking Ritalin, or whatever drug performs best for him or her, the core symptoms of the disorder will return. Fortunately, it appears that stimulants in particular are quite safe and can be used for many years with relatively few side effects. Generally speaking, antidepressants are also safe when used correctly. Nevertheless, the decision to take any medication is a serious one that should be made only after you have carefully weighed the risks and benefits with your doctor.

TO MEDICATE OR NOT

Before you and your doctor conclude that taking ADD medication is right for you, discuss the following issues together:

Make sure it is safe for you to take ADD medication. "I was very worried about taking a stimulant on a regular basis," admits Ruben. "High blood pressure runs in my family, and I wasn't sure how it would affect me over the long term."

Ruben was right to be concerned. Any medication—even an over-the-counter drug—has the potential to alter your body chemistry and thus exacerbate an underlying health problem. In addition, there are certain drugs that may be dangerous when taken in combination with one another or when taken with alcohol or, in some cases, with certain kinds of food.

Before prescribing any medication for you, then, your doctor should study your medical history and check your current health status to make sure you are free of any medical condition that would be adversely affected by ADD medication. And it's up to you to tell him or her about every drug—prescription, over-the-counter, or recreational—you're taking, as well as your eating and drinking habits. Such information will allow your doctor to prescribe the safest and most effective drug regimen for you.

Be willing to form a partnership with your doctor. As discussed in Chapter Three, successful treatment for ADD requires a particularly close relationship between doctor and patient, and this is especially true with respect to devising and implementing drug therapy. Indeed, you may well find it necessary to consult with your doctor quite often during the first few months after drug therapy is initiated and then on a fairly regular basis for as long as you take medication.

Outline your goals and expectations and share them with your doctor. Although ADD may certainly affect several aspects of your personality and lifestyle at the same time, it is likely that some symptoms of the disorder trouble you more than others. Before you begin drug therapy, it can be very helpful to target those symptoms you would most like to see improve. That way, you can measure how well the medication is working by seeing how well you are able to cope with what had been your major difficulties.

"I wanted to get my office into some kind of order," Sam, the photographer, remembers. "I was tired of leaning on my assistant so much for my schedule and my correspondence.

About two weeks after I started taking Ritalin, I felt like I had some control over my professional life. Not only did I know what was going on from day to day, but I could also make definite plans for the future. I knew that the drug was working because I could see my work life beginning to change."

At the same time, taking the time to outline your goals with your doctor will provide you with an opportunity to evaluate your expectations. Some adults recently diagnosed with ADD find themselves thinking that medication will be a total cure. When their problems do not disappear overnight, they are often far too quick to give up on themselves and on the medication.

Weigh all the benefits and risks of drug treatment. In the section below, the potential physical side effects of the various drugs used to treat ADD are outlined. In the meantime, there are some emotional and practical issues you should consider when discussing with your doctor whether or not drug therapy is right for you:

Will I have to take this drug every day for the rest of my life? The truth is, the effects of medication for ADD only last as long as the drugs are in your body; in the case of Ritalin, that means you'll derive its benefits for only about three to four hours at a time. Other forms of ADD medication may last longer (antidepressants are often effective for much longer periods of time), but none "do the trick" for any sustained length of time. Most adults with ADD for whom drug treatment is successful take medication every day for many years.

However, that's not to say that taking medication has to be a rigid, unalterable matter. Although one should always follow drug prescriptions carefully, missing a dose or two of Ritalin or taking one or two extra doses should not cause any harm. In fact, many people decide with their doctors to take "drug holidays" to see how they do without any medication or otherwise alter the amount of drugs taken as circumstances dictate.

Marion, for instance, decided to take a two-month leave-of-absence from work after finishing a major campaign for one of her clients. "While I was on vacation, I just didn't feel the need to take Ritalin every day because I didn't have the same need to focus and stay prepared. My doctor told me to feel free to stop taking it altogether, then talk to him again when I wanted to go back on the drug. I felt fine the whole time."

After a year or two on Ritalin, Bonnie worked with her doctor to tailor a medication schedule that worked best for her. Now when she has a party to go to or a particularly important meeting at work to attend, she'll take an extra dose of her medication. If her day is going to be a quiet one during which she'll be alone and away from distractions, on the other hand, she often decides to skip taking any medication at all—and without experiencing any adverse side effects.

In some cases, adults with ADD decide to stop taking medication altogether, usually after spending a period of time learning new skills that the effects of medication made possible. When medication is withdrawn, they have found they have learned enough practical skills to thrive without drug therapy.

"The combination of Ritalin and Prozac kind of snapped me into focus," admits Amy. "It lifted my depression and, at the same time, helped me to concentrate and relax a little. I worked with a fantastic therapist who helped me to build some communication skills and get my finances and professional life organized. Over a period of about four or five months of real success in holding things together, I asked my doctor if I could stop taking medication. He said sure. I haven't felt the need to go back to it yet. But I am glad to know it's there."

As these examples show, drug therapy for ADD is often a give-and-take, trial-and-error affair and it is often necessary for you and your doctor to experiment a bit in order to find a dosage level and schedule that works best for you.

Will taking ADD medication make me a drug addict? Many people worry that stimulants and antidepressants are addictive.

Although it is true that all drugs have side effects and some have the potential to be abused, medications typically used for ADD are generally safe and nonaddictive. The stimulants, for example, tend to be quite short-acting (in and out of your body in a matter of a few hours) and, when taken as prescribed, do not cause feelings of euphoria or intoxication that could become psychologically addictive. Again, address any questions you may have about medication to your doctor.

What if I have a substance abuse problem? Many adults with ADD first visit a mental health professional because they suffer from drug or alcohol addiction. Depending on the severity of your addiction, your general health, and other considerations, your doctor may decide that you must cope with your dependence before you begin therapy to treat ADD. In our clinic at the University of Massachusetts Medical Center, we generally suggest that a patient with a clear substance abuse addiction get treatment for this problem first, and then come in for an ADD evaluation after six months of sobriety. Only then are we able to make a definitive ADD diagnosis. In fact, once the addiction problems are alleviated, some patients find that their ADD symptoms have improved or disappeared as well.

On the other hand, if the substance abuse problem is relatively mild and the patient appears to be self-medicating in an attempt to alleviate his or her symptoms of ADD, we may decide to treat the ADD with medication and recommend psychotherapy to help eliminate their substance abuse. As is true for so much about ADD, decisions like this one are highly dependent on individual circumstances and can only be made after a careful psychological and physical examination is performed.

What if I have a coexisting condition such as depression, anxiety, or obsessive-compulsive disorder? Your doctor will attempt to target a drug that will best serve all of your needs, but depending on your symptoms, you may need to take more than one type of medication. Certain combinations of medications have been found to be useful in treating ADD and other psychological problems at the same time. If you do take more than one drug, it is particularly important that you inform all the health professionals you visit about the medication you have been prescribed.

Taking Charge

Again, the most important point to keep in mind as you think about these matters is that the decision to take medication—today, tomorrow, and in the future—rests with you and you alone. If there ever comes a time when you feel, for whatever reason, that medication is not right for you, then by all means let your doctor know. Unless he or she believes that your health would be seriously impaired—for instance, if you were in the depths of a major depression—it is likely that he or she would quickly accede to your wishes.

The good news, of course, is that it is very likely you'll benefit a great deal from taking medication for ADD and experience few if any side effects. However, before you decide to take any drug, you should take the time to learn as much as you can about its specific effects and potential side effects. By doing so, you'll be better prepared to monitor how the drug works for you once you start taking it. At the same time that your doctor provides you with a prescription, he or she should take some time to describe how the drugs are supposed to work, when to expect to experience results, and what to look for in terms of possible side effects. Listen carefully and take notes on what you hear. Read all informational material provided by your doctor or that comes with the prescription itself, and follow the directions carefully. Always remember that you have a right to know everything about the drugs you take and their expected effects and side effects.

In the meantime, here are short descriptions of the most

commonly, and most successfully, used drugs to treat ADD (see Table 4A). These descriptions are meant only to give you a general idea of the way the medication works and what to watch for in terms of side effects. How you'll be affected will depend on a host of factors, including your unique body chemistry and treatment goals. In general, you and your doctor have three options when attempting to minimize these side effects: Change the dosage, alter the schedule, or switch to another drug. As stated, about 70 percent of adults with ADD at our clinic find that their symptoms improve with medication, but finding the right drug in the proper dosage can be a challenge. Fortunately, there are at least three stimulants, several antidepressants, and several other types of medication to try.

TABLE 4A A Quick Look at the More Common ADD Drugs

Name	Dosages	Benefits	Possible Side Effects
Ritalin (methyl-phenidate) [stimulant]	5, 10, and 20 mg pills, each lasting about 4 hours; 20 mg sustained-release pills lasting about 7 hours	improved concentration; reduced restlessness and impulsivity	short-lasting; difficulty sleeping, decreased appetite, irritability; not recommended for those with motor tics or family history of Tourette's Syndrome
Dexedrine (dextro-amphetamine) [stimulant]	5 mg liquid and tablets, each lasting 3 to 4 hours; 5, 10, and 15 mg sustained-release capsules, each lasting 8 to 10 hours	improves same symptoms as Ritalin	high doses can lead to decreased appetite, difficulty sleeping, irritability, headache, stomachache

Cylert (pemoline) [stimulant]	18.75, 37.5 or 75 mg tablets, each lasting 12 to 24 hours	improves same symptoms as Ritalin; long-lasting; taken only once per day	same as other stimulants; also may interfere with liver function; should not be taken by anyone with hepatic or renal problems
Norpramin (desipramine) & Tofranil [antidepressants]	10 to 300 mg a day 50 to 150 mg a day	both alleviate impulsivity and hyperactivity; long-lasting	may cause dizziness, high blood pressure, dry mouth, constipation, sleepiness; can be fatal if taken in large amounts
Prozac [antidepressant]	20 mg capsules; usually 20 to 40 mg a day	controls impulsive behavior and feelings of restlessness and agitation; helpful for those with low-grade depression	diarrhea, anxiety, drowsiness, weight loss, and insomnia

NOTE: All of these drugs are affected if other drugs are being taken simultaneously. Please read the appropriate sections in this chapter carefully and be sure to talk to your doctor about any medications (over-the-counter or prescription) that you are taking.

A GUIDE TO DRUGS USED FOR ADD

Stimulants

Stimulants are the most common drugs used to treat the symptoms of ADD. They act upon neurotransmitters to activate or stimulate the central nervous system, primarily the frontal lobes of the brain. Stimulants tend to help improve focus and attention, and may also help to reduce hyperactivity and impulsivity.

All stimulants have the same set of potential *side effects*. Some patients complain of feeling nauseous or headachy at the outset of treatment, but find that these side effects pass within a few days. Others find that their appetites are suppressed and/or that they have difficulty sleeping. In our experience, however, these side effects are quite rare. More common, especially if the stimulant dosage is too high, are feelings of nervousness, agitation, and anxiety. In rare cases, increased heart rate and high blood pressure can result with the use of stimulants, especially if the patient has an underlying predisposition toward hypertension.

Ritalin: The most widely prescribed drug used to treat ADD in both children and adults, Ritalin appears to work by stimulating the production of the neurotransmitter dopamine. The benefits of Ritalin include improved concentration and reduced distractibility and disorganization.

Dosage: Ritalin is available in 5, 10, and 20 milligram pills. Each dose generally lasts about four hours and hence must be taken several times a day in order to provide continuous symptom relief. A typical schedule might be one 10 mg dose just before breakfast, another before lunch, and a third during the late afternoon. (Most patients find it helpful to take Ritalin about thirty minutes before meals). This schedule can be revised as one's needs dictate. Some patients, for instance, prefer to take a fourth 5 mg dose with dinner if they are working in the evening or have social obligations. Others require a higher or lower dosage throughout the day. Ritalin 20 SR (sustained-release) is a long-acting form of the drug that lasts up to eight hours. The sustained-release formula tends to have a less even and predictable effect on some patients who take it, however.

Special Considerations: In some patients, Ritalin is metabolized so quickly that its effects are fleeting, in which case another stimulant, such as Dexedrine or Cylert, should be considered. Another common complaint resulting from its fast-acting nature is called the "rebound effect." Some patients find that as the drug wears off, they feel especially edgy and distracted until the next dose kicks in. The rebound effect can be minimized, usually by taking smaller doses of Ritalin more often during the day.

Drug Contraindications: If Ritalin is taken with certain other drugs, the effects of either could be increased, decreased, or altered in some way. Check with your doctor if you take any of the following medications:

MAO inhibitors (antidepressants such as Nardil, Parnate, and Marplan)
Anticoagulants (such as Coumadin)
Anticonvulsants (such as Dilantin or Tegretol)
Tricyclic antidepressants (such as Tofranil and Norpramin)

Dexedrine: This drug acts to stimulate frontal lobe activity by helping the brain make the most out of available dopamine (unlike Ritalin, which acts to increase dopamine production). Although Dexedrine appears to work in a slightly different way than Ritalin, it helps to improve the same symptoms, primarily the distractibility and agitation common to many adults with ADD. Dexedrine is considered to have a greater potential for abuse than Ritalin.

Dosage: Dexedrine is available in liquid, tablet, or sustained-release capsule form. The liquid and tablet forms are given in 5 milligram doses that last about three to four hours. Long-acting capsules in 5, 10, or 15 milligram strengths last from eight to ten hours. Generally speaking, adults require a little more than half as much Dexedrine as they do Ritalin. A typical schedule might involve three 5 milligram doses five hours apart starting first thing in the morning.

Special Considerations: The common side effects of Dexedrine are similar to those of Ritalin. Most of them are short-lived and those that are not are usually dose-related. Too much

Dexedrine in the system can lead to decreased appetite, difficulty sleeping, and excessive restlessness or irritability. Rapid heartbeat and high blood pressure may also result and should be monitored carefully throughout treatment with the drug. Some patients may experience nausea, dry mouth, diarrhea, or dizziness. If these side effects persist for more than a few days, contact your doctor immediately.

Drug Contraindications: There are a host of drugs that can interfere with the action of Dexedrine. It is extremely important that you advise your doctor about all drugs—prescription or over-the-counter—you are taking. Among those medications requiring special attention when combined with Dexedrine are the following:

> Antipsychotics (such as Haldol, Thorazine, and Lithium)
> Diuretics (such as Diuril and Reserpine)
> Antiseizure medication (such as Dilantin)
> Narcotics (particularly Darvon and Demerol)

Cylert: Specifically designed to treat ADD in children, Cylert appears to have the same beneficial effects in adults. Like Ritalin and Dexedrine, Cylert works best to decrease distractibility and restlessness. Because it is very long-acting (twelve to twenty-four hours), it need be taken only once a day and there is rarely any rebound effect.

Dosage: Cylert is available as an 18.75, 37.5, or 75 milligram tablet. Most patients take one tablet a day of either strength.

Special Considerations: The long-acting nature of Cylert has its advantages and disadvantages. On the plus side, Cylert produces sustained symptom relief and requires only one dose a day. What this means, however, is that the dosage and the schedule cannot be altered as often as they can with either Ritalin or Dexedrine. In rare cases, Cylert can cause liver function or kidney problems. Therefore, periodic liver function tests are recommended when using Cylert.

Drug Contraindications: Talk to your doctor before you combine any of the following drugs with Cylert:

Antiseizure medications (such as Tegretol)
Stimulants (including Ritalin and Dexedrine)

Antidepressants

Antidepressants, like stimulants, work to restore a proper balance of neurotransmitters in the brain, thereby allowing messages about concentration and behavior to be properly delivered and received. They do so by acting to increase the available amount of the neurotransmitters serotonin and/or norepinephrine.

There are three major classes of antidepressants—tricyclic antidepressants, SSRI's (often referred to as serotonin reuptake inhibitors), and MAO (monoamine oxidase) inhibitors. Antidepressants are often chosen for ADD patients who experience adverse side effects from stimulant medication or who have concurrent depression, anxiety, or another mood disorder.

Each type of antidepressant has its own set of actions and potential side effects. However, all remain active in your system for twenty-four hours or longer, thereby alleviating the need to take several doses of medication during the day or experiencing any rebound effect. Some patients find the long-acting nature of antidepressants a boon; others prefer to have more control over when and how much medication is in their system.

In general, the side effects of antidepressant medication include dry mouth (decreased saliva), excessive sleepiness, appetite suppression, and constipation. Like those experienced with stimulant medication, these side effects are generally short-lived and mild. Antidepressants should be taken with caution if you have a heart condition or high blood pressure, as these conditions may be exacerbated.

Norpramin and Tofranil: These are two common tricyclic antidepressants prescribed to ADD patients today. Tricyclic antidepressants appear to work by readjusting the level and use of the neurotransmitters norepinephrine and serotonin. Because norepinephrine is a powerful chemical that works on several other systems of the body, tricyclic antidepressants can cause some annoying side effects, such as dizziness and high blood pressure.

Dosages: The usual dosage for Norpramin to treat depression is about 100 to 200 milligrams a day. However, some patients with ADD have had success by taking a much lower dose—about 10 to 30 milligrams a day; others find that a higher dose of 75 to 300 milligrams is effective. With Tofranil, the daily dosage for ADD usually ranges from about 50 to 150 milligrams. Both drugs come in tablet form.

Special Considerations: Both Norpramin and Tofranil can be fatal if taken in large amounts, so it is essential to follow the prescription to the letter. Because these drugs can build up in your system, your doctor may perform periodic blood tests to measure the level of the drugs in your body. In addition, they may have a tendency to make you a little sleepy, especially when you first start taking them, so it is recommended that you do not drive until you are sure of how the drug will affect you. People who take antidepressants known as MAO inhibitors (see below) should not under any circumstances take tricyclic antidepressants at the same time.

Drug Contraindications: Taking any drug in combination with another can cause the action of either or both to be altered, sometimes in a dangerous way. The following drugs, among others, are particularly problematic when taken with tricyclic antidepressants:

Anticholinergics (such as Cogentin)
MAO inhibitors (such as Marplan, Nardil, and Parnate)
Sedatives (such as Halcion and Valium)
Antianxiety medications (such as Xanax)
Decongestants (such as Sudafed)
Thyroid medications (such as Synthroid)
Ulcer medications (such as Tagamet)
Other antidepressants (such as Prozac)

Prozac: Prozac (fluoxetine hydrochloride) is a relatively new antidepressant that works by increasing the amount of the neurotransmitter serotonin. Unlike other antidepressants, however, Prozac does not affect the action of norepinephrine and hence tends to cause fewer side effects than other types of antidepressants do. Prozac can be useful in helping ADD patients control impulsive behavior and feelings of restlessness and agitation, although research on Prozac and ADD remains largely anecdotal. ADD patients with concurrent low-grade depression are often treated with Prozac in combination with Ritalin.

Dosage: Prozac comes in 10-milligram and 20-milligram capsules. Most patients take one 20-milligram capsule a day, usually in the morning, although some prefer a second dose in midafternoon.

Special Considerations: There has been a great deal of publicity about Prozac, including highly exaggerated reports about its potential to cause violent or suicidal behavior. Further research has shown that this is an extremely rare side effect, but careful monitoring by a health professional is necessary with this and all prescription drugs. Diarrhea, anxiety, drowsiness, weight loss, agitation, and insomnia are among the most reported side effects of Prozac. As is true for the other drugs used to treat ADD, these side effects are usually short-lived. If they persist, your doctor will most likely attempt to treat you with one of the other drugs.

Drug Contraindications: Talk with your doctor about taking Prozac in combination with any medication. Among those that may cause difficulties are the following:

MAO inhibitors (such as Parnate, Nardil, Marplan)
Sedatives (such as Valium and Halcion)
Anticoagulants (such as Coumadin)
Other antidepressants (such as Elavil)

In addition to those drugs outlined above, there are several others that have been used in the treatment of ADD when other medical or psychological problems are present. Tegretol (Carbamazepine) is an anticonvulsant drug that may also relieve ADD symptoms in those patients who suffer with epilepsy or

other seizure disorders. An antihypertensive drug called Cloni-
dine (Catapres) is especially helpful for those ADD patients
who also have Tourette's Syndrome and/or are particularly aggressive or highly impulsive. It may also be an option for people
unable to take stimulants and for whom antidepressants do
not alleviate ADD symptoms. Two antidepressants, bupropion
(Wellbutrin) and nortriptyline (Pamelor) have also proven useful in the treatment of ADD. The drug Anafranil (Clomipram-
ine) appears to be helpful for ADD adults who also suffer from
obsessive-compulsive disorder. Finally, a new drug is now being
developed specifically to treat ADD. Called ADDeral, this medication is a combination of Dexedrine and Ritalin and is designed
to be longer-acting than others currently in use.

Before taking any medication, make sure your doctor knows
if you are:

- pregnant or are intending to become pregnant
- breastfeeding
- taking any other prescription medications
- using any over-the-counter or illegal drugs
- drinking alcohol in any amount

No matter what medication or combination of medications
you are prescribed, take the time to learn as much as you can
about the effects, side effects, and intended actions. You're the
only one who can tell how the medication makes you feel or
how well it acts to alleviate your symptoms, and it's up to you
to report those feelings to your doctor.

We have emphasized the intensely individualistic nature
of ADD. Because each of us has a different body chemistry and
physical makeup, and because each person with ADD suffers
from a different combination of symptoms, treating ADD with
medication often takes a trial-and-error approach. In the following section, we'll discuss some of the most common issues and
strategies involved in successful ADD drug therapy.

⌐ MEDICATION MANAGEMENT

Trial and error. Hit or miss. Patience. Perseverance. Dedication. Open communication. These words and phrases are among those heard most often by adults who use medication as part of their treatment for ADD. Indeed, drug therapy for ADD remains a highly imperfect science, one that requires energy and commitment from both doctors and their patients.

That said, it is worth repeating that medication has proved to be very successful in alleviating the symptoms of ADD for a majority of adult patients. Most people are happy to say that coping with some mild side effects and/or trying out a few different drugs or drug dosages is a small price to pay for the benefits medication ultimately provides. And, because so many adults with ADD have been willing to share their experiences with other patients and their doctors, some effective medication management strategies have been, and continue to be, developed.

"My life was saved at a support group meeting, or at least it felt that way at the time," says Marion. "I had such a hard time remembering that I was supposed to take medication four times a day—in order to improve my memory, ironically enough! The first couple of weeks were very erratic. I'd forget to take one in the morning, or I'd forget the second dose if I had to prepare for a business lunch. Then, at a support group meeting, someone told me that they used a watch with a timer that went off every time a dose was due. So simple, really, but I never knew about it. I haven't missed a dose—or a support group meeting—since."

Here are some other tips and hints for managing your ADD medication:

Keep a drug diary: Many patients keep a daily diary of symptoms and side effects to help them evaluate the effects of their ADD medication (See Table 4B, page 96). Whenever you experience a symptom or side effect, write it down in a notebook,

TABLE 4B A Sample Drug Diary Entry

Symptom	Date & Time	Last Dose of Medication Taken . . .	Sleep Problems? (yes/no)	External Stressors? (yes/no)	Last meal was . . .
irritability	1/5/95 8:00 a.m.	6:00 a.m.	yes	no	7:00 a.m. (cereal, coffee)
Notes:	tossed and turned all night				
Notes:					

noting the time of day it occurred, when the last dose of medication was taken, and any other details that might be relevant, including when and what you last ate, how you slept the night before, and what kind of external stress you were under at the time. Then you'll have a complete record of events to show your doctor, who will appreciate this information when assessing how drug therapy is working for you.

Mark, whom you met earlier, monitored his drug therapy very carefully, especially when he first started taking Ritalin. "I had a few rough months with Ritalin," Mark remembers. "Just two days after I started taking it, I called my doctor to complain about stomachaches and feeling jittery. He told me to give it a couple more days. Sure enough, I felt better. But after a few more weeks, I felt like the drug wasn't working as well. At my next appointment, my doctor upped the dosage a bit. But then I felt anxious and had trouble sleeping."

After Mark's doctor suggested that he keep a drug diary, Mark noted that his medication tended to "kick in" about thirty to forty-five minutes after he took it, and its effects lasted about three hours. He and his doctor decided to try this approach: Instead of waiting four hours to take the next dose, Mark took a slightly lower dose of Ritalin every three hours and took the last dose at 6 P.M. instead of 8 P.M.

"That seemed to do the trick," Mark reports, "but then I got tired of having to take a pill so often. We're now looking into a sustained-release form of Ritalin, since that drug tends to last longer."

Mark's experience not only shows how useful keeping a drug diary can be, it also illustrates the second tenet of successful medication management:

Be patient and flexible: By taking ADD medication, you are working to reestablish a proper balance of neurotransmitters in your brain. Needless to say, that is a difficult and often unpredictable enterprise that requires a great deal of finesse on the part of your doctor and, unfortunately, a great deal of patience on your part.

"I couldn't believe it," Rich admits. "Finally, someone told me that what I had been feeling all these years was real. And that there was medication that would most likely help me. But then it turned out that I couldn't tolerate Ritalin—it made me even more hyper—and Norpramin put me to sleep. I was so frustrated, I felt like screaming. Finally, we gave Prozac a shot and, though it isn't perfect, it has calmed me down enough to allow me to focus more and relax a little. I can finally get something done at the office, and my wife tells me I'm much easier to be around."

Like Rich, you may find that you need a little patience and perseverance, especially at the beginning of drug therapy. That's why good communication is essential.

Communicate with your doctor and with fellow ADD patients: We've already discussed the medical necessity of maintaining an honest, forthright dialogue with your physician. By telling him or her about your symptoms and side effects— those that are minor as well as the more serious ones—you'll be able to work together to find the most effective drug and drug schedule for you. By talking with your fellow ADD sufferers, you can learn techniques and tips that will help you better manage all aspects of ADD, including drug therapy.

In fact, what you're bound to learn—from fellow patients, from your doctor, and from your own experience—is that no matter how successful drug treatment may be, you'll still face emotional and practical challenges as a result of having ADD. Which brings us to the final tip to keep in mind about drug therapy for ADD:

Understand the limits of medication: The men and women quoted earlier describe the remarkable and positive effects of medication on the symptoms of ADD. As millions of Americans across the country can certainly attest, Ritalin, Dexedrine, Prozac, and other drugs can change one's day-to-day life in often dramatic ways. Suddenly, people are able to spend two hours paying bills instead of putting the task off until creditors are at the door. Suddenly, they can communicate in an honest and intimate way with their spouses instead of flipping from one subject to another, snapping, or clamming up altogether. Finally, they can attend the symphony without fidgeting throughout the evening.

As terrific as you're bound to feel if you meet with similar success, however, you should be aware that you face other challenges—challenges that drug therapy alone will not allow you to meet. Remember, you have struggled for many years with the symptoms of ADD without even knowing your enemy had a name. Your sense of self-esteem may be scarred, you may have learned bad habits to compensate for your condition, or you may have damaged relationships that you wish to repair. To deal with these issues and many others related to ADD, you may decide to seek further counseling from a therapist. In Chapter Five, we'll outline for you the many types of therapy available and help you sort out your own goals for counseling and how best to reach them.

IMPORTANT QUESTIONS AND ANSWERS ABOUT CHAPTER FOUR

Q My husband takes Ritalin to alleviate his symptoms of ADD. For a while, he took two doses a day, but now he takes one only if he has something really important that takes a lot of concentration, such as doing our taxes or attending an important meeting at work. Is it okay to take medication so sporadically?

A In the case of Ritalin, most people gain maximum benefit from taking it on a regular basis. However, there is no harm in varying your schedule and taking it only at times that are particularly challenging or stressful to you. Your husband should be sure that his doctor is aware of and has approved his medication schedule, however.

Q I'm a forty-eight-year-old man who has had two mild heart attacks. I was recently diagnosed with ADD and my doctor put me on a relatively low dose of Ritalin. But I know it's a stimulant. Am I putting myself at increased risk of another heart attack?

A This is clearly a question for your own physician and/or cardiologist. However, anyone with a serious, concurrent medical condition should work very carefully with his or her doctor before taking any medication. Make sure that your doctor has full access to your medical records and is well aware of any other medication you are taking for your heart problem or any other condition.

Q I take Dexedrine to treat my symptoms of ADD. I find that it works much better on some days than others and I'm not sure why. Is that normal?

A Both the symptoms of ADD and the drugs that are used to treat them tend to have different effects on every individual. Indeed, some variability is common and may stem from different emotional and environmental factors. If your experience with Dexedrine is so unpredictable that it keeps you from being productive, talk to your doctor. There is probably another drug that will work more consistently for you.

Chapter Five

THE
BENEFITS
OF THERAPY

Knowledge Is Power. As common as that adage may have become, it remains an essential truth. The more we know—about ourselves, about the world around us, about the situations in which we find ourselves—the better able we are to meet life's demands and attain our personal goals. A related sentiment is the old Boy Scout motto, Be Prepared. Once we have an understanding of the challenges we face, it's up to each of us to gather the tools we need to meet those challenges and flourish to the best of our abilities. Psychological therapy, led by a trained health professional with experience in treating the behavioral side effects of ADD, is one of the best and most useful tools available.

When an adult is diagnosed with ADD, the first adage—Knowledge Is Power—is satisfied, perhaps for the first time in that person's life. Questions long unanswered—about potential, about ability, and about the invisible barrier that has kept him or her from success—are now resolved. A truer picture of the self emerges from the confusion and the chaos that had reigned for so long. Suddenly, the terrain of the future is a bit clearer, and with this knowledge, an adult with ADD can begin to prepare him- or herself for what lies ahead.

In Chapter Four, you read about one of the most important tools in the treatment of ADD: medication. For most ADD patients, drug therapy represents a first and often major step on the journey forward. The effects of medication help many patients to absorb the vast amount of information that comes with a diagnosis of ADD, as well as to begin the skill-building process. In some cases, medication remains the single most important agent of change and growth for an adult with ADD.

Because Medication Is Rarely Enough

A majority of ADD adults require other tools and guidance systems in order to navigate successfully through this new terrain. For one thing, the burden of the past often hinders their progress, and help is needed to relieve the disappointment, frustration, and nagging sense of self-doubt that often weighs upon them. Some arrive at this threshold suffering from low-grade depression or anxiety, others with a dependence on alcohol or drugs, and most with low self-esteem and feelings of helplessness or even hopelessness.

"For me, medication was a double-edged sword," Amy says. "I was thrilled that Prozac lifted the cloud that had covered me for so long and, later, Ritalin helped me to better focus on the day-to-day business that needed to get done. But with that cloud cover gone, I was left facing my feelings, my *real* feelings, for the first time. I felt all the hurt I'd been avoiding, all the shame that had festered inside. And, on the positive side, I felt hope that things were going to change. I knew I could do it, but I realized I'd need a little help along the way."

Sam's challenges were far more practical in nature. "Although I felt frustrated a lot about my career and some financial issues, I've always been a pretty happy guy. So I didn't really need much emotional support. Thanks to Ritalin, I knew I *could* focus on my business plan, scheduling, billing, etc., but I simply didn't know how because I'd never done it before. I needed someone to show me how."

Both Amy and Sam decided to pursue further therapy once they received their ADD diagnoses, but for two completely different reasons. Amy had substantial emotional and psychological wounds to heal, while Sam wanted to concentrate on behavior strategies and skill building. In fact, all of the people we've introduced in this book have sought out some form of therapy, each for his or her own unique reasons and at different stages of the treatment process.

Mark, for instance, was so impressed with the effects of Ritalin that he believed medication could be the complete answer to all of his problems. "Within a year of taking my first dose of Ritalin, I earned enough credits to graduate from college—after trying for almost fourteen years. I thought I was in control. But I still had these mood swings when flashes of anger would overwhelm me. I still found it hard to sit and talk about my feelings with my wife. Finally, I went back and asked my doctor to suggest a family therapist for me and my wife to see."

Ken sought continued treatment for his alcohol and drug dependencies, Bonnie visited a counselor who helped sort out her problems with intimacy, and Ruben took advantage of the services offered by a vocational counselor. As these examples show, every person with ADD has different needs and priorities. Some people find that they can handle the issues that arise by themselves, with just a little guidance from their diagnosing doctors. Others have problems and challenges they feel should be handled with help from another trained professional.

Later in this chapter, we'll outline some of the types of therapy considered most useful to an adult with ADD. In the meantime, it may be helpful to explore the deeper purposes and benefits of the therapeutic process, no matter what shape or form that process takes.

DEFINING THE GOALS OF THERAPY

Therapy for ADD really begins at the moment of diagnosis, when you learn the name of the condition with which you have suffered so long. In fact, the primary aim of therapy is to help patients fully understand the disorder and how it manifests itself in their lives. From this knowledge stems all other benefits and goals of treatment. By learning as much as you can about the disorder—from your doctor, from pamphlets and articles, and from books like this one—you will be able to trace the effects the disorder has had on your past and in your present. And with every piece of knowledge about ADD that you acquire, the more capable you become of changing the behaviors or circumstances you dislike and enhancing your strengths and assets.

A second and most crucial part of the education process involves informing those around you about the disorder and its effects. Just like you, family members, friends, employers, and colleagues have been playing roles in the drama called ADD without ever being aware of it. Explaining how the disorder may have affected your relationships will go a long way in repairing any past damage as well as paving the way to a more stable, fruitful future.

Reframing the Past and Erasing Negative Messages

Another benefit derived from knowing as much as possible about ADD is that you are able to *reframe the past* in a more positive and realistic light. You now understand that you were not totally responsible for the problems you had in grammar school and that your junior high school teacher was wrong when he called you "incorrigible and mean-spirited." Your spotty employment record has had far more to do with a neurobiological problem than with your attitude or aptitude. You are not, in fact, unlovable or unable to give love, you simply have to work at finding and sustaining intimacy in a different way than most other people.

During your course of education and therapy for ADD, you'll discover more and more about how the disorder may have affected your past behavior, decision making, and resulting circumstances. As you do so, you'll hopefully find yourself able to *erase negative messages* left to you by your parents, teachers, employers, lovers, and friends. If you're like most adults with ADD, you've made a kind of internal tape of all the criticisms, reprimands, and disparagements made about you by others, and you've been replaying them again and again. You hear them every time you start a new project or relationship, every time you forget to attend a meeting or pay a bill, every time you dream a new dream of success.

"Whenever I miss a deadline, I hear my father yelling—not at me, but at my mother—about how lazy and unmotivated I am," confesses journalist Rich. "Mind you, he yelled those things when I was only seven or eight years old, but I've never forgotten them. I cringe when I think how much they might have held me back. But now it really helps to hear them for what they were: the frustrated rantings of a father who didn't know what was wrong with his son. Although I understand that on an intellectual level, I still have a hard time forgiving him or trusting him. But I'm trying."

In attempting to heal the breach between him and his father, Rich has had to learn new communication skills and strategies that have served him well in many other aspects of his life. "The Ritalin and the counseling combined have made a huge difference in my personal life," Rich says. "You could see it first in my work, of course, but then when my relationship with my father became an issue, my counselor helped me find new ways to talk to him. For the first time, I could stop myself from saying something that would get us into a fight. I could slow down and explain what I really meant to say. And these same techniques worked when I went to ask my boss for a raise. I didn't get one, but at least I asked for one in the right way!"

The Retraining Process

What Rich has begun to do is to *retrain* himself, a process sure to become an integral part of your therapy for ADD. Retraining involves several steps. The first requires you to "unlearn" some of the behaviors and thought processes that have held you back in the past. Whether that includes stuffing bills in the back of a drawer because you can't sit down long enough to pay them, the way Marion often did, or snapping at people with whom you're trying to communicate, the way Rich did, it is likely that you have one or more patterns of behavior that need to be deconstructed and rejected.

The second step consists of developing new, more effective skills and behaviors. With help from any number of professionals, including psychologists, stress management experts, time management consultants, and career counselors, you can now move forward into the next phase of life equipped with the right tools to meet the challenges ahead.

"I know it sounds silly," Marion admits. "But instead of going into long-term therapy, I simply hired someone to come into my house and really *organize* it, then teach me how to maintain some order. Ritalin was getting me to think more clearly than ever before, but I felt overwhelmed by the piles of confusion I'd collected. So I hired a woman who helped me rearrange my closets, straighten out my desk drawers, and set up a kind of filing system for bills and papers that made it easy to see what needed attention and when. She wrote everything down so clearly that even I could follow it. I then had her come in and do my office. I made some mistakes, but after a while I got the hang of it."

Indeed, all the other steps in the retraining process can be summed up in one word: *practice*. As we'll emphasize in Chapters Seven and Eight, new skills cannot be learned overnight and improvements are bound to be made in fits and starts rather than in a smooth progression. As you begin the retraining process, it is important to anticipate setbacks and disappointments. Over time, however, your goal will be to create successful new behavior patterns that become an automatic part of your daily life.

"Sure, there would be times when I'd scrawl a phone number on a scrap of paper and lose it almost immediately," says Marion. "But more often than not, I'd pick up my notebook and write it down in its appropriate place. After a couple of months, I never went anywhere without my book in hand. It really worked for me."

Building Self-Esteem

Every time you learn a new skill and, especially, every time such a skill results in success, the more your sense of empowerment and accomplishment will increase. To *build self-esteem*, then, is another goal—and ultimate benefit—of ADD therapy. We've already discussed the many ways that one's spirit may be crushed by a lifetime of struggling against an unseen enemy such as ADD. If you persevere in your journey forward, you'll eventually be able to replace those negative messages of failure, guilt, and self-blame with ones that speak of achievement, mastery, and potential.

If you haven't been able to do so before, your improved sense of self-esteem may allow you to better emphasize the positive aspects of ADD. With proper skills training, you may find yourself better able to turn what might have been perceived as biting sarcasm into sparkling wit, scattered thinking into creative brainstorming, dangerous risk taking into a love of great adventure. The truth is, no matter how much therapy— psychological or drug-related—you receive, ADD will always be a part of your life. You'll always have an ADD brain which, if you learn to cope properly, may become a significant asset instead of a shameful drawback.

Setting Realistic Goals

Which brings us to the ultimate benefit of receiving therapy for ADD: learning to *set realistic goals*. No matter where in the process of self-discovery you find yourself or what kind of impediments you have faced, you must finally come to terms with who you really are and what you have to offer. As discussed, there remains no cure for ADD; as effective as medication may be, you may still experience some difficulties caused by the disorder. Sometimes it will be possible to match your skills with your ambitions, and sometimes you must amend your dreams to correspond with your abilities.

Back in Chapter Three, we referred to this stage of the coping process as "accommodation." Learning about ADD and its effects on the way you think and behave is an important part of accommodation. Working with your doctor and/or with a host of other professionals experienced with ADD, you'll be in a position to recognize and promote your strengths and learn to compensate for your flaws.

CHOOSING A THERAPEUTIC APPROACH

Until recently, the idea of psychotherapy of any kind seemed to go against the grain of most Americans. Unless you suffered from a serious mental or emotional illness, you should be able to pull yourself up by your bootstraps and get on with your life—or so the Puritan work ethic upon which this country was founded prescribed. Even today, some of us remain influenced by this kind of thinking.

Starting in about the 1970s, though, it became clear that many individuals could benefit from counseling for less severe and far more practical challenges. At the same time, new schools of therapy arose, offering a wide variety of approaches to, and techniques for, learning, self-awareness, and growth. Slowly but surely, the concept of helping yourself by accepting help from others has become more and more accepted.

All of this is good news for adult ADD patients searching for ways to gain control over the disorder and the effects it has on their lives. Although there remains a serious shortage of health professionals trained in the complexities of ADD in adults, the opportunities to secure the help you need to meet your particular challenges are more numerous than ever before. Fortunately, as more becomes known about the adult ADD syndrome, even more specific therapies and techniques are sure to be developed. For now, the main options open to you include:

- individual counseling
- group therapy
- family therapy/marriage counseling
- vocational counseling.

Within these larger categories exists a wide range of approaches and services from which you can choose. In order to decide what kind of help you need, you and your doctor should target the symptoms you most want to alleviate, just as you did while determining a course of drug therapy. With this information, you will be better prepared to find the right therapeutic approach and the right therapist for your needs.

Below is a brief overview of the many types of therapy available to you. If you're interested in one or more of these options, discuss the matter with your doctor.

Individual Counseling

For a variety of reasons, one-on-one sessions with a psychologist, social worker, or psychiatrist can be of enormous benefit to an adult with ADD. First, many adults with ADD are genuinely helped simply by being able to talk about their problem with a professional who truly understands them.

"No kidding, all my doctor had to do was nod at me and say, 'I know what you mean,' and I felt better," says 34-year-old Ben. "I'd been to a lot of other doctors who didn't have a clue as to what was going on, and I always felt more misunderstood and miserable when I left. When I finally met someone who really knew what was going on, it was such a powerful experience. All I wanted to do was talk and have him listen. And that's what we did for a while. For three or four sessions, he just let me vent for most of the hour, and then we'd get down to figuring out what I could do about all my frustrations."

In many cases, adult ADD patients find that a few intensive sessions with their diagnosing doctors, followed by regular "checkups" every month or two, provide enough support and guidance for their needs. During the first appointments, they receive information about ADD, are evaluated for drug therapy, outline their goals, and work through some strategies to meet them. Follow-up meetings monitor progress, readjust medication, add or alter treatment approaches, and work on improving specific areas of difficulty.

Other ADD patients, on the other hand, require more extensive therapy. The doctor who diagnosed Ben's ADD, for instance, decided that Ben's problems, which involved both deep-seated issues of intimacy and perhaps a low-grade depression, required more intensive psychotherapy. He recommended that Ben see a psychiatrist, but offered to continue to monitor his progress on the ADD front.

"I felt okay about it," Ben remarks. "By that time, I knew a lot about ADD and how it was affecting me. But there was a lot of stuff, about my brothers and my parents, that I needed a different kind of help with. I'm sure ADD had a lot to do with the problems I was having, but it didn't explain everything. My psychiatrist helped me see what else was going on."

The psychiatrist Ben went to see practiced what is known as *traditional psychotherapy*. There are probably as many types of traditional psychotherapy as there are therapists and patients. In fact, the chemistry between doctor and patient creates its own dynamic and influences the therapeutic process to varying degrees. That's why it is so important to choose a doctor with whom you feel comfortable, as we discussed in Chapter Three.

In very general terms, traditional psychotherapists work with patients to explore past hurts, failures, and traumas that still fester within and prevent patients from living full and satisfying lives. These issues are examined during appointments that are scheduled for at least once a week—traditional Freudian analysis often requires four or five sessions weekly.

Although traditional psychotherapy is helpful to many people, it is not useful for most adults with ADD unless, like Ben, they have other problems that can be relieved through such a process. Instead, treatment for ADD usually requires a much more active and pragmatic approach on the part of both therapist and patient. The goal of treatment, as discussed above, is to change behavior and thought patterns as they exist today. *Behavioral therapy* and *cognitive therapy* are two forms of individual counseling considered particularly useful to adults with ADD, and many therapists who specialize in treating ADD combine the two approaches.

Behavioral therapy, as its name implies, focuses on changing one's behavior by acquiring new tools and skills. It is a very pragmatic approach that deals directly with alleviating specific symptoms in order to meet specific goals. If you, like so many others with ADD, put off tasks or chores that seem overwhelming, a behavioral therapist will teach you "tricks" to get you started and keep you focused. One especially useful strategy, which we'll discuss in more depth in Chapter Seven, involves breaking down a large project into several smaller tasks, each of which can be accomplished with less feeling of intimidation and dread. Every completion is a success, reinforcing the newly learned skill and enhancing your sense of control and ability.

Another important behavioral technique involves creating a system of "rewards" for "good" behavior. If you promise to treat yourself to a manicure or a movie every time you balance your checkbook or finish a project for work, the task may seem less onerous now and in the future. After a time, you may even begin to look forward to it, not only for the external reward but for the sense of satisfaction you derive from a job well done. You're also likely to enjoy the positive responses your prompt and efficient actions elicit from the people in your life.

Improved time management, organizational abilities, and communication skills are among the many benefits of behavioral therapy. In Chapters Seven and Eight, we'll discuss more techniques and strategies that work to change your behavior in positive, constructive ways.

At the same time, we'll introduce some of the principles of *cognitive therapy*, which attempts to correct faulty behavior by changing our thought patterns. As discussed, most adults with ADD come equipped with a rather unpleasant internal tape recorder that plays back negative scripts—some self-composed, others written by teachers, parents, spouses, and employers. A cognitive therapist works with patients to erase those messages and replace them with ones of encouragement, affirmation, and optimism.

Another strategy of cognitive therapy involves "self-talk" designed to influence behavior. If you tend to blurt out inappropriate remarks without thinking first, a cognitive therapist may teach you to silently repeat the phrase "Stop and think" before speaking. With practice, you'll find that you interrupt or speak inappropriately much less often.

As you can see, working on a one-to-one basis with a therapist—traditional, behavioral, cognitive, or some combination of all three—can help you meet all of the goals described earlier in this chapter. In addition, there are several other approaches that may support your efforts to gain control over ADD.

Group Therapy

Misery loves company, or so the saying goes. If you're like most adults with ADD, however, you never knew—until recently—that millions of other adults suffered from the same symptoms of distractibility and restlessness, the same feelings of failure and frustration as you have—and for the same reason. Had you known, you might well have been able to lift some of the burden you carried when you were alone by simply sharing your feelings and experiences.

Fortunately, the benefits of group therapy for adult ADD patients go far beyond the worthwhile but limited act of catharsis. With an experienced therapist leading the sessions, a group therapy situation can be likened to a laboratory where skill-building methods of all kinds are tested and adapted, coping strategies are explored, feedback is provided, and management techniques are shared. Because most groups include people in different stages of the therapeutic process—from newly diagnosed patients to veterans with several years of coping skills—some patients can serve as role models, mutual support is exchanged, and everybody tends to feel better about themselves and their situation.

Depending on where you live, it may be difficult to find a group specifically devoted to adults with ADD at this time. However, chances are good that you'll be able to find a support group organized by an association like CH.A.D.D. or A.D.D.A. Support groups differ from group therapy situations in that they usually are not conducted by a psychologist or other health professional and thus often lack a certain structure and organization. This lack of structure can sometimes be frustrating to an ADD patient who, by his or her very nature, craves order and direction. However, because of the many opportunities they provide for emotional and educational exchanges, support groups can be an invaluable component of any treatment plan for ADD. You'll find more information about support groups in your area in the Appendix.

Family Therapy or Marriage Counseling

No man—or woman—is an island, and that certainly holds true for many adults with ADD. As we'll discuss in further depth in Chapters Eight and Nine, finding and sustaining healthy intimate relationships may be one of the biggest challenges an adult with ADD faces. For this reason, family therapy and/or marriage counseling is often recommended for a recently diagnosed adult who has experienced difficulties in this area of life.

As your own spouse or intimate partner probably can attest, living with an ADD adult can be extraordinarily difficult. Until they understand the dynamics of ADD, partners of ADD adults often feel hurt and frustrated by what they consider to be the willful misconduct, insensitivity, and/or forgetfulness on the part of their husbands, wives, or lovers. The same feelings are certainly shared by others in the family, including children, parents, and even adult siblings.

"I was devastated when I realized that my son thought I didn't care about him," recalls Rich. "I was always so distracted and, because I procrastinated, always behind a deadline, that I frequently missed his basketball games. He thought he wasn't important, that I had better things to do, when it was just that I was lousy at scheduling my time. When we finally all sat down with a counselor to talk it through, I could see how relieved he was. That's not to say I don't have a lot to make up to him, but at least some of his resentment is gone."

Later during the course of therapy, Rich invited his sister, Beth, to come to a session. Estranged for many years, Beth and Rich had many issues to resolve, many of which involved ADD-related problems. "Our parents used to fight all the time about me and my lousy behavior," Rich explains, "and Beth had enormous resentment about that and about the fact that I took attention away from her. By coming to therapy, she found out how hard I had struggled during my childhood, and how much I blamed myself. We still have a ways to go, but we're finally getting a little closer."

By educating family members and intimate partners about ADD, an experienced family therapist can help all the people involved reframe their difficulties within the context of ADD. Slowly but surely, anger, blame, and frustration can be replaced with optimism and commitment to change. In Chapter Nine, we focus on these issues in more depth.

Vocational Counseling

With or without ADD, matching one's ambitions to one's abilities is a tricky task. Although there are a few supremely fortunate individuals who claim they are ideally suited to their jobs, the rest of us still harbor dreams of discovering the perfect career, the one that underscores all our strengths and assets and dismisses as unimportant our weaknesses and flaws. Vocational counselors, professionals trained in the art of matching people to careers, are there to help us all.

For the adult who suffers from ADD, the challenges involved in finding and remaining in a satisfying job are intensified. In fact, many adults with ADD have spotty employment records marked by frequent dismissals, mutual partings, and/or resignations. Sometimes the difficulty lies with the lack of organizational and communication skills of many people with ADD. In other cases, the need for constant stimulation leads those with ADD to feel bored and frustrated at work, and hence more likely to quit or fail to flourish in their position.

Along with a diagnosis of ADD comes a great opportunity for those who have never found the right employment niche. First, medication and/or behavioral therapy may significantly improve job skills and productivity. Second, when adults learn exactly how ADD affects their behavior and thought processes, they often will be in a better position to make more sensible and ultimately more satisfying career choices. Enlisting the services of a vocational counselor to explore career options, identify strengths and weaknesses, and help to match skills and abilities with the right job can be a terrific opportunity for adults recently diagnosed with ADD.

By describing the many therapeutic options open to you, we hope to increase your sense of empowerment and optimism and to encourage you to follow through with treatment. The most important message we want to impart is that you are not alone: There are health professionals who understand and can help you and there are millions of fellow ADD patients with whom you can share feelings, experiences, and coping strategies.

As we observed earlier, Knowledge Is Power. The more you know about ADD and its effects, the better prepared you'll be for the challenges it presents. In Part III of this book, we show you ways to put this knowledge to good use by acquiring the skills and tools you need to outmaneuver ADD's symptoms and side effects. In the meantime, Chapter Six offers some hints and advice about aspects of daily life that are often overlooked in a discussion of ADD: what you eat, how you exercise your body, and the ways in which you relax, or fail to relax, on a regular basis.

IMPORTANT QUESTIONS AND ANSWERS ABOUT CHAPTER FIVE

Q I've been in counseling for several years, mainly because of my difficult relationships with family members. Now that I know that ADD has contributed to some of my personal problems, I want to help make it up to my parents and my sister. What should I do?

A In Chapter Nine, we'll discuss family issues in more depth. But for now you should know that troubled family relationships are common among ADD patients. The first step in mending those relationships is to educate yourself and your family about how ADD may have affected you all. The second may involve family therapy if you so choose. Ask your doctor for advice.

Q I've been taking Ritalin for two months now, and I know that my ADD symptoms are improving, but I still feel depressed and anxious much of the time. Should I switch to another medication?

A If you are feeling depressed and anxious, talk to your doctor. Although another medication either instead of, or in combination with Ritalin may help you, it is possible that you would also benefit from some psychological counseling. It may be that your struggle with ADD has left you with less than ideal self-esteem. Or your symptoms may have nothing to do with ADD—remember, a diagnosis of ADD can and often does coexist with other psychological conditions, such as mood and anxiety disorders, as well as substance abuse.

Q When I first found out I had ADD, I thought I'd need lots of therapy. But my doctor suggested I get help from an organizational expert and a financial planner, and to keep my regular once-a-month appointments with him. Is he right, or should I look into other kinds of therapy?

A It depends. This is really a question for you and your doctor to answer together. Many adult patients with ADD are well adjusted and productive. With some behavioral therapy and guidance, like the kind you would receive from an organization expert and a financial planner, they are able to truly thrive in their environment. Others will need more intensive and ongoing therapy. As for your case, see how you feel after a few months. If you feel you have deeper issues to resolve, you can always seek further help at that time.

Chapter Six

CREATING A BALANCED LIFE:
Diet, Exercise, and Stress Management

By now, chances are you've already received a diagnosis of ADD, started on the journey through the coping process, and made some decisions about medication and psychotherapy. You may have even begun to change the patterns of thinking and behavior that have held you back in the past. At this point, it may also be helpful for you to examine some of your day-to-day habits and how they might be affecting—for better or worse—your health and sense of well-being.

So often in books like this one, you'll read about a specific diet or exercise plan designed to make you healthier and stronger than ever before. Here, however, we will make no such claims. So far, no data exist to support the notion that any particular food causes—or cures—ADD, or that exercise can eliminate symptoms or side effects over a long period of time. Although learning to meditate and relax one's body can certainly help alleviate the distractibility and restlessness that is so much a part of ADD, such methods are unlikely to be either foolproof or particularly suited to all adults with ADD.

On the other hand, there is no question that eating a balanced diet, exercising regularly, and reducing stress promotes general health. And—with or without ADD—we all need to provide our bodies with the raw materials they need to function properly. Those raw materials include the food we consume, the oxygen we breathe, the work we provide our muscles during exercise, and the rest we give our bodies and minds.

THE ELEMENTS OF A HEALTHY LIFESTYLE

For many Americans, the whole subject of diet and exercise has become fraught with tedium, frustration, and often anxiety. A newspaper headline proclaims the virtues of using margarine instead of butter, then—practically the next day—the same newspaper runs a story about the dangers of trans-fatty acids, a common essential ingredient in margarine. One report claims that exercise is beneficial only if you exercise at your target heart rate three times a week for thirty minutes; another maintains that fitness can be achieved by simply increasing your daily physical activity an extra ten or fifteen minutes.

Because new information emerges every day that changes yesterday's rules, it's safe to say that no one really knows *exactly* what it takes to stay healthy and fit. Nevertheless, there are some general prescriptions to follow that will help keep us all on the right path. Some of those prescriptions are presented later in this chapter.

In the meantime, it's important to stress that the purpose of changing your daily habits is not to add frustration or anxiety to your life. As an adult with ADD, you've probably suffered enough of those negative emotions to last you a lifetime. Instead, your goal should be to add these three elements to your lifestyle:

1. **Balance:** In the *Random House Dictionary*, one definition of the word *balance* is "a state of stability, as of the body or the emotions"; another refers to *balance* as "a state of harmony."

By attempting to alleviate the symptoms and side effects of ADD—with medicine or through behavioral techniques alone—you are in essence attempting to reestablish the balance that has been lost. Without this balance, you are too easily distracted, overly impulsive, hyperactive.

At the same time, it is likely that other aspects of your life are out of balance as well. Perhaps you work constantly and feel you have no time to exercise or relax. Maybe your eating habits are out of whack: You forget to eat lunch because you're trying to meet a deadline at work, or you overeat in an attempt to soothe your anxiety and restlessness.

As you look for ways to bring the rest of your life back into balance, take the time to stabilize your eating, exercise, and relaxation habits as well. You may find that the connection between a healthy, balanced body and a healthy mind is closer than you think.

2. *Structure:* Perhaps more than any other single feature, structure is what has been missing from the lives of adults with ADD. Distracted and overwhelmed, you are unable to schedule events, finish projects on time, or even estimate how long a task will take or how much effort will be required on your part. A chore meant to take thirty minutes takes all afternoon. A report due on Monday is not completed until Wednesday, despite working fourteen-hour days. Bills due on the first of the month somehow aren't paid until warning notices are sent. As hard as you try, you always seem to be behind schedule and overworked.

If you're like many of your adult peers with ADD, this long-standing state of affairs has left you unable to set limits for yourself. Meals are created and eaten haphazardly; exercise sessions canceled, rescheduled, then canceled again; time set aside to relax is filled with anxiety or overtaken by work commitments that took longer than anticipated.

The benefits of adding structure to your life as you learn to cope with ADD cannot be underestimated. Not only will you be able to better manage the practical aspects of your life, but, as difficult as it may be to believe in today's fast-paced world, you may well learn to enjoy a greater sense of peace and tranquillity the more structured and consistent your days become.

3. *Satisfaction:* Attaining a sense of balance and adding structure to your days are admirable goals for any adult attempting to cope with ADD. But, in the end, what matters most is that the life you create for yourself is a satisfying, fulfilling one. It is likely that you've spent much of your life feeling disappointed with at least some aspects of your life. You've had a nagging feeling that the way you lived wasn't "right" somehow or that you haven't achieved all that you know you are capable of.

Today, however, you can make a fresh start. You know better than ever before the challenges you face and how to meet them with a greater chance of success. Now is the perfect time to reassess what it is you *really* want out of life and how you want to live it. As you do so, keep in mind that establishing a healthy lifestyle should never be a chore to be dreaded or despised. Instead, think of it as an opportunity to provide your body and soul with the raw ingredients needed to thrive and flourish. If your diet leaves something to be desired, create an eating plan that includes foods you enjoy and that make you feel good. If you're looking to start an exercise program, choose physical activities that bring you pleasure as well as burn calories or build muscle. And if stress and anxiety are constant companions, explore avenues of relaxation that emphasize your sense of self-awareness and internal balance.

If you are interested in making extensive changes to your lifestyle, talk to your doctor about setting some safe, realistic, and manageable goals. In the sections below, we offer some tips about eating, exercising, and relaxing that you may find helpful. Keep in mind that this is just a brief overview of a few basic strategies for you to consider.

THE FOOD CONNECTION

Food is nourishment. The nutrients in the food you eat every day are the catalysts for millions of major and minor miracles— the beating of your heart, the birth of an idea, the appreciation of taste and smell—that take place within the chemistry lab that is your body.

Food is also a source of pleasure. We do not eat merely to ingest the various vitamins, minerals, and other substances we need to survive. Instead, eating is a supremely sensual activity: We smell food's aromas, taste its flavors, admire its colors and textures, and feel its consistency inside our mouths. Depending on the circumstances, our sense of hearing may be equally stimulated by the conversation of our table-mates or the sounds of soothing dinner music.

As you consider your dietary habits, ask yourself these questions:

- Do you take the time to enjoy the sensual aspects of eating or do you simply think of food as fuel for the body?
- Do you eat only those things that taste good without considering their nutritional value?
- Are there foods that you enjoy eating but which seem to exacerbate your ADD symptoms or otherwise upset your system?

If you can answer yes to any of these questions, it is likely that your daily diet could use a little readjustment.

The Caffeine Question

As discussed, there is no clinical evidence to suggest that the consumption of a particular food either causes or cures ADD. However, because ADD most likely involves a disturbance or imbalance of brain chemicals, it is possible that—for some people—certain foods may aggravate symptoms while others appear to help relieve them.

For instance, caffeine is commonly linked to ADD, in both positive and negative ways. "Like I said before, caffeine always made it easier for me to concentrate," recalls Ken. "I didn't really know that it was doing that at the time; it just made me feel better."

Ken is not alone. Many people with ADD can claim a long history of heavy coffee drinking. The reason? Caffeine is a stimulant that works directly to stimulate certain neurotransmitters in your brain and throughout your body. In some individuals, this increased stimulation makes it easier to focus and sustain attention—somewhat in the same way that a dose of Ritalin or Dexedrine does. For someone struggling to compensate for the effects of ADD, such a side effect can be a blessing.

For others, however, caffeine has the opposite effect. "I never understood why people drank coffee," says Bonnie. "It always tasted horribly bitter to me, and made me even more hyper and irritable than usual. And now that I'm taking Ritalin, one sip of the stuff and it seems like I'm on another planet."

As Ken and Bonnie's experiences illustrate, one man's nectar is another's poison. Some people are highly sensitive to certain foods, or substances in food, that may worsen their symptoms. In addition to caffeine, substances most often cited as problematic among a minority of those with ADD include sugar, food preservatives, and food additives.

However, current research indicates that these substances do not play a role in the development of symptoms or in the treatment of ADD for *most* ADD patients. As with many other aspects of this disorder, the food connection to ADD varies considerably from one person to another. If you are concerned that your symptoms are affected by any of the foods you eat, talk to your doctor. He or she may suggest that you keep track of your diet and symptoms, writing down the foods you eat, when you eat them, and the symptoms that arise over the course of a day. After a few weeks, a pattern may—or may not— appear.

"Much to my surprise, I found that drinking caffeine-free diet soda really upset my system," remarks Marion. "I thought that because it didn't have any caffeine, it wouldn't be a problem for me. But when I kept track, I found that I felt edgy and distracted about an hour after drinking a couple of sodas. My doctor had no clear explanation for it, but thought maybe the artificial sweeteners or the preservatives were causing problems. In any case, he gave me a perfect piece of advice: If it makes you feel bad, don't eat it!"

In the end, then, Marion's doctor's advice is the best we can offer to you as well: Eat the foods that contribute to your general health and sense of well-being, and avoid those that appear to heighten your symptoms or otherwise upset your system.

Rules to Eat By

As you structure an eating plan that's right for you, keep in mind these general goals:

Balance your diet: Maintaining a balanced diet means more than simply giving your body its share of required nutrients. It also means having a healthy, balanced relationship to food. Here are some tips for developing a balanced diet:

• *Follow the Pyramid Plan.* The United States Dietary Association (U.S.D.A.) recently developed a new way of devising a healthy daily diet. According to this plan, each day you should eat the following:

— 6 to 11 servings of complex carbohydrates (bread, cereal, rice, and pasta)
— 2 to 4 servings of fruit
— 3 to 5 servings of vegetables
— 2 to 3 servings of protein (meat, fish, eggs, beans, nuts)
— 2 to 3 servings of low-fat dairy products (milk, yogurt, cheese)
— Fats and sugars are to be consumed sparingly.

If you need more information about proper nutrition, see the Appendix for suggestions or talk to your medical doctor.

• *Maintain a healthy weight.* Because many adults with ADD tend to be impulsive about everything—including their eating and exercise habits—weight control can become a challenge. If you need to lose or gain weight, talk to your therapist about some behavioral techniques that might help you get your eating habits under control.

• *Consume all good things in moderation.* Unless you have a specific allergy or sensitivity, no food is off-limits for you in terms of coping with ADD. However, in order to maintain a healthy and fit body and mind, limit the amount of fat, sugar, caffeine, and alcohol you consume on a regular basis.

Structure your mealtimes: Eating on the run, skipping or forgetting to eat meals, and compulsive eating are particular problems for the adult with ADD. Adding structure to your daily life will help you improve your eating habits as well.

• *Set regular times for your meals.* In Chapter Seven, we'll be outlining some time management techniques that will help you better plan—and stick to—a daily routine. As you begin to structure your days with more consistency, give priority to your mealtimes. Schedule them as if they were business appointments that cannot be broken—not the last on a list of "things to do." And give yourself enough time to sit down and really enjoy the food you eat rather than just grab something on the run.

• *Plan and cook ahead.* Time has a way of flying by—even for those of us without ADD. If you make the effort to plan ahead by creating a menu, shopping, and even cooking ahead of time, you'll be able to resist the temptation to pick up whatever food is at hand—regardless of its nutritional value or even its appeal to your taste buds. Again, the time management techniques you'll learn here and through therapy will help you structure your meal times more effectively.

• *Plan special meals and treats.* Although we should all aim to eat healthy, wholesome foods as often as possible, many of us have cravings for foods that are less than ideal and we should never try to permanently deprive ourselves of these foods. By building some occasional indulgences into our diets, we can satisfy those cravings without undermining our otherwise healthy eating plans. Depending on your weight, health, and personal tastes, you might want to plan to eat a special dessert once a week or a cheeseburger lunch with all the trimmings once a month.

Satisfy your appetites: As discussed above, food is more than just a combination of nutrients; it should also be a source of pleasure and satisfaction. In order to make the most of your meals:

• *Add variety to your diet.* By eating lots of different kinds of foods during the day, you'll not only improve your chances of getting all the nutrients you need, you'll also probably find yourself enjoying your diet more than ever before. At least once a week, try a new food—an exotic fruit or vegetable, for instance—or cook a different dish. Although many adults with ADD tend to shy away from cooking because of its perceived difficulties, you may be pleasantly surprised at how easy and enjoyable cooking can be.

• *Take time to enjoy the sensual aspects of eating.* Too often we find ourselves gulping down food without really tasting its flavors or enjoying its textures and aromas. Eating food on the run also means denying ourselves the pleasure of setting an elegant table and lingering over a fine meal in the company of family and friends. At least once in a while, take the time to make eating an experience to be savored rather than an automatic activity.

• *Eat foods that leave you feeling healthy and well.* Pay attention to how you feel after you eat your meals. If you're often groggy and uncomfortable, you may be eating too much, failing to eat a balanced diet, or consuming food that doesn't agree with your particular body makeup. Nutritious food, prepared well and eaten in a relaxed atmosphere should nourish your body and your soul. If you need further information, ask your doctor or a nutritionist for more advice.

Now that you've assessed your dietary habits, it's time to move on to another subject of interest to anyone looking to establish a healthy, vibrant lifestyle: exercise.

EXERCISE FOR BODY AND MIND

The benefits of physical activity are almost too numerous to mention. In addition to reducing your risk of developing heart disease, stroke, high blood pressure, some kinds of cancer, and a myriad of other diseases, exercise can dramatically improve the *quality* of the life you live today. It allows you to connect with your physical body in an intimate way: You'll feel your heart beat harder, your muscles grow stronger, and the tension of the day slip away. At the same time, you may well find that your mind—and all the thoughts that seem to race through it constantly—takes a bit of a break while your body does most of the work. Indeed, many adults with ADD who exercise claim that it is the one time in their day when they feel truly free of the disorder.

"When I run," Rich explains, "I'm not *thinking* about anything. Not about my work, not about paying bills, or even about something pleasant like a vacation. And I certainly don't think about ADD. I'm just breathing, stretching, sweating, and *feeling*. I run for about thirty minutes every day at lunch and I truly believe it keeps me sane. I really need to expel the excess energy that always seems to be there."

At this time, no research has been done to show exactly how and why exercise seems to help people with ADD better cope with the disorder. Plenty of anecdotal evidence exists, however, that clearly links regular activity with an alleviation of ADD symptoms. Adults with ADD claim that they not only feel better physically, but also have a renewed sense of emotional well-being both during and in between exercise sessions.

Part of the reason for these benefits is that certain brain chemicals called *endorphins*, known to dull pain and invoke mild euphoria, are released whenever the body feels pain, including during vigorous exercise when the muscles begin to tire and "burn." Produced in the spinal cord and the brain, endorphins may explain the reason that exercise appears to reduce anxiety and stress in those who undertake it on a regular basis. Smokers who exercise find it easier to quit, therapists frequently prescribe exercise to their depressed patients, and adults with ADD feel more able to concentrate and focus.

Rules to Exercise By

It is important to note that exercise need not be demanding or elaborate to be effective: Moderate exercise—defined as thirty minutes a day of light activity such as walking and gardening—is almost as beneficial to one's health as higher levels of exercise, such as high-impact aerobics and jogging. As you develop an exercise plan, keep in mind that people who learn to make exercise a habit in their lives also often increase their self-esteem by setting and reaching new goals.

Balance your energy: To exercise or not to exercise, that is the question so many of us ask ourselves every day. Part of our resistance comes from the idea that exercise requires us to devote our lives to getting and staying in shape. In fact, however, exercise should fit into our lives in a natural, balanced way, as the tips below indicate:

• *Exercise is not an all-or-nothing proposition.* If you're like many of your peers with ADD, you may have a tendency to be a bit perfectionistic in your thinking and behavior. If so, you may think that, to see results, you must run every single morning or make every evening's aerobics class at the gym. If you can't manage these demands, so the thinking goes, there's no point in even trying. But this is an outdated mode of thinking. Exercise can consist of a brisk walk to the market, an afternoon of gardening, even an hour of vigorous vacuuming—any activity that requires your body to move and your mind to take a backseat to the task at hand.

• *Set realistic goals.* If you've been sedentary for a number of months or years, deciding to train for next month's marathon by running ten miles every morning would be counterproductive and even dangerous to your health. After failing to meet the unrealistic goal, or straining your muscles trying to do so, you'd become frustrated and probably decide not to exercise at all. It is important to set goals you know you can meet, or perhaps ones just slightly out of reach. Achieving them will give you a sense of pride and self-confidence sure to keep you motivated.

• *No pain, no gain is a myth.* Performed improperly, any kind of exercise can cause serious injury. Pain is a warning system, a message from the body that something is wrong and needs attention. At the very least, if exercise causes you pain or leaves you feeling achy and sore, you're likely to end up discouraged and disappointed rather than stimulated. You should feel challenged by the effort you make during exercise, but you should never feel pain of any kind. If you are just starting an exercise program, ask your doctor or a fitness instructor at a local YMCA or health club for advice.

Structure your activities: In the end, the ultimate goal is for you to make exercise a habit, not for you to treat exercise as an occasional, and dreaded, assignment. The following tips will help you on your way:

• *Schedule time to exercise.* For many people, exercise is often last on a long list of "things to do." For adults with ADD, that can spell disaster for any exercise program. Consider your exercise session like a business appointment you've made with yourself, an appointment you can break only under very special circumstances. As you learn other time management techniques in Chapter Seven and through therapy, make scheduling regular exercise one of your priorities.

• *Join a gym.* If they can afford it, many people find it easier to start exercising at a gym or health club. The support of fellow exercisers is often welcome, as is the structure provided by participating in classes and the technical advice offered by instructors.

• *Seek convenience and variety.* As you plan an exercise program, eliminate as many excuses as possible for not following through. If you join a health club that is open only during hours you are at work, for instance, then obviously you're setting yourself up to fail. To alleviate boredom, you may want to alternate activities, taking a dance class one session, bicycling outside for forty-five minutes the next, performing yoga postures every other morning. By varying your routine, you'll be more likely to keep it going on a regular basis.

Satisfy body and mind: Nothing will sabotage an exercise program faster than boredom and/or frustration. In order to maximize your potential for success, follow the tips provided below:

• *Choose activities you enjoy.* Perhaps the most important element in the design of your exercise program is choosing activities you will enjoy over the long haul. Many people with ADD enjoy high-intensity sports, such as singles tennis or racquetball, because these activities satisfy their cravings for excitement and competition. Others prefer the quiet intensity of slow stretches and yoga postures. Experiment with a few different types of exercises to see which provide you with the most enjoyment.

• *Focus on the way you feel during and after you exercise.* Breathing deeply, working your muscles, and concentrating on meeting new challenges all add to the intensely personal experience of exercise. Indeed, exercising should bring you closer to truly understanding the unique structure of your own body, closer to understanding its limits and its potential.

• *Build self-esteem along with muscle.* Every time you make it to the gym for an exercise class, every mile you run, every inch you lose in fat (or gain in muscle) will add to your sense of accomplishment and empowerment. Allow yourself to feel the pride that comes along with meeting each and every one of your goals.

LEARNING TO RELAX

Stress. It's a fact of life for most people living in late-twentieth-century America and a special burden for the millions of men and women who also have ADD. But what exactly is stress? And why is it so harmful to our bodies and minds?

The second question is much easier to answer than the first. In fact, a great deal is known about the way the body reacts to situations, emotions, or events considered stressful. When your body perceives that it is in any kind of danger—from a missed deadline at work to something quite physical like an oncoming car—it reacts to protect you through the "fight-or-flight" response. Your heart beats faster, your blood pressure rises, your muscles tense, and your breathing quickens. These reactions occur in order to prepare you to either stay and fight, or run away. Once the threat has passed, your bodily functions should return to normal.

Although many people with ADD claim to function better under a certain amount of stress, this constant pressure eventually may cause irreparable harm. Chronic high blood pressure, heart disease, and a variety of other serious health problems all have been linked to unrelieved stress.

Now that you know what stress can do to your body, it might be helpful to know exactly how to identify stress and thus learn to avoid it. That goal, however, is a little harder to meet. The difficulty in defining stress is threefold. First, except for extreme situations, like the death of a loved one or the threat of imminent physical harm, a clear definition of stress is not available. Everything that occurs in your life or exists in the atmosphere is technically a *stressor* (a stress-causing stimulus) because it affects you in some way. Even a positive occurrence such as getting married or getting a new job may be considered a stressor.

Second, not everyone responds to stress in the same way. Some people become outwardly aggravated over the slightest mishap, while others never blink an eye even when disaster occurs. It should be noted, however, that the outwardly calm person may be actually seething inside, perhaps negatively affecting his or her physiology even more than the person who expresses anger and frustration in a more open way.

Third, and even more significant, stressors vary from person to person. For some people, a day spent lying on a beach is completely relaxing, while for others (especially high-energy seekers), such forced leisure is sheer torture. White-water rafting or skydiving is much more likely to relax someone with a need for constant stimulation than would watching a movie or reading a book.

Indeed, how you as an individual perceive an event or situation determines how your body reacts to it. Working with your therapist and your medical doctor, find out if stress is affecting your state of mind or your health in a negative way. Are you irritable and anxious more often than not? Do you have high blood pressure? If so, chances are certain aspects of life are causing undue stress on your body and mind.

Developing the Relaxation Response

Fortunately, there are ways to improve the way you cope with the stressors in your life, no matter what they are. Your body can learn what is known as the "relaxation response," so named by Herbert Benson, M.D., to counteract the fight-or-flight response during times of stress, bringing the body back into balance quickly and efficiently. In fact, there are many physical exercises you can do that will result in some significant physical and psychological benefits within a relatively short period of time.

We've chosen to show you two types of relaxation exercises, but there are many other methods of relaxation available. You should feel free to continue your research using other books (listed in the Appendix) or by asking your doctor for advice.

Deep breathing: Have you noticed that when you are distressed, your breathing becomes rapid and shallow? When you're more relaxed, you're probably breathing more slowly and regularly. When you are tired, have you noticed that taking a deep breath makes you more alert? Or when attempting to concentrate, that breathing in helps to improve your performance? By learning to breathe deeply and regularly, you can bring your body and mind back into balance whenever you need to focus and/or relax.

The object of the following exercise is to completely fill and empty the lungs. The rhythmic quality of the breathing, over time, will bring about a state of relaxation, deeper concentration, and increased energy.

Exercise #1

1. Sit on the floor, cross-legged or in any comfortable position. Make sure your back is straight (not arched or leaning forward), your head is erect and facing forward, and your arms are relaxed, with your hands resting on your thighs or on the floor.

2. Close your eyes and attempt to concentrate only on your breathing. Leave behind the worries or joys of your day and think only of this moment in time, when you are feeling the energy and power of your breathing.

3. Visualize your lungs as consisting of three parts: a lower space located in your stomach, the middle part near your diaphragm (just beneath your rib cage), and the upper space in your chest.

4. As you breathe in, picture the lower space filling first. Allow your stomach to expand as air enters the space. Then visualize your middle space filling with energy, light, and air, and feel your waistline expand. Finally, feel your chest and your

upper back open up as air enters the area. The inhalation should take about five seconds.

5. When your lungs feel comfortably full, stop the movement and the intake of air.

6. Exhale in a controlled, smooth continuous movement, the air streaming steadily out of the nostrils. Feel your chest, your middle, and your stomach gently contract.

7. Make about four complete inhalations-exhalations in a minute, resting about two or three seconds between breaths. Rest for twenty seconds or so, then repeat the process until you feel more relaxed and in control.

8. If you like, add a self-affirmation to your relaxation session by saying to yourself, "I am in control," "I am relaxed," "I will concentrate," or another positive, motivating sentence every time you exhale.

Progressive relaxation: Progressive relaxation is a technique used to induce nerve-muscle relaxation and involves tensing one muscle group and then relaxing it, slowly moving from one muscle group to another until every muscle group in the body has been affected. In addition to reducing stress and tension, progressive relaxation appears to have psychological benefits as well: Self-esteem is raised, depression lessened, and sleep problems alleviated in patients who practice this relaxation method over a period of several weeks.

If you decide to use progressive relaxation, it is helpful to learn to recognize when you become most tense and where in your body the tension is centered. After you have more experience with progressive relaxation, you will be able to relax individual muscle groups from a standing or seated position. At the start, it may be best to work through your body, from head to foot.

Exercise #2

1. Lie down on the floor with your knees bent and your feet flat on the floor; make sure that the small of your back is

on the floor so that you do not risk straining those muscles. If you like, support your head with a small pillow.

2. Take a deep breath and tighten the muscles of your feet by clenching your toes.

3. As you exhale, relax your feet. Notice the difference in the way your feet feel.

4. Breathe in again, and tighten the muscles of your calves. Hold the exertion for a few seconds.

5. As you exhale and release your calf muscles, say to yourself, "I feel relaxed."

6. Continue the process, with your knees, thighs, buttocks, stomach, chest, arms, shoulders, neck, and face. Each time you tighten and release the muscles, feel yourself sink deeper and deeper into a state of relaxation.

7. When you have finished the process, breathe steadily and deeply for five minutes, enjoying the sense of relaxation.

8. Repeat the exercise daily.

As you learn more about your body and the way it reacts to stress, you may be able to attain the relaxed state more quickly and directly. For example, you may be working at your desk and notice that your shoulder muscles are tense. To relax them you can tense them further, and then let them relax. When you focus on the warm, relaxed sensation of your shoulder muscles, you may feel your entire body, and spirit, relax as well.

Rules to Relax By

As mentioned, it may seem strange to you to have to learn to relax, or to practice relaxation techniques. But the fact remains that in today's fast-paced world, relaxation is considered a luxury, not the requirement for physical and mental health that it truly is.

Balance your spirit: Depending on your particular lifestyle, leisure activities that lead you to a genuinely more calm state of mind may be few and far between. These tips may help you get started:

• *Choose activities that stimulate as well as relax.* There's often a fine line between relaxation and lethargy, especially when it comes to the all-American pastime of watching television. Although watching a few television shows may take your mind off the pressures of the day, studies have shown that the longer this passive activity lasts, the *less* relaxed it makes you feel. Instead of calming down, you become more irritable, guilty, and frustrated the longer you sit in front of the television. Reading, learning a new hobby, or even walking to a movie theater to catch a flick are much better choices.

• *Beware of high-risk behaviors.* Too many of us tend to try to relieve stress and pressure by partaking in some rather unhealthy habits, such as smoking, drinking too much, or over-eating. Although you may feel that these activities help to relax you, they are, in fact, increasing the stress on your body by forcing it to cope with the ill effects of these substances and behaviors.

Structure times of peace: Having enough time and energy just to get through the "must do" chores of the day is challenge enough for most people. If you need help in adding relaxation to your routine, follow these hints:

• *Plan to relax.* When you know a deadline is coming up, or the week ahead is going to be particularly busy and stressful, try to schedule some time—even just a few minutes—every day to perform one of the relaxation methods described above or simply to take a walk to relieve the pressure. Chances are, you'll return to the task at hand feeling rejuvenated and better able to focus your attention.

Satisfy your spirit: Relaxation should never be a chore, but instead a release and a joy. These simple hints will help you find peace and avoid frustration:

• *Create space.* Choose a room in your home, or at least carve out a space within a favorite room, to be your private space where you are not to be disturbed. Use it as a sanctuary from the confusion and chaos that is apt to spring up all around you.

• *Increase your sense of self-esteem and control.* Learning that you have power and control over your internal environment and realizing that you can make successful, positive changes in your physical and mental health will automatically raise your self-esteem and give you a new sense of self-confidence.

• *Remember to laugh.* Although it may have become a bit of a cliché, laughter truly is one of the best medicines known to man. Humor provides a healthy balance to all the hostility, anxiety, and tension we feel every day. If you can look at the world and yourself with a bit of humor and a touch of whimsy, you'll find that your mind is not so cluttered and your stress is not so great.

Eating well, exercising regularly, and taking the time to relax should help you feel healthier and more satisfied generally. In the next section of the book, we'll focus on strategies to help you cope with some of the specific symptoms and side effects of ADD. We include tools to help you organize your time more efficiently, relate to the people in your life more honestly and intimately, and plan for a fuller, more productive future.

IMPORTANT QUESTIONS AND ANSWERS ABOUT CHAPTER SIX

Q I find that when I go to the gym on a regular basis I feel much better and my symptoms tend to be far less severe. Sometimes I don't even feel like I need to take my medication. Is this all in my head, or is there a correlation between exercise and symptom relief?

A Although no studies have yet been done to show a specific link between ADD and exercise, anecdotal evidence exists to suggest that the brain chemicals called *endorphins* released during exercise help improve focus and concentration in people with ADD. In addition, exercise burns excess energy, thereby helping to reduce the edginess and restlessness so common in ADD patients. Finally, when performed on a regular basis, exercise has been shown to improve self-esteem and elevate mood, two other benefits of particular significance for those with ADD. Although exercise can be beneficial, it is not considered a substitute for medication, and it is highly likely you will continue to need medication.

Q I know that meditation is supposed to help me relax and improve my concentration. But whenever I try, I feel like I'm going to jump out of my skin. Is there something else I can do?

A Don't despair. Meditation doesn't help everyone. Some patients with ADD find that exercise—either aerobic or weight training—helps clear their minds and brings their bodies into a more relaxed state. At the same time, it may help you to try some simple deep-breathing exercises like the one described in this chapter to help you relax during times of stress when exercising is not an alternative.

Q I've been taking Ritalin for about six months now. Suddenly, I find that whenever I drink coffee I feel jittery and nervous and can't sleep very well. What's going on?

A It could be that between the Ritalin and the caffeine, your body is overstimulated. Let your doctor know about this side effect. He or she may well recommend that you drink decaffeinated coffee for a while to see if that will resolve the problem, or if you need to reduce the amount of Ritalin you're taking.

OUTMANEUVERING

ADD

Chapter Seven

TAMING THE
ORGANIZATIONAL
DEVIL

Chaotic. Unpredictable. Frenetic. Exhausting. For a great many adults with ADD, these words quite accurately describe the quality of their lives on a daily basis. They plow through their days rushing to perform tasks and meet goals, but all too often their energies are misdirected or usurped by the internal engines that drive them. Fortunately, this cycle of commotion and wasted energy can be broken and replaced with one of clear direction and accomplishment. With proper medication and new skill-building techniques, adults with ADD can add words like *productive, inspiring,* and *satisfying* to their lexicon.

Generally speaking, the problems faced by adults with ADD fall into two broad categories: those concerning organization and time management, and those involving communication and interpersonal relationships. In this chapter, we tackle the first category of challenges by helping you get yourself, your work life, and your home into a more ordered and structured state.

If you're like many of your ADD peers, you've been fighting

what we call the "organizational devil" for much of your life. This devil seems to be everywhere at once, circumventing your every effort to maintain order and structure. He's there in your closet, shoving one shoe into an inaccessible corner. He's in the front hall, dropping your keys behind the coat rack. He's in the office, stashing the sales figures under a pile of last week's unopened mail. He's in the kitchen, leaving the frying pan in the food pantry. He's in the study, scattering monthly bills underneath the desk, between the pages of a magazine, and on top of the television set.

THE FIRST STEP TOWARD TAKING CONTROL

In order to really take control of your life, you've got to recognize one undeniable truth: The organizational devil that has been sabotaging your very existence lives inside of you. It is not simply "the way of the world," or cosmic fate, or bad luck that keeps you from running your daily life with any kind of order or structure. Instead, the physical effects of ADD have made it difficult for you to concentrate long enough to follow through on tasks or manage your time with any consistency. Over the years, you've learned patterns of behavior that have kept this organizational devil alive and kicking and ready to disrupt your life at any moment.

The good news is that you'll be able to tame your internal devil by teaching yourself new tricks and techniques. Slowly but surely, with time and practice, you'll be able to replace chaos with order. You'll be able to make plans and set goals with a greater degree of confidence and self-assurance.

"Medication helped bring things into focus for me," Marion remarks. "And what I saw when I focused both terrified and motivated me. I finally recognized how much of the chaos of everyday life could be avoided by simply setting up a little structure for myself. I realized I had to rush to work every morning not because I overslept, but because I couldn't figure out what to wear, or find my keys or briefcase. At work, I'd forget to return phone calls because I stuffed my messages into the folder I had been looking into for another reason. My projects were always late because I'd underestimate how long they should take, then panic when I realized how far behind I was. Once I started to look at things a little more logically, everything seemed to get much easier to handle."

In this chapter, we offer suggestions that may help you get a better grip on your own particular organizational problems. First, we address the basic skills you'll need to add more structure to your life in general. Later in the chapter, we'll provide some tips about coping with your organizational devil in the workplace and at home.

Before we get started, it's important to reiterate that coping with the effects and side effects of ADD is a process, not an all-or-nothing event. Medication may be part of that process, as may psychotherapy. The skill-building techniques you'll be learning in this and the next chapter are part of a process as well: a process of trial and error, of setbacks that result in ultimate success, of frustration that finally leads to confidence. Patience is not only a virtue when it comes to conquering ADD, it is a prerequisite.

This chapter is divided into six sections:

• *Prepare Yourself for Success* explains how you can increase your odds of accomplishing your goals by laying some fundamental emotional and physical groundwork.

• *Set Priorities for Change* teaches how to establish specific, realistic methods for accomplishing your goals.

• *Learn to Manage Your Time Better* outlines several effective time management strategies that will take the guesswork and anxiety out of completing important tasks and projects.

• *Build Your Organizational Skills* describes several techniques for handling paperwork, establishing efficient filing systems, and increasing office and household organization.

• *Organize with ADD at Work* shows you how to apply time management and organizational strategies to professional challenges.

• *Celebrate Success* stresses that the overall purpose of building organizational skills is to bring you closer to meeting your personal and professional goals, as well as to increase your confidence and self-esteem.

As you read each of these sections, keep in mind that the behavioral and cognitive therapy techniques described are only suggestions. You may well find other methods—recommended by your therapist or members of a support group, or which you develop on your own—that are better suited to your purposes or personality. Feel free to experiment.

PREPARE YOURSELF FOR SUCCESS

• Do I constantly put down my efforts to
  succeed?   _____

• Am I all too ready to give in to failure?   _____

• Am I surrounded by chaos?   _____

• Do I feel alone in my efforts to grow and
  change?   _____

• Do I believe in my heart and mind that I
  cannot succeed?   _____

Chances are, you answered many of the above questions with a resounding Yes. Like most other adults with ADD, you probably have a built-in "negation system" that thwarts your attempts to modify your behavior, recognize your strengths, and move forward. First on your agenda for change, therefore, is reorganizing the way you think about yourself and your prospects for progress. In effect, you must learn to *plan* to succeed. In Chapter Five, we mentioned the Boy Scout motto, Be Prepared, as a watchword worth remembering. Indeed, careful planning on many levels offers you the best prospect of attaining your goals in the long run.

Prepare Yourself Emotionally

A lifetime of feeling out of step and behind your peers may well have left you lacking hope that a more productive and satisfying future is possible. But without optimism and confidence, you'll probably also lack the energy and commitment it will take to learn more successful patterns of behavior. Starting today, you must lay a new emotional foundation upon which to build a positive and practical approach to life.

As discussed in Chapter Five, the first step on the path to emotional preparation involves erasing any negative messages left on your internal self-talk tape. For instance, if your first response to picking up a pile of mail is "I'll never get through this today," it's very likely that you'll be right. After reading this chapter and learning the techniques described here, you'll be able to change that tape to play positive affirmations. Even before you're *really* sure you can handle a task, say to yourself, "With practice, I can do anything."

And that leads to another important tip for remaining emotionally prepared for your new life: Accept the reality of setbacks. There are bound to be lessons you must relearn, often more than once, before any new behavior pattern becomes automatic and entrenched. It is essential you do not equate a setback—even a serious one—with failure but instead view it as an opportunity. Remember that you can always learn from setbacks and apply that knowledge to future experience.

Prepare Your Physical Environment

If you are surrounded by clutter and disarray—as is likely if ADD-related disorganization has been part of your life for many years—it may be very difficult for you to become more organized and capable, even as you learn new skills. Instead, it's best to start with a clean slate by clearing away some of the extraneous material filling up your closets, file drawers, and kitchen cabinets. Later in this chapter, you'll learn tips to help you do just that.

In addition, we encourage you to find or create work spaces that are conducive to the way you best perform. If you tend to concentrate best in a brightly lit room with music playing in the background, it only makes sense to try to work as much as possible within such an environment.

"In college, I discovered that I needed complete quiet in order to focus on my work," Bonnie recalls. "I'd close myself up in a study room at the library. That's how I became an engineer. But at home, I'd forget that somehow, and I'd try to pay my bills while watching a movie or listening to rock and roll. A chore that would have taken an hour or two in the right space ended up taking a whole afternoon; and I never managed to send out all my bills on time, and my checkbook never balanced."

Once Bonnie recognized what she needed from her environment in order to perform tasks efficiently, she created a soothing place for herself to work at home. "I knew I wouldn't actually go to the office or to the library on my day off to pay bills or write letters," Bonnie admits, "so I turned a spare closet into a teeny little study, with one file drawer, a narrow table, and a comfortable chair. It is my own little world, and it works great. As long as I get myself in there, I work much better and much faster."

Prepare the People Around You

If you're like most adults with ADD, you've attempted to "go it alone" throughout much of your struggle with the disorder. Hurt by others' comments and unable to trust your own judgment, you may have withdrawn from your family, friends, and colleagues. Instead of reaching out and asking for help, you've attempted to hide your disorganized thought and behavior patterns from the rest of the world—and lived in fear that your terrible secret might be discovered.

Now, thankfully, you know the truth and you can begin to

let other people in on the not-so-terrible truth about ADD and the way the disorder is affecting your life. You can tell your friends and family that ADD is highly treatable, and how much can be gained by simply taking the time to learn about its effects and side effects. (Using care and good judgment, you may even be able to tell your boss and your colleagues about ADD, although that is a subject you must consider carefully first. More about this later.) You may discover the people in your life will be relieved to know the truth about you, and excited about the prospects for growth and change that the diagnosis offers.

On the other hand, you should prepare yourself for the fact that not everyone may sympathize or empathize with your news. Because ADD in adults is a relatively new phenomenon, there remains a great deal of ignorance about the disorder and its effects. You may be accused of adopting the "disease of the month" or of making excuses for being lazy or unmotivated. In such cases, it is helpful to have some literature—a pamphlet or newspaper article—to show the doubtful people in your life the truth about your condition.

On a related note, you may find it very helpful to enlist a coach or partner in your efforts to come to terms with the disorder—a trusted person who can monitor the effects of medication, guide you through skill-building techniques, and help you through the periods of frustration that are bound to crop up. Coaches can help remind you of your long-range goals, while gently keeping you focused on the tasks at hand. A coach can be particularly helpful at work, especially when you're first learning new skills and techniques.

Some people choose to have their therapists act as their coaches, especially if they meet every week to monitor progress. Others elicit help from someone a little closer to home, such as a spouse or best friend. No matter whom you choose, make sure the person has a terrific sense of humor, the ability to use positive reinforcement instead of negativity, and a great deal of patience. With time and effort, your partnership may well bear some very organized and efficient fruit!

Prepare Your Mind

Creative visualization is a fancy term for a simple technique: If you picture in your mind what you want to accomplish before you begin, the task will be easier to perform and more likely to be finished than if you simply plunged ahead. This technique works for many people for two reasons. First, by envisioning the chore or goal completed in your mind's eye, you provide yourself a bit of extra confidence in yourself and your abilities. Seeing is believing, if you will.

Second, as you imagine working to your goal step by step, you may be able to prepare yourself on a practical level as well. You will know better what tools you'll require to complete the task and what challenges you are likely to meet along the way. Right now, for instance, you may be imagining yourself living an organized and structured life, free of clutter and confusion. Picture yourself sitting in a clean office, with color-coded files filled with appropriate papers and an up-to-date, accurate appointment book on your desk. Know that you can do it— and continue to read this chapter to see just how.

Five Tips for Preparing Yourself for Change

- Say to yourself, "I can and will be more organized."
- Work in an environment that plays to your strengths, not your weaknesses.
- Educate your friends, family, and colleagues about ADD.
- Work with a coach or partner who can help keep you on track.
- Picture the life you want to lead, and believe you can live it.

SET PRIORITIES FOR CHANGE

- Am I overwhelmed and aggravated by the disorganized state of my home and my office? _____

- Is there a pattern to my disorganization? _____

- Do I feel that I'm the only one who can do a job right? _____

Rome wasn't built in a day, as the saying goes; nor can you reorganize your life from top to bottom in a few hours or even a few weeks. Instead, you must learn to be patient—a trait unfortunately in short supply among most adults with ADD—as you slowly but surely conquer each of your organizational foes one at a time.

Deciding where to start is your first challenge—and you would be wise not to underestimate it. In fact, choosing among many competing priorities may seem like an overwhelming prospect to you, as it is for many adults with ADD. Your whole world may seem so confused and disorganized, you're likely to think there's no point in even trying to sort it out.

That's where you're wrong. Every single problem that you solve—no matter how little or insignificant it may seem—will help you gain more control over your environment. For example, let's say you have trouble getting to work on time in the morning. By the time you arrive at the office, you're already behind. You fail to make a few important phone calls, you stash the mail instead of opening it and dealing with it, you make mistakes typing up an important report. By the end of the day, you're further behind than ever: Your desk is a mess, your files are out of order, and your report will be late because you have to redo it.

Examine the Situation

Now, let's look at one way to begin to solve your widespread organizational problems. You are often late in the morning because you have a hard time getting dressed and out the door in a reasonable amount of time. Your closet is a disaster area and nine mornings out of ten you spend at least twenty minutes looking for your keys. What if, say, you laid out your wardrobe the night before? Or better yet, organized your closet so that you could find matching garments more easily? What if you put a hook right next to the door and hung your keys there as soon as you entered your home? The hour or so you save getting ready in the morning could well translate into a more efficient, less frustrating day at work.

On the other hand, you might be able to live in a disorganized home quite well—for the time being, anyway—if only your office ran more smoothly. Being a little late wouldn't matter so much if you had systems that you could count on already in place. Instead, you stumble through the day taking on more and more tasks and never really finishing anything, at least not on time. But what if you set aside one hour, every day at the same time, during which you returned telephone calls and another hour during which you filed? What if you made a deal with yourself that you wouldn't leave the office until your desk was clean and your priorities were set for the next day? Even if that meant staying late once in a while, wouldn't tomorrow be so much easier to face?

Keep in Mind the Three Goals

As you attempt to come to terms with your organizational needs, it may be helpful for you to keep in mind the three goals established in Chapter Six: balance, structure, and satisfaction. Many adults with ADD truly work best when surrounded by a *little* bit of clutter or with *some* deadline pressure upon them. Force them into an overly organized or controlled environment, and they feel trapped and stymied—and as unproductive as ever. In the end, like so much else about ADD, finding the right balance between order and chaos or planning and spontaneity is a highly individual process. Only you can tell how neat the house has to be before you feel comfortable and relaxed in it. Only you know when time management techniques have begun to tyrannize you, making you feel overscheduled and overwhelmed.

So where do you start in your quest to find balance, structure, and satisfaction? By finding out what activities and habits most disturb, annoy, or hinder you on a day-to-day basis. Here's one way to do that:

Beginning Your Quest for Satisfaction

1. Tonight before you go to bed, *think about everything that happened to you today*, starting from the moment you woke up.

2. *Write down what you were doing every time you felt confused, frustrated, or rushed during the day.* For example: "Couldn't find my other black shoe." "Tripped over the pile of newspapers near the kitchen." "Missed calling a customer back because his number was in the Rolodex I left at home."

3. *Divide the day's frustrations into two categories:* those that tend to be material in nature—scattered paperwork, jumbled clothing, messy desk—and those involving time management—running behind schedule, overcommitting yourself, losing track of time, etc. Notice that these problems usually overlap. You're behind schedule because you couldn't find your other black shoe in the cluttered closet, or, conversely, a project is late because you underestimated the time it would take to complete it.

4. *Prioritize the problems within each category according to the amount of aggravation they cause you.* Apply the number 1 to those things that drive you completely nuts or disrupt your activities, number 2 to habits or difficulties that are only mildly upsetting, and number 3 to problems that would not hinder you if the rest of your life were more organized. You'll probably want to find ways to alleviate those difficulties labeled 1 first, then attack the 2s, and then decide if the others need attention at all.

To begin to solve your organization and time management problems you can do the following:

Learn new skills and habits. The time management techniques and organizational tips described in the sections below will help you better plan your days and arrange your belongings. Over time, and with practice, you'll become more efficient and organized.

Learn to delegate. With or without ADD, none of us is capable of handling every task that comes before us, nor are we expected to be able to do so. Instead, we must learn to trust the people around us to provide help and support. If there's a chore you find particularly difficult or unpleasant, see if your spouse or a friend or colleague would be willing and able to perform it for you. In exchange, perhaps there's a task he or she finds disagreeable that you could take over.

Another option—if you can afford it—is to hire a professional. If housekeeping isn't your strong point, for instance, hire a maid or cleaning service to tidy up once a week or once a month. The money it costs may well be worth the bother it saves you. Take advantage of messengers and delivery services to handle some of your errands if you feel constantly pressed for time. Use grocery stores and pharmacies that take orders over the phone. Hire a hairdresser or personal trainer to come to your office once in a while if you feel trapped by work demands and are employed in a company that allows you to schedule such activities during office hours.

Later on in this chapter, we'll describe ways for you to begin to organize your time, living space, and work life. Once you've got a handle on the basics, you can prioritize each chore as it comes up, handling some yourself and delegating others to friends or professionals. In the meantime, your top priority should be to remember to stay patient and flexible. After years of feeling scattered and confused, it may take some time for you to accept the need to organize and structure your time and space. Indeed, as strange as it may sound, you've grown accustomed to disorder, and any habit—even a harmful one— is hard to break. Also keep in mind that no system is infallible; you'll likely need to make constant adjustments as you go along. That's especially true as your needs and obligations change.

Five Tips for Setting Priorities for Change

- Aim to eliminate as many irritations in your life as possible.
- Remember your ultimate goal: to establish balance, create structure, and attain satisfaction in your daily life. Do not tyrannize yourself with too many rules and systems.
- Plan to revisit your list of priorities after a few weeks or months. See how many you can cross off because you've managed to tackle them.
- Learn to recognize your talents and strengths. Build upon them as well as learn new skills.
- Learn to delegate to others as many aggravating or difficult tasks as possible.

LEARN TO MANAGE YOUR TIME BETTER

- Do I often forget or lose track of appointments, meetings, and other activities?   _____

- Am I able to accurately estimate the time it will take to complete a project?   _____

- Do I procrastinate for fear of falling short of perfection?   _____

- Is my concentration often interrupted by thoughts of impending tasks?

- Am I constantly fluctuating between
  frantic activity and periods of total
  inertia?   ____

Do many of the questions listed above relate to your life?
If so, you're not alone. Many of your fellow adults with ADD
count among their most pressing problems the inability to structure and control their time. Time management is particularly
problematic for adults with ADD for the following reasons:

- Disorganized record keeping translates into last-minute
attempts to catch up, missed appointments and deadlines, and
backtracking to make up for lost time and effort.
- Because they are so easily sidetracked from the tasks at
hand, adults with ADD often cannot accurately estimate the
time it will take to complete a project.
- An inability to sustain attention for long periods of time
makes it difficult for many adults with ADD to carefully plan
and prepare for an activity or project. Unexpected delays often
crop up under these circumstances.
- The tendency to feel overwhelmed by the size or number
of tasks requiring attention frequently results in procrastination.
For many adults with ADD, procrastination is the best way to
avoid what they are certain will be another failure.
- More often than not, the eyes of those with ADD are
much larger than their time or energy capacities. Many adults
with ADD tend to take on more tasks than anyone could possibly
complete, either because they impulsively dive in without considering the consequences or because they are unable to say no
to others who request their services. In either case, they often
have more things on their "to do" list at the end of the day
than they had at the beginning.

The ultimate result of experiencing one or more of these
ADD-related difficulties is, quite simply, a time management
nightmare. Nothing seems to get done on schedule, at home
or at work, and planning—even for something pleasant like a

vacation—appears to be impossible. In addition to the obvious practical implications of living such an unpredictable life, the emotional fallout can be heavy as well. The people around you often feel unable to trust you to meet your responsibilities or even show up on time for an event. And their lack of faith in you only reinforces your own. What's the point of even trying, you say to yourself, when I know I'll just end up feeling like I'm back where I started?

Fortunately, there are several time management techniques that can work for even the most out-of-sync men and women with ADD. As long as you are willing to put in some time and hard work, one or more of these systems will help you gain more control over your time and energy.

The Art of Keeping Track

It seems so simple on the face of it: Just write down appointments and deadlines in a date book and you'll always know where you are supposed to be and what you are supposed to be doing. If you're like most people with ADD, however, you've never quite figured out how to make appointment books or planners work for you. After a few days or weeks of sporadic attempts to jot down important dates and tasks, you become frustrated and bored. Months later, you find your date book stuffed behind the sofa, at the bottom of your purse or briefcase, or you simply lose track of it altogether.

"I can't tell you how many different kinds of calendars and appointment books I've tried to use," photographer Sam confesses. "For about six years in a row, my wife would buy me a terrific leather-bound appointment book. And every New Year's Eve, I'd make a resolution to use the thing regularly, and for about two weeks, I would. But then I'd get bored or frustrated with it, and it'd end up in the bottom of my desk drawer before Valentine's Day. My wife would seethe every time I missed an appointment or was late for a date with her."

After Sam was diagnosed with ADD, however, he decided

to take the bull by the horns and learn to manage his time. "A friend of mine is a management consultant for small companies and knows lots of tried-and-true methods for scheduling and organizing time. With his help, I devised a system that ended up really working for me."

The Time Management Plan

The approach to time management that Sam and his friend devised is a simple one that may work for you, too. It involves two components: a wall calendar and a three-subject notebook. The wall calendar will help you keep track of major events such as birthdays, project deadlines, holidays, vacations, and appointments. Many people find it helpful to buy one of the larger calendars that show the entire year, month by month, on one sheet of plastic. Not only do these calendars have plenty of space in which to note important dates with an erasable colored marker, but they provide a long-range perspective on the weeks and months ahead.

"Knowing a report was due on, say, November third had no real meaning for me until I could picture it in relation to other deadlines and events," explains ad executive Marion. "Using a year-at-a-glance wall calendar helped me really to grasp that the November third deadline was just two weeks after an important conference that would take up lots of my time, and three weeks before Thanksgiving. It put time into some kind of realistic perspective."

The second part of this time management system involves scheduling and tracking your daily activities. Although there are many tools available for this purpose—including Filofaxes, Day-Timers, and other commercial products—you may well find that these more elaborate appointment books are too confusing and overwhelming over the long term. Instead, try using the three-subject notebook method we describe here.

In this notebook, you will track your tasks and activities by creating three different lists: the *Master List*, the *Daily Schedule*, and the *Project Planner*. Let's take them one by one.

The Master List

In the first section of a three-subject notebook, create a running Master List. Every time you think of a task or activity that requires your attention, add it to the Master List. Keep this section of the notebook free-flowing and nonspecific: It doesn't matter if the task is a personal one (like "Make appointment for haircut"), professional in nature ("Call XYZ company tomorrow"), or household-related ("Change kitty litter"). Simply write it down as soon as it occurs to you. If there is a certain deadline attached to the duty, make a note of it, e.g., "Order liquor for Christmas Party on 12/18."

Let's take a look at a recent entry from Sam's notebook to see what a Master List might look like:

Sam's Master List 12/2 (A.M.)
Photo shoot at South Beach, 10:00 tomorrow
Prepare for end-of-year business review.
Fix garbage disposal.
Make appointment for haircut.
Call Joseph about Thursday's photo shoot.
Write Ted and Eileen.
Create marketing plan.
Pick up dry cleaning.
Prepare contact sheets for Hawthorne meeting at 3:00.
      Confirm with phone call to Hartmann.
Meet June for dinner, 8:00, Ambrosia.
Make arrangements for Christmas party 12/20.

At the end of every day, Sam reads the items on his Master List and decides which tasks must be completed the next day, which can wait until another time, and which require further planning. The items in the first category are placed on the Daily Schedule, while those that involve further planning are considered in the section devoted to Project Planning. As soon as a task is transferred to another section of the notebook and a notation is made indicating its new location in the notebook, it is crossed off, leaving only those chores that can wait for another day on the Master List. Here's what Sam's list looked like after he assessed it on the evening of December 2:

Sam's Master List 12/2 (P.M.)

~~Photo shoot at South Beach, 10:00 tomorrow.~~ (Daily Schedule)

~~Prepare for end-of-year business review.~~ (Project Planner)

Fix garbage disposal.

~~Make appointment for haircut.~~ (Daily Schedule)

Call Joseph about Thursday's photo shoot. (12/5)

Write Ted and Eileen.

~~Create marketing plan.~~ (Project Planner)

~~Pick up dry cleaning.~~ (Daily Schedule)

~~Prepare contact sheets for Hawthorne meeting at 3:00.~~
~~Confirm with phone call to Hartmann.~~ (Daily Schedule)

~~Meet June for dinner, 8:00, Ambrosia.~~ (Daily Schedule)

~~Make arrangements for Christmas party 12/20.~~ (Project Planner)

Tasks that are left over, which should be less pressing tasks such as "Fix the garbage disposal" and "Write Ted and Eileen," remain on the Master List until Sam can figure out when he'll have a chance to perform them. Once he has cleared some time, he will transfer them to the appropriate Daily Schedule. "Call Joseph about Thursday's photo shoot" also remains on the Master List until Sam schedules it in his daily planner on 12/5.

The Daily Schedule

The second section of the notebook is devoted to the Daily Schedule. On each page, you'll list the tasks you intend to perform on a given day, including meetings, appointments, telephone calls, and errands. If possible, schedule a time for each activity. To give you an idea of how a Daily Schedule might look, we've reproduced another page from Sam's notebook. This schedule includes tasks derived from his Master List, but does not yet include chores related to major projects, which will be covered in the next section.

Sam's Daily Schedule 12/3
Appointments/Activities

9:00 Make phone calls

9:30 Leave for photo shoot

10:00 South Beach

10:30   **Important Calls**

11:00   Hair salon: 555-6638

12:00   Hartmann: 555-7878

12:30 Lunch/office

1:00

2:00 Prepare contact sheets

2:30

3:00 Hartmann meeting   **Expenses**

3:30 $12 gas

4:00 $20 dry cleaning

4:30   (check #256)

5:00   **Notes**

Evening

     Pick up dry cleaning.

     Meet June at Ambrosia, 8:00.

Every night, Sam makes up a new page just like the one above, then fills it in with tasks and appointments from his Master List. "I consider the Daily Planner like the guidebook to my day," Sam says. "If I pay attention to it—and I did have to train myself to use it faithfully—I find I can get more done during the day, with so much less anxiety and stress. In fact, the whole notebook system has become a way of life for me. I never go anywhere without it. I use the Master List as a warehouse for all of my random thoughts and obligations, the Daily Planner to organize my days, and the Project Planner to work out the details of larger tasks. As long as I take a little time every day to go through all three sections of the notebook, I can stay on top of life. It feels great."

The Project Planner

Preparing for a year-end business review. Organizing a party. Planning a vacation. Cleaning out the garage. Rearranging the filing system. What all of these disparate activities have in common is their complexity—a complexity that often overwhelms the adult with ADD.

"What held me back in my job as an account executive was not a lack of creativity," Marion says. "In fact, I've come up with some pretty hot ideas, if I do say so myself. But I couldn't manage to put together an entire ad campaign with all of its separate components on time and in order, mainly because I didn't understand the fundamentals of planning. I'd lose track of who was working on the copy and when he or she needed to get it to the art department, what materials the art department required, and when the job needed to get to the printer to be finished on time. Until I learned to break down the larger project into its separate components and schedule them carefully, I never met a deadline and I always felt anxious and sick about my job."

Marion's description of successful project planning is a good one, one you might find helpful in organizing your own responsibilities. The first step is to break down the larger project into smaller, more manageable tasks that can be handled in about an hour or two. Sam's Project Planner for the month of December is a good example of how such a system might work.

The two major projects on Sam's agenda for the month of December include a year-end business review and an office-client holiday party. Each one of these larger projects can be broken down into several smaller tasks that must be scheduled and executed in an orderly way. As each task is completed, the larger project comes closer to being completed—on time and with a minimum of stress and anxiety. Let's see how Sam broke down his projects:

Sam's December Project Planner
Year-end Business Review (12/28)
1. Clean out files

   A–F week of 12/3
   G–L week of 12/11
   M–N week of 12/18
   O–Z week of 12/25

[Sam broke this down further by scheduling a half hour every day to clean out one or two files at a time.]

2. Provide accountant with figures for quarterly audit by 12/8. [Sam knows the accountant needs at least three weeks to complete audit. He checks this page every day and adds the following tasks to his Daily Schedule within the next few days.]

   • Organize January–October receipts (2 hours).
   • Add up November's receipts (4 hours).

3. Review previous marketing plan (2 hours).

Plan Holiday Party (12/22)
1. Call Cathy about caterer ASAP.
2. Establish guest list (1½ hours).
3. Send guest list to printer for invitations by 12/8.
4. Arrange for liquor to be delivered, week of 12/18.

As long as Sam takes a few minutes every day to go over the Project Planner, adding new tasks and crossing off those he completes, he is able to keep the tide of activities flowing in the right direction—and for the first time in his life.

"This system may seem pretty elaborate, but taking the time to break a big project down like this is so much less overwhelming than not really knowing what's supposed to happen and when," Sam explains. "Once you get the basics, it ends up saving you so much time and energy."

On the evening of December 2, Sam took a look at his Project Planner and added some tasks from it to his December 3 Daily Schedule:

Sam's Daily Schedule 12/3

Appointments/Activities

9:00　Make phone calls

9:30　Leave for photo shoot

10:00　South Beach

10:30　｜

11:00　｜

12:00　↓

12:30　Clean A–B files/lunch/
1:00　　office

2:00　Prepare contact sheets

2:30　　↓

3:00　Hartmann meeting

3:30　｜

4:00　｜

4:30　Start working on party
5:00　　guest list

Evening

Pick up dry cleaning.

Meet June at Ambrosia, 8:00.

Important Calls

Hair salon: 555-6638

Hartmann: 555-7878

Caterer: 555-3990

Expenses

$12 gas

$20 dry cleaning
(check #256)

Notes

Hartmann pleased with layout.

Shot four rolls at South Beach.

Call caterer back.

The three items under "Notes" were written during the day as Sam completed tasks or made observations about his activities. When he sits down to review his Master List, Daily

Schedule, and Project Planner, he'll use these remarks as reminders and guideposts for future planning.

Make Planning a Habit

It should be noted that this time management system is only one of dozens. Some people choose to keep their schedules on computer, others find making notes into a tape recorder more helpful, still others find commercial date books sufficient for their needs. You may find an altogether different way to keep track of your responsibilities and activities, one that is suited to your own unique personality and requirements.

No matter what method you choose, however, it is essential that you learn to make it a part of your everyday life. Sam, for instance, considers his planning notebook a permanent part of his wardrobe and never goes anywhere without it. At some point, usually at the same time every day or every other day, he spends a half hour or so going over his Master List and transferring activities and tasks to their appropriate places in the notebook. You may choose to gather your thoughts and plan your daily activities first thing in the morning or in the evening before you go to bed. The most important thing is to make planning a regular habit in your life.

After a few weeks or months of practice, you'll probably come to depend on this system of time management to help you meet your responsibilities and plan more efficiently for the future. You are also likely to find the increased structure and discipline it lends to your daily life both comforting and encouraging.

Making and Meeting Deadlines

How often have you looked at your watch only to be shocked at how much of the day has passed without your being aware of it? For most adults with ADD, the answer to that question is, "Quite often." Perhaps because your mind tends to be filled with so many different thoughts and priorities, you've never been an accurate judge of time. Hours, days, even weeks, seem to slip by and you're not sure where they've gone or what was accomplished during them.

The old adage, Keep Track of the Pennies and the Dollars Take Care of Themselves, can easily be applied to the minutes and the hours of the day. Once you get a handle on how long fifteen minutes really are, and what you can accomplish in that time frame, the better you'll be able to make and meet accurate deadlines. Like all the other habits discussed here and in other chapters, however, this one will take practice and perhaps a little outside support in order to master it.

"People thought I was irresponsible because I was constantly underestimating how long something would take me," says Mark. "It wasn't that I was lying or overconfident; I really just didn't know. Then my therapist told me to perform a simple experiment: Keep track of what I was doing every single minute of the day for a few days in a row. It took a little time, but I learned so much from it. I found out that I don't spend 'a few minutes' reading the newspaper in the morning, I spend about a half an hour. It doesn't take me fifteen minutes to get to the office, it takes about twenty. So now at least I know why I'm getting docked for being late nine mornings out of ten. And I can work on ways to change it."

If you are unsure of where the time goes during many of your days, you might want to perform the same experiment. Create a Daily Schedule like the one devised above, only break it down further into fifteen-minute increments. For two days, keep track of everything you do—from showering and eating breakfast in the morning to brushing your teeth at night—and how long it takes you. Be as honest and as accurate as possible: If you spend an hour chatting with a co-worker instead of writing a marketing report, write it down. At least you'll understand why the report isn't finished when you expected it would be, and can plan your time more efficiently and accurately in the future.

Another trick to help you keep better track of time during

the day is the good old-fashioned egg timer, an alarm clock, or a newer device, the watch alarm. If you set aside an hour to read through a complicated report, set an alarm to alert you that you've reached the time limit. Otherwise, you may find yourself so immersed in a project that you fail to meet other scheduled commitments during the day.

Finally, it is important to understand your own personal limitations when learning to make and reach deadlines. One of the more endearing, but ultimately frustrating, qualities shared by many adult ADD patients is the inability to say no when others ask them for help. Unfortunately, the consequences of adding too many other unexpected tasks will eventually spell disaster for your carefully constructed Daily Schedule, and probably result in disappointing far more people than you satisfy. In Chapter Eight, we'll offer you some tips on how to communicate your priorities and needs directly and firmly to the people in your life—an essential skill in the art of time management. In the meantime, try to limit as much as possible the amount of time you spend performing unplanned activities.

The Principle of Delayed Gratification

"Another problem I used to have when it came to getting anything done on time was thinking of about a billion other things I had to do, or wanted to do, at the same time," Mark admits. "I'd start to clean out the garage, but then I'd think about fixing my son's bicycle or starting dinner or planting shrubs. By the time I stopped myself, I'd have started all three things, finished none of them, and it'd be the end of my Saturday afternoon."

Mark is learning to halt the torrent of disruptive thoughts and conflicting priorities by carrying his three-subject notebook wherever he goes—even to the garage on Saturday afternoons. "As long as I write it down," Mark explains, "I know I'll get it done eventually, and I can finish what I've started."

On the other hand, many adults with ADD find that they need to take some kind of break during the performance of a particularly challenging or time-consuming task. If they fail to do so, they are apt to become frustrated and give up long before the job is finished, or, even worse, start another complicated project to burn off their excess energy.

If you often feel yourself getting itchy or restless during the day, try one of the following "distractions" to see if it helps you return to your task with renewed energy and focus:

Five Distractions of Five Minutes or Less

- Practice deep breathing exercises such as the ones described on pages 133–135.
- Take a brisk walk around the block or around your office building, or perform ten or twenty jumping jacks. Time yourself.
- Turn on the radio and listen to one song. If you're alone, and it's appropriate, dance to it.
- Stand up, walk away from your desk or the task at hand, and stretch your body from head to toe.
- Make yourself a cup of tea and sip it while leafing through a magazine. Time yourself.

Planning for Procrastination

As we've mentioned, a certain amount of pressure is often helpful to an adult with ADD. You may find that you're able to focus better and work harder when there's just a little tension over an upcoming deadline or goal. Consciously or unconsciously, you may put off beginning a project or task just to attain that "deadline high" that comes from being under the gun. However, it is *essential* that you enter the procrastination mode only after you've carefully thought through every step of the project you're putting off.

"Like many writers, I tend to work best under a deadline, and sometimes I push against the limits a bit," says Rich. "Most of the time, I'm okay. But more than once I've been caught short because I didn't have all the facts I needed before I sat down for the crunch. One time I waited until three hours before deadline to start a story. It would have worked out all right except that I failed to get an essential quote from a principal in the story and couldn't get in touch with him in time. Boy, was that a tough thing to explain to my editor. When he asked me why I waited until the last minute to start, I had no real answer."

In the end, the key to success in the time management game appears to be *planning*: careful, consistent planning. The better prepared you are to meet your obligations, the more freedom you'll have to work in a style that best suits your capabilities and talents, and the more free time you'll have to enjoy some well earned, carefree leisure time.

Five Tips for Managing Your Time

- Use your chosen time management system faithfully.
- Break down large projects into smaller, more manageable tasks.
- Know your limitations and learn to say no.
- Schedule time for blowouts and goof-offs.
- Procrastinate wisely by planning ahead.

BUILD YOUR ORGANIZATIONAL SKILLS

- Do I find it impossible to throw anything away?   _____

- Am I constantly searching for lost items?   _____

- Am I surrounded by piles of paper and unopened mail?   _____

- Do I have enough storage space, and do I use it well?   _____

- Do I fail to put away things (groceries,
  laundry, mail) as soon as I bring them
  into the home or office?   _____

"Time management has never been much of an issue with me," says engineer Bonnie. "My work life is pretty regular and not particularly cluttered with appointments or deadlines. My biggest problems that stem from ADD, I think, have always been communication issues—I've never felt very comfortable around people—and how to organize the *stuff* in my life—papers, clothes, knickknacks, magazines, you name it. It truly upsets me when I ruin my clothes because I don't have the patience to care for them properly. And when I realize that one of the main reasons I never entertain at home is that I just know I could never clean the house properly, I feel like such a failure."

Does Bonnie's situation sound familiar to you? Did you answer many of the questions above with a resounding Yes? If so, don't despair. The problems you, Bonnie, and millions of other adults with ADD have with organizing your physical environment are not unsolvable. In the past, the symptoms of the disorder have prevented you from grasping how and where even to start building some structure and order into your home and/or office. Now that you know the source of your trouble, you will be better able to learn some new, effective strategies to tame the "organizational devil" set loose by ADD.

Getting Started

Your first step on the organizational journey involves revisiting the list of priorities you were asked to make earlier in the chapter (see "Set Priorities for Change," pages 149–153). What did you discover were your most pressing organizational problems? Chances are, these problems fall into one of two major categories: *Paper Chaos* and *Stuff Disorder*. If you're plagued by Paper Chaos, you're probably surrounded by piles of bills, letters, memos, reports, newspaper and magazine clippings, even junk mail advertisements (for goods and services that might just come in handy *someday*), to say nothing of important documents such as birth certificates, deeds, wills, and passports. Stuff Disorder, on the other hand, involves everything else—from clothes to tools to mementos and knickknacks—and may be found in every room of the house and every corner of the office.

Later in this chapter, we provide hints for managing each category of organizational challenges. If your first priority is to clean out your home or office files, you may want to read the section "Managing Paperwork" first (it starts on p. 170). But if "Stuff Disorder" is making you crazy, feel free to go on to the tips discussed under "Organizing Your Personal Belongings" (pages 174–177).

In the meantime, there are some general rules and strategies to keep in mind as you attempt to add structure and order to any aspect of your environment:

Use your planning notebook: Add your organizational goals and priorities to your Master List and/or Project Planner, then work out a logical, manageable schedule to meet them.

Break down larger challenges into more manageable tasks: As discussed earlier, it is essential for you, as an adult with ADD, to avoid becoming overwhelmed by the size or complexity of a project as much as possible. "Clean out clothes closet," for instance, may be too big and complicated an order to fill. Instead, aim to "sort and store winter clothes" one day, and save "arrange shoes, scarves, and accessories" for another time. "Establish filing system for bills" is a far more attainable goal than "Straighten out finances." In addition, keep in mind that how you feel as you approach large tasks is crucial. Instead of looking at the potential pitfalls, be positive about your capabilities. .

Strive for simplicity and comfort: The object of the organization game is to make your life easier and to minimize the stress and frustration that stem from disorder. It is not to make you feel tyrannized by any rigid, artificial system. You may well function at your best with a little clutter on your desk, or feel cheered and inspired by seeing mementos and photographs lining your shelves and bookcases. As long as you and the people around you are comfortable, any environment that allows you to feel motivated and productive is an organized one.

Start by cleaning up your environment: If organization has been a problem for you for some time, it is likely that you're both surrounded by external clutter and burdened by internal messages of self-doubt. Try to clean away as much of the disorganization and as many of the negative thoughts as possible. Fortunately, achievement in one area tends to reinforce our efforts in the other. In other words, the more messes you clean up, the more confidence you will have in your organizational skills, and vice versa.

MANAGING PAPERWORK

Phase I: The Cleanup

In order to "conquer the paper tiger," as organization expert Stephanie Winston puts it in her book *Getting Organized*, you'll need the following tools and equipment in order to begin Phase I, *The Cleanup*:

- a filing system
- a wastebasket
- three file folders or small boxes labeled "To Do," "To File," "To Store"
- your planning notebook
- ruthless determination

"My wife threatened to divorce me—or worse—if I didn't do something about my study," admits Mark. "And, frankly, I can't blame her. Not only did it look like an unholy mess, but I've lost—apparently forever—more than one important document. In fact, we had our phone shut off not because we couldn't pay the bill, but because I lost it and then forgot to pay it."

Mark's first priority was to clean out and organize his desk. Armed with the materials listed above—including ruthless determination—he attacked the task drawer by drawer. Every piece of paper he put his hand on ended up in one of the following files:

"To Do": Any material requiring action or attention within the next three to four weeks should be placed in this category. In Mark's case, the "To Do" file held unpaid bills, letters to be answered, an invitation to a wedding two weeks hence, and a magazine subscription renewal notice.

"To File": Items relating to pending projects or projects coming up from one to six months in the future should be placed in this category. Mark placed in his "To File" file a summer school catalog, several magazine articles and advertisements about a car he was thinking of buying, recently paid bills and receipts, and his grades for last semester's classes.

"To Store": Important records belong in this file, including passports, birth certificates, wills, deeds, and other legal documents. In addition, Mark finally decided to store all receipts, canceled checks, tax returns, personal letters, and souvenirs (such as playbills and postcards), and other papers that were more than two months old and no longer pending.

The Wastebasket or "Circular file": With any luck, this category will be the largest one of all, and ruthless determination is important here. Adults with ADD tend to be pack rats and hoarders for a number of reasons, including their fear of being caught unprepared because they've discarded an important object or piece of information. Another reason for the presence of so much paper chaos in the lives of adults with ADD is the sheer number of projects and schemes they either become involved in or think about getting involved in "sometime in the future."

But now is the time to be realistic about what you really need to keep. Will you ever join the yoga class offered at the community center? If not, toss the two-year-old pamphlet for it into the circular file. Same goes for the 1982 series of *National Geographic* articles, which you always thought you'd get around to reading, about the rare breed of South American turtle. Mark finally forced himself to dispose of baseball yearbooks from the previous three seasons (he was never *that* much of a fan), brochures for a cruise offered five years previously (he did add the number of the cruise line to his telephone directory), and several old grocery lists and To Do lists he had kept for who knows how long or for what reason.

Phase II: System Creation

Once Mark had a drawer or two completely free of paper, he began Phase II of the organizational plan, System Creation. With his planning notebook in hand, he carefully went through each of the active files. Based on what he found there, he established the following:

1. A *filing system* for pending projects/activities: Such a system is highly individualized and depends on the kind and complexity of records one needs to keep on hand. For some people, an accordion file to sort current bills and personal letters is enough structure for their needs; others require something more elaborate. Mark's desk contained a drawer for which he created about fifteen separate files, including one for his children's current school records, one for up-to-date insurance policies, one to hold information about the car he was planning to buy, and one marked "Pending Projects" for miscellaneous ideas Mark thought might deserve future consideration.

2. *Permanent storage* for obsolete but important documents: The only rule for creating this system is that you must mark clearly what is in every box of papers you decide to store. The woman Marion hired to help sort her things had Marion

write on a piece of paper every document she placed in a given storage box, then tape the list on top of the box. In addition, she had Marion write the general category of components with a colored marker, in large letters, on the side of every box. One read "Personal Letters 1994," another "Tax Returns and Receipts 1990–1994." Because Marion lacked a cellar, attic, or other out-of-the-way storage facility, she chose to purchase attractive floral boxes and stacked them neatly in the corner of her den. Mark, on the other hand, followed the same system, but used less expensive cardboard boxes and stored them in his basement.

3. A *schedule* for performing pending tasks and projects: Here's where your time management tools come in. It is likely that you'll find things to add from each of the active files you created as you began the organization process. Mark added the date of the wedding to his wall calendar, for instance, and made a note in his Project Planner about buying a car within the next few months. He added several tasks to his Master List, including "Write Fred and Beth," "Pay bills 12/15," and "Renew *Newsweek* subscription."

Phase III: Working the System

Once a degree of organization has been achieved, and structures like filing cabinets and storage boxes are in place, Phase III: Working the System begins—and never ends. Indeed, Phase III lasts for the rest of your life as you attempt to maintain the order you've finally created for yourself and your paperwork.

"The one thing I never fail to do is go through the mail within twelve hours of it entering my house," Marion explains. "I take it to my desk, which has a file cabinet, a wastebasket, and my planning notebook right near it. As I read each piece of mail, I decide immediately what to do with it: throw it away, file it, or do something about it. I write lots of reminders in my planning notebook so I don't lose track of what went where. And that's especially important for any work I bring home with me. So far, it's worked great. That's not to say I haven't lost the occasional bill or misplaced a file, but I'm getting much better."

Perseverance and practice are the qualities you'll require to successfully carry out Phase III of the paperwork management plan. Fortunately, the very same skills it takes to tame the paper tiger will help you organize other "stuff" in your life.

ORGANIZING YOUR PERSONAL BELONGINGS

"Long ago, I made a deal with my wife," Mark explains. "I'd handle the family finances and correspondence, and she'd take care of the rest of the household. Needless to say, until recently, all of the burden was on her. But now that I've gotten the paperwork under control and have a handle on ADD in general, I'm finding out that I can help her—and want to help her— with the rest of the household organization. I used to just leave the children's toys lying around the house and wait for my wife to pick up. Now we've worked out a pretty good system, one that's easy to follow and doesn't leave my wife doing all the dirty work. We both feel much better. She likes the help I give her, and I like not feeling guilty all the time."

In Chapter Nine, we'll discuss some of the issues Mark brings up about sharing responsibilities among all family members. The important message for this chapter involves the desire and willingness Mark now has to set up systems for organization and to work to maintain them. He and his wife both felt that the clutter left behind by their two children, due in large part to a lack of storage space for toys and clothing, was the main obstacle to order in their household. "I added 'Put up closet shelves' and 'Buy toy box' to my Master List and got around to completing those tasks within a couple of weeks. Once we had created space for all the things that needed putting away, we had a long talk with our kids. For the first time, they really had some direction, from *both* of us, about keeping things neat and orderly. Although it took some work, we all felt better. There was so much less tension in the house."

Like Marion, Bonnie decided to hire a personal consultant to help straighten out her living situation—starting with her clothes closet but eventually involving every room in the house. "What I discovered was that a room didn't have to be sterile and empty to look uncluttered and clean," Bonnie says. "It just had to make sense. Everything had to have a place, and I had to learn to put it back if I moved it. After a while, it really wasn't a big deal. I felt so much less overwhelmed when it came time to clean the house for a dinner party. Sure, things get messy sometimes, but at least I know how it is *supposed* to look—and I know what to do to get it back there."

The 3-Step Process

The process for bringing order to your personal belongings is almost identical to the one used to manage paperwork. It involves the following three steps:

1. *Throw away (or give away) what you no longer need.* Many organization experts suggest using the one-year rule—if you haven't worn or used something in more than a year, chances are you'll never wear or use it again. Exceptions exist, of course, for such things as wedding dresses, special china or silver services, and mementos and gifts. But again, you must be a bit ruthless if you want to really make a dent in your clutter. Do you really need to save every one of your child's stuffed animals— especially now that she's sixteen years old? The rack of size-fourteen clothes that you haven't worn since you lost weight three years ago can certainly be of use to someone else. And the woodworking set that your father-in-law gave you last Christmas, and which you never even opened, could be donated to the local YMCA or Boys' Club rather than take up space in your garage.

2. *Store things for future use or for sentimental purposes.* On the other hand, not everything you want out of sight need end up out of the house forever. Arm yourself with a few sturdy cardboard boxes or garment bags as you sort through your belongings. Perhaps there are some articles of clothing that you'd like to keep for a while, even if you haven't worn them for some time. Your matchbook or porcelain collection may no longer belong in your living room, but instead might find a place in storage until you have a proper showcase for it. Just as you did for the paperwork you stored, mark each box carefully so that you can keep track of where things are in case you need to retrieve them quickly.

3. *Find the most logical and accessible space for everyday items.* Logic is the key here. Once you've identified an organizational problem, look to find the most immediate and uncomplicated solution. If you're constantly misplacing your keys, keep them on a hook by the door and train yourself to deposit them there as soon as you enter the house. If you're constantly tripping over your paperback book collection, give some of the books away, store them in boxes, or build enough shelves to house them.

As you can see, building your organizational skills is a process and a goal, not a simple task. The goal is not to become perfectly organized overnight, but rather to make small, incremental steps in the right direction. The methods described here are only a few of the many available. No doubt you'll develop your own techniques, perhaps with the help of your therapist, your spouse, a hired professional, or through the tips provided in one or more of the many excellent books on organization and time management. (See Appendix for more information.) The main thing is to stick with it, not get discouraged if you have a setback, and really believe you can beat the organizational devil once you put your mind to it.

Five Tips for Building Your Organizational Skills

- Don't allow yourself to be overwhelmed by the "big picture." Tackle problems one by one, breaking each down into manageable pieces.
- Learn to be ruthless about obsolete paperwork or useless items. Throw them away or donate them to charity if appropriate.
- Use logic when designing space for your paperwork and personal belongings, but let your own unique personality shine through.
- Deal with each new item immediately. Sort mail within twenty-four hours and put away clothes as soon as they come out of the laundry, out of store packages, or off your body.
- Stop and think before you add new items to your home or work environment. Don't undermine the progress you've made by simply adding more stuff to the mix.

ORGANIZE WITH ADD AT WORK

- Are you often unsure and anxious about your responsibilities and duties?   _____
- Do you often lose track of time at work?   _____
- Is your work space organized in a way that inspires creativity and/or productivity?   _____
- Do you have someone at work who can act as your coach?   _____

For many adults with ADD, functioning within the work environment poses significant challenges. Generally speaking, work involves structure, rules, and schedules, against which adults with ADD usually chafe. And excelling at work usually requires patience, compliance, and consistency, qualities often in short supply within the ADD population. Although many adults with ADD are highly successful in the business world, many others can point to a long history of employment disappointments and setbacks. And, successful or not, a great majority of adults with ADD describe a work history marked by struggle—struggle to compensate for their shortcomings, to hide their fears and insecurities, to fit into a world that they don't quite understand or feel a part of.

In Chapter Ten, we'll discuss ways for you to reconsider your current career in the context of your ADD diagnosis. Now that you know about the disorder and how it may be affecting you, it may be possible for you to choose a line of work that more effectively utilizes your strengths and assets than does your present occupation. In addition, we'll help you to identify some goals and ambitions that may be buried beneath layers of ADD-related self-doubt and anxiety.

Until then, the next section outlines some of the ways you can make effective use of time management, organizational, and behavioral strategies within the work environment.

Learn the Rules and Procedures

As you may well know, structure can be either the bane of your existence or your very best friend, and this is all the more true within the work environment. Mark, who has held jobs in construction and manufacturing, speaks for many adults with ADD when he explains his view of structure in the workplace: "I get along just fine when the rules and procedures are made very clear to me from the beginning. As long as I know what's expected of me, I do okay most of the time," he says. "But when the regulations seem arbitrary or aren't enforced consistently, or if my job responsibilities aren't clearly defined or don't make sense to me, I get really frustrated, lose my temper, and end up walking off the job or getting fired more often than not."

Marion, who works in the relatively liberal and unstructured environment of advertising, also finds that having a specific set of job guidelines and office procedures makes her feel more comfortable and productive at work.

"It really helps me to have something to *follow* when I'm working, like a system or a form or a course of action," Marion says. "The president of my current agency made up a checklist of all the elements involved in a complete ad campaign and what order they should come in. I keep one copy of the list tacked up on my bulletin board, and use another to focus on as I go along. In a strange way, the guidelines are liberating; they provide a context in which I can take chances I might be too afraid to take in a completely free atmosphere."

Although some adults with ADD thrive in less organized environments, if you think you might benefit from having more structure in your job, try following one or more of these suggestions:

• Read the employee handbook or departmental/project guidelines and make lists of helpful rules and procedures. Tack the lists on a bulletin board for quick reference.

• Ask your employer to provide you with a list of your job responsibilities. Make sure you understand exactly what is expected of you and ask questions if you don't.

• Request regular evaluations from your supervisor. Feedback, whether in the form of encouragement or constructive criticism, is extremely helpful for an adult with ADD who can easily get lost in his or her own often unrealistic expectations and assumptions. Ask your supervisor to be specific in his or her comments and, if possible, to provide concrete examples of expected behavior and performance. This process will reduce miscommunication and help keep you on track.

Managing Time on the Job

No matter what type of work you perform, from construction like Mark to high-tech engineering like Bonnie, your employer no doubt expects you to make efficient and productive use of your time on the job. Arriving at work on time, staying focused on the task at hand, and consistently meeting your job responsibilities are just a few of the ways that time management is important in any work environment. If your job involves making and meeting deadlines, scheduling appointments, and/or tracking several ongoing projects, the need for good time management skills is especially crucial.

The techniques described earlier in the chapter—such as setting realistic goals and priorities, breaking down large projects into more manageable tasks, and using your planning notebook on a regular basis—can certainly be adapted for use at work. In addition, some of the following tips might come in handy:

• Use bright-colored Post-its tacked to your desk or bulletin board to remind you of important meetings or deadlines.

• If you have flexibility in setting your work schedule, plan to tackle especially creative or intellectually demanding tasks during times of the day when you're apt to be most focused and efficient.

• Try doing more than one nondemanding task at the same time: Open the mail while returning telephone calls, jot down some notes while waiting for a meeting to begin or for the copy machine to be free.

Managing Paperwork in the Workplace

In most offices across the country, there is a virtual avalanche of information cascading onto the tops of desks every day. For workers who suffer from ADD, Paper Chaos can get truly out of hand in this environment, and so it is especially important for you to follow the guidelines of paper management described earlier. Other tips that may help you "tame the paper tiger" include:

• Try to sort through your In box at least once a day, preferably at the same time. Otherwise, you'll end up under the heap of papers before the week is out.

• Create an efficient system for paperwork. Throw away all nonessential documents, place those that require action on your part in a folder marked "To Do" and all those that should be filed in a "To File" folder. If necessary, set up other categories, such as "To Read" or "For General Circulation."

• Handle paperwork only once whenever possible. Shuffling papers from one folder to another is a waste of time, energy, and space. Whenever you pick up a piece of paper, tag it with a pencil mark. If you see more than two or three marks on any piece of paper, it's time to deal with it, file it, pass it along, or throw it away.

Take Advantage of Technology

Computers, fax machines, calculators, answering machines, and voice mail—these are all amazing devices with the capacity to save time, eliminate paper chaos, and help organize our schedules. Unfortunately, many adults with ADD tend to feel anxious and incapable of mastering technology, mainly because they've never felt particularly adept at learning *anything* new.

Since you've made it this far in the book, however, we assume that you have more confidence in your abilities than ever before. If you haven't discovered the power of the computer or the art of the fax machine, it's time to at least get on the "on ramp" of the much-touted "information superhighway." Find someone at work to introduce you to the basics, or take a class offered at a local high school or college. You'll be surprised at how much time and energy you'll end up saving.

Find Support

As discussed earlier, telling your boss and colleagues about your ADD may or may not be wise, and it is difficult to advise anyone about such an important matter without knowing the exact situation. However, if at all possible, you should tell at least one person at work about your condition, and preferably someone highly organized and willing to act as your coach during the work day. He or she can help keep you on track and focused, remind you of important appointments and meetings, as well as encourage and cajole you should you become frustrated or overwhelmed. Needless to say, you should be able to communicate easily with your coach, and to trust him or her implicitly.

Five Tips for Organizing at Work with ADD

- Understand your job requirements and the expectations of your employer.
- Use your planning notebook consistently.
- Maintain an efficient, orderly work environment.
- Take advantage of technology.
- Enlist the services of a "work coach."

CELEBRATE SUCCESS

- Do I often lose track of tasks I complete and instead concentrate on those things still to do?
- Do I feel that any time off is wasted time?
- Am I as aware of my strengths as I am of my shortcomings?

It is all too easy in these stressful, overscheduled times to lose sight of the small but significant advances we make every day on the climb up our personal mountains. Instead we tend to focus on the challenges left unmet and the miles of the journey still ahead. The effort you are making to learn to manage the symptoms of ADD is a brave one, and one that takes a great deal of energy and commitment. It is essential that you take the time to recognize and reward yourself for every bit of success you achieve along the way.

That's not to say that you should buy a mink coat because you organized your closet or take a vacation every time you finish a project on time. Fortunately, there are several less expensive and far more appropriate gestures you can make in honor of your progress.

"I know you'll think it sounds silly," Marion admits, "but I put a gold star at the top of my Daily Schedule whenever I've had a particularly successful day, like if I cross everything off the To Do list or handle an unexpected job at work without going nuts. When I flip through the notebook, I get a little thrill when I see all the stars."

Crossing things off your list as you complete them, taking a moment to admire an organized closet, even awarding yourself a gold star for finishing a project are just a few of the concrete ways to celebrate your accomplishments. Rich displays a framed copy of his first front-page story on the wall near his desk to remind him that "if I could do it once, I can do it again and again," while Bonnie keeps a before-and-after picture of her once-cluttered, now pristine living room taped to the refrigerator door.

"I go for something a bit more self-indulgent," remarks Sam. "When I deliver finished proofs to a client—on time—I take myself out for a big, juicy hamburger at my favorite diner. It's a small extravagance, but one I've learned to feel that I deserve."

You too should learn to indulge yourself with some well-deserved rewards and time-outs when you've reached a certain goal or worked a particularly long day. If you're like most adults with ADD, you have lots of excess energy and if you try too hard to control and focus it, you'll end up burning out instead of moving forward. The following list is offered to show you how easy and inexpensive it can be to reward yourself. It's up to you to start believing that you really deserve it.

Ten Rewards Worth Two Hours and Ten Dollars (or Less)

- Take an aerobics class during your lunch hour or after work.
- Visit a local museum on a free afternoon. Choose to view the works of just one artist or from one period.
- Take your spouse out for coffee or your best friend for an ice cream cone—right in the middle of a work week if you can manage it.

- Get a manicure (men, too!).
- Play a game of tennis, racquetball or other high-energy, competitive sport.
- Go to a movie—and walk to the theater if possible.
- Stroll briskly through your local park or favorite neighborhood. Take the time to really appreciate the beauty around you.
- Call your best "out-of-town" friend—no matter where in the world he or she lives—and talk for fifteen minutes.
- Buy (or pick) a bouquet of flowers for the room in which you spend the most time during the day.
- Simply goof off and do absolutely nothing of importance for one solid hour. Time yourself.

Perhaps the most meaningful reward you can give yourself is the credit for learning to organize your time, meet your obligations, and make your deadlines. Through your talent, intelligence, and understanding of ADD and its effects, you are now able to set some goals and work toward them with energy and commitment. Even if you've had some setbacks—and you'll have a few more in the future, no doubt—you are now able to see your time management and organizational challenges more clearly and with more optimism than ever before.

Five Tips for Celebrating Success

- Never lose sight of your accomplishments.
- Prepare a list of appropriate rewards and indulge in one whenever you reach a goal or finish a major task.
- Believe that you are deserving of rewards.
- Consider setbacks opportunities for growth.
- Concentrate on your assets, not your liabilities.

In the next chapter, we'll tackle the other side of the ADD behavior coin: communication. For many adults with ADD, symptoms of the disorder have formed what may seem like an impenetrable barrier between them and the rest of the world. Relationships of all kinds are affected by their difficulties in conveying their emotions, making clear their objectives, and accurately interpreting the verbal, visual, and sensory messages sent to them by others. Chapter Nine will help you better understand how ADD may be affecting your ability to establish meaningful relationships with colleagues, friends, and lovers, as well as provide skills and techniques for improving your communication skills.

IMPORTANT QUESTIONS AND ANSWERS ABOUT CHAPTER SEVEN

Q Although my office may look pretty messy on the outside, I always know where everything is. But at every staff review, my boss strongly suggests that I straighten it up. Shouldn't I be allowed a little clutter if that's how I work best?

A In an ideal world, we'd all be able to choose to live and work in the atmosphere best suited to our personal needs and tastes. The reality is, however, that in order to get along and progress, we often must learn to compromise with and conform to certain standards at work and in society at large. Your boss may have very good reasons for wanting your office to look neat: Is it visible to visitors and clients? Is it distracting to other workers? Are you sure that you don't occasionally lose important documents in the clutter?

If the answer to those questions is no, on the other hand, you may want to revisit the issue with your boss. Is he or she aware that you have ADD? Is he or she well educated about its effects? If not, and the issue of office neatness is a significant problem for you, you may want to consider broaching the subject with your boss, especially if you think he or she would be more willing to accommodate your needs under such circumstances.

In the end, however, it may be easier simply to tidy up your office using the strategies outlined in this chapter. You may well find—as have many of your adult ADD peers—that you are more productive and less anxious the more organized you become.

Q I freeze up when I'm faced with a deadline, even a small one, like paying a bill on time or making a phone call at a specific time. It's not like I'm overwhelmed by the size of the task, or even its importance. What's happening, and what can I do about it?

A It sounds as if you may be resisting deadlines because you've missed so many in the past. In other words, you may be so afraid of failing because of past negative experiences that you don't want to even try today—despite the fact that you may have learned some valuable time management and organizational skills in the meantime.

One piece of advice: Keep trying to meet those small deadlines. This is where a system of rewards may come in handy. If you make the phone call in time, buy yourself a magazine to read at the end of the day. If you get the bill in the mail on time, reward yourself with an extra half hour at the gym over the weekend. With each success and reward, your confidence in your own strength and capabilities will increase and, chances are, you'll feel better able to conquer ever larger tasks on time and with far less anxiety.

Chapter Eight

BRIDGING THE COMMUNICATION GAP

Communication. Derived from the Latin word *communicare* meaning "to share," communication is the process by which we exchange information, ideas, and feelings. It is the essence of all human interaction and the basis upon which individual relationships are built, business transactions conducted, and societies formed.

The symptoms of Attention Deficit Disorder pose special challenges to this process for many adults, challenges addressed at length in this chapter. In the first half of the chapter, "ADD Roadblocks to Intimacy," we'll describe the ways ADD may have affected your communication skills, and thus your ability to form and maintain healthy, successful relationships. In the second half, "Clearing a Communication Path," we'll outline strategies and techniques to help you improve your skills as a listener, speaker, and observer.

It should be noted that social skills training and skill-building can benefit almost everyone with ADD. However, even those who know or are aware of how to behave in social situations may lack the ability to follow through and perform those skills. Simply possessing or acquiring these skills does not always translate into appropriate use of them. In this sense, ADD can be viewed not so much as a skills deficit problem, but more of a skills performance problem. Indeed, as Dr. Russell Barkley, a leading researcher on ADD, has said, "ADD is considered to be not a disorder of not knowing what to do, but rather a disorder of not doing what you know." Nevertheless, learning and practicing social skills, communication skills, organizational skills, and other self-management skills remain a crucial aspect of treatment for most adults with ADD.

ADD ROADBLOCKS TO INTIMACY

Many of the qualities necessary to communicate successfully—including patience, attention, empathy, and an understanding of one's own emotional and intellectual motives—are often in short supply among the ADD population. Hence, many adults with ADD must struggle just as hard to create satisfying social and intimate lives as they do to establish order and structure in their physical environment.

Communication and ADD

I have trouble getting along with people.   _____

I feel misunderstood most of the time.   _____

I frequently lose my temper.   _____

I am perceived by others as being cold and
    unfeeling.   _____

It is difficult for me to be intimate with
    another person.   _____

"I never could figure out what I was doing wrong," says Amy. "But ever since I can remember, I've felt like I lived behind some kind of opaque screen that distorted everything I said and heard. It's only now, since I've learned about ADD, that I understand some of the obstacles I've had to face, like completely missing the point of a conversation because I didn't read body language very well or didn't recognize someone's tone of voice. Or when I got so frustrated with myself and my shortcomings that I snapped at the person I was talking to or turned away because I was embarrassed. It's hard work, but I'm finally able to sort through some of these issues. Finally, that screen is being lifted and I feel like a part of the world for the first time in my life."

If you've been living with ADD for most of your life, chances are good that you can relate rather well to Amy's experience, as well as to the statements made above. Many adults with ADD describe feeling isolated and "different" from their non-ADD peers. *Anxiety* and *avoidance* are words commonly used by those with ADD to characterize their feelings about establishing and maintaining meaningful relationships.

"By all appearances, I have lots of friends," says Bonnie. "I'm pretty outgoing and don't have much trouble meeting people. But something short-circuits along the way. In the past, before I realized the impact ADD could have on my relationships, I thought that I just got bored with everybody. I cringe when I think about how rude and impatient I could be, sometimes without even realizing it. And even when I did realize it, I just assumed it was because *they* couldn't keep up with me. The truth is, no one could keep up with me, not even me! Half the time, my mind was racing so fast, I couldn't follow what anybody else was saying. And I can't tell you how often I'd have absolutely no memory of having a conversation with someone, even a deeply personal one. No wonder I've never had many really close friends. And my love life, well, that's a whole other story."

As Amy and Bonnie's honest descriptions of their social difficulties reveal, the symptoms of ADD can disrupt the communication process in several different ways. Some people with

ADD have trouble following conversations because they become distracted by their own thoughts and/or by outside stimuli. Others, like Amy, have difficulty properly interpreting the messages sent to them because they fail to notice body language, intonation, and other nonverbal clues. Social skills are perhaps most difficult to master for those adults who suffer from the impulsivity so often a part of ADD. Even if they know and accept standard rules of behavior, they are often unable to control themselves enough to follow them.

Although having deficient communication skills is often a part of the ADD syndrome, it is important to underscore an important point: The way you express yourself is a unique feature of your personality, a part of you that you should neither want nor expect to completely change. Instead, you should aim to recognize, and then work to improve, those aspects of the communication process that are troublesome for you. Later in this chapter, we outline some specific strategies that address some of the most common communication problems among adults with ADD. First, however, let's examine exactly how the symptoms of ADD may affect your ability to form healthy, strong relationships of all kinds.

Recognizing the Roadblocks

In Chapter Seven, we looked at ways that the symptoms of ADD might affect your ability to organize the physical world—to balance your priorities, structure your time, and establish an orderly, productive environment at work and at home. In fact, the very same symptoms can interfere with your ability to communicate effectively with the people in your life. Hyperactivity, inattention, and impulsivity are the three major roadblocks to effective communication, while other ADD-related behaviors—such as poor anger control, thrill-seeking, and low self-esteem—may cause additional difficulties.

ROADBLOCK #1: HYPERACTIVITY

I find myself constantly fidgeting during
    conversations and/or feel the need to
    get up and walk around.   _____

I'm often told I appear nervous and
    distracted.   _____

I find it difficult to spend quiet time with
    my friends and family.   _____

"People have forever been mistaking my restlessness for boredom and rudeness," journalist Rich remarks. "And who can blame them? I used to be always tapping my foot or playing with a rubber band or even getting up and walking around in the middle of a conversation. It often caused problems on the job when I'd inadvertently distract or even insult someone I was interviewing. Now, with medication and some behavioral training, I'm able to sit still and feel comfortable for much longer, which has really helped at work."

Hyperactivity, one of ADD's cardinal symptoms, is a common roadblock to successful communication in many venues, as you may well have experienced. Feeling agitated and restless makes it difficult to engage in any kind of meaningful dialogue, at work, at home, or in social situations. It is especially upsetting to the development of intimate relationships, where quiet times and moments of reflection and serenity are often desired, but just as often circumvented by this symptom.

"I know I've had trouble with this one," Bonnie admits. "I can think of many times when my erratic behavior undermined a relationship. I remember one moment in particular when I realized how tedious I must be to be around. A guy I was seeing brought over some Chinese food and a couple of videos. I was okay for about an hour and then I kept getting up from the couch, clearing away dishes, then doing the dishes, then moving some magazines from the end table, then making some coffee, then cleaning up after the coffee, then fluffing the throw pillows.

Here he was trying to get romantic, and I was acting like some deranged Suzy Homemaker. And I just couldn't help it."

Three Strategies to Control Hyperactivity

• Try to exercise or otherwise release excess energy before an important meeting or quiet date.
• If you must fidget, try to do so discreetly. Tap your foot beneath a desk or table. Walk around only when you are speaking.
• Hyperactivity can also mean talking too much or too fast. Ask a trusted friend to warn you when you are talking too much.

See "Clearing a Communication Path," pages 204–206 for details.

ROADBLOCK #2: INATTENTION

I find it difficult to follow fast-paced
conversations.   _____

I often fail to hear or remember important
details after they are told to me.   _____

I'm often accused of not respecting someone
else's opinions.   _____

Nothing is more upsetting than realizing in the middle of a conversation that you haven't been paying attention to what has been said to you and so have no idea what to say next. At the same time, the person with whom you are talking feels equally at sea, and sometimes downright offended, when he or she realizes that you've been somewhere else all along.

As someone with ADD, you may have noticed that inattentiveness can cause a variety of problems. First, if you fail to pay close attention, you will undoubtedly miss hearing and remembering important information. At work, this can result in missed meetings, overlooked or improperly performed tasks, and unmet expectations. In personal relationships, inattention may have particularly distressing consequences, including hurt feelings, broken promises, and feelings of neglect and inconsideration.

"I can't tell you how many times I've seen hurt and disappointment in my wife's eyes," admits Rich. "And not just because I'm always late for everything or forget her birthday. It's worse than that. I've hurt her because she feels I don't care about her opinions and feelings, that I don't listen because what she's saying isn't important to me. Of all the things I'm looking forward to now that I know about my ADD, making that up to my wife is the most significant to me."

Three Strategies to Combat Inattention

- Reduce distractions during conversations. Shut off the television, close the office door, choose a quiet restaurant.
- Make frequent eye contact. This will help bring you back into the conversation.
- Focus on body language and vocal intonation to gain deeper understanding.

See "Clearing a Communication Path," pages 204–206, for details.

ROADBLOCK #3: IMPULSIVITY

I often find myself saying things without
thinking.   _____

I often walk away from a discussion if I
become bored or frustrated.   _____

People tell me sometimes that they find me
too opinionated or overbearing.   _____

The difficulty many adults with ADD have in curbing their verbal and physical responses to stimuli can be very disruptive, especially within the work environment. Generally speaking, office protocol does not allow mouthing off to your boss, snapping at your staff, or suddenly walking out of a meeting because you feel bored or annoyed. Such behavior not only tends to undermine others' trust in you, it may eventually even destroy your own confidence in yourself and your capabilities.

"I'm okay at work, for the most part, mainly because I'm by myself most of the time," Bonnie explains. "Where I get into trouble is in larger groups, when I'm more nervous. I find myself saying the first thing that pops into my head, and it's not always appropriate in tone, or content, or timing. Especially when it comes to politics, or other subjects I have strong opinions about, I don't always know when I've gone too far. I do know that people sometimes find me overpowering because I'm always interrupting."

Three Strategies to Harness Impulsivity

- Before taking your turn in a conversation, ask the person speaking if he or she is finished.
- Don't feel you have to fill every second with conversation. Remember, silence *can* be golden.
- Take a mental time-out from a conversation if you feel you're becoming overstimulated and out of control. Simply find the right moment to excuse yourself and take a break.

See "Clearing a Communication Path," pages 204–206, for details.

RELATED ADD ROADBLOCKS

My mood changes constantly; I never know
how I'm going to react—and neither
does anyone else. ____

I'm known for my quick and explosive
temper. ____

I like to "push people's buttons" during
discussions.   ____

I rarely feel confident about myself or my
ability to hold my own in
conversations.   ____

In addition to the three cardinal symptoms of ADD, other common ADD symptoms and behaviors may also influence the course of relationships because of their impact on communication. You may well have trouble creating and maintaining solid relationships if you are one of the many adults with ADD who experience frequent *mood swings*, for instance. Never knowing what emotional state you'll be in from day to day, or even from hour to hour, makes it difficult for both you and the people in your life to establish a healthy rhythm and pattern to your association.

A symptom of ADD closely related to mood swings is *poor anger control*. Many adults with ADD tend to have quick and explosive tempers due to the high degree of frustration with which they live as they try to cope with their symptoms. The lack of patience and understanding they exhibit frequently alienates co-workers, friends, family members, and lovers.

"Although I also have a pretty quick temper, what really drove my first wife crazy was my need to take huge chances all the time," says Mark. "Driving too fast, drinking a little too much, spending too much money. It plain wore her out, I think. On top of all that, I think I also pushed the edge of the envelope verbally, too. I got some kind of rise out of seeing someone get shocked or offended by what I was saying. It wasn't like I didn't know what I was doing, or couldn't stop myself. I actually thought it was kind of fun. Until, of course, I'd ruin another friendship or lose another job."

Like Mark, a small subset of adults with ADD are predisposed toward highly stimulating, *thrill-seeking* behavior. Although such conduct often masks itself as enthusiasm or a healthy zest for life, a little of it often goes a long way when it comes to most relationships. As Mark's first wife can certainly attest, there tends to be a fine line between thrill-seeking and self-destructive behavior, a line often crossed by adults with ADD.

Finally, what probably interferes most in the communication process for many people with the disorder is their chronic *low self-esteem*. Needless to say, it is hard to form healthy relationships if you are unable to appreciate your own good qualities. After years of feeling out-of-place and inept, many adults with ADD lack the self-confidence to enjoy social interaction or to participate on an equal basis with others.

Three Strategies to Bolster Emotional Stability

- Accept emotions as a natural part of life. Try to focus on the positive rather than the negative.
- Learn to identify your feelings as they occur and see if there is a pattern to your mood swings or a trigger to your angry outbursts.
- Once again, concentrate on your assets, talents, and accomplishments. The more confidence you have in yourself, the better you'll be able to communicate with others.

See "Clearing a Communication Path," pages 204–206, for details.

Recognizing Unhealthy Patterns

The symptoms and related behaviors of ADD, especially low self-esteem and a high degree of frustration, frequently result in the creation of unhealthy patterns within relationships of all kinds. See if you recognize yourself in any of the following statements:

I often feel like the deck is so stacked against me that I could never be someone's true equal in a relationship. _____

I have my own way of doing things, and it's
    difficult for me to change for anyone
    else.   ____

I'm so frazzled and disorganized. I really need
    someone in my life to help me stay
    on track and on top of things.   ____

I've been hurt so often in relationships that
    I have a hard time trusting anybody.
    Sometimes I think it would be better if
    I just stayed alone.   ____

As an adult with ADD, you run a higher risk than some of establishing a negative or problematic self-image which, in turn, may be damaging to your relationships. In fact, the way you see yourself and your capabilities has a great impact on the quality of all of your relationships.

Whether or not ADD is involved, no association between two or more people, no matter how sound and well balanced, is based on complete equality. We each bring our own individual strengths and levels of commitment to every association we develop. Both in the business world and our personal lives, one person generally has a little more interest in the relationship than the other and/or holds a position of greater or lesser power. In most relationships, this balance shifts at various points as time passes and circumstances change.

It is also true that it is quite natural for people to assume certain roles within relationships, partly based on their particular talents and proclivities, partly on gender differences, and partly on the chemistry between the people involved. "I think I first noticed the role-playing things with my parents," Rich recalls. "Before they got divorced, my mother always seemed to be in so much control, not only as a disciplinarian with us kids, but also in her manner and style. My father was the freewheeling one. But after he left, my mother loosened up so much. Maybe that was because a source of tension was gone, but I think it was also because people in relationships tend to seek a kind of balance with each other. If it's done in a healthy way, it's great, but when it requires you to change too much of yourself, it can be a disaster."

Needless to say, relationships can become unbalanced and unhealthy for any number of reasons, and ADD is only one of them. However, there is no doubt that ADD may add special pressure and constraints to relationships of all kinds. Fortunately, the symptoms of ADD are often mild enough—or the person with ADD adept enough at compensating for them— to mitigate some of these pressures. In other cases, however, the relationship is profoundly influenced by the presence of the disorder and its effects, both practically and emotionally.

THE EMOTIONAL ROLES OF ADD

In the next chapter, we'll take a look at some of the practical issues raised within couples and families when one or more members have ADD. In the meantime, it's important to recognize some of the emotional roles adults with ADD may take on within relationships.

The Victim

All of us, at one time or another, feel as if the entire world has turned against us, that nothing is going right, and that there's nothing we can do to change it. For many adults with ADD, however, this refrain may become a litany that is repeated endlessly until it becomes almost a self-fulfilling prophecy.

"I went into so many relationships—at work and in my personal life—with such a big chip on my shoulder that it's a miracle anybody talked to me at all," Ken admits. "I was the king of all victims. Nothing was ever my fault, not my substance abuse, not my failure to follow through on commitments, not my crummy attitude. I blamed my parents, the woman I was with, life in general. Even now that I know about ADD and am working to change it, I still find myself feeling this way sometimes."

What happened to Ken happens to many other adults with ADD who consciously or unconsciously cast themselves in the role of victim. Their poor self-image is reflected in their relationships often in negative ways. If you project the image of someone who is always on the wrong end of bad news or a regular casualty in the war of bad luck, for instance, employers may well think of you as someone unreliable and apt to make mistakes. Your family may draw back from you a bit to avoid being touched by your misfortune too often. Friends and mates may be more difficult to come by, and the ones with whom you become involved may well take on certain unhealthy roles to balance your own.

In fact, some "victims" end up surrounded by people who fulfill that claim by taking advantage of them. Others find themselves paired with a friend or lover who plays the role of "savior," constantly feeling the need to rescue you from certain doom—a doom you create for yourself. As long as that person keeps saving you—or until you both get tired of the constant struggle—you will stay stuck in a victim role forever.

Three Ways to Avoid the Victim Role

- Stop assigning blame for your problems. Instead, work on strategies to solve them.
- Make a list of your accomplishments and successes. Every time you start to complain or blame, recount one of your triumphs instead.
- Insist upon taking more responsibility for yourself. As you learn new skills, introduce them into your relationships.

The Controller

"I can't tell you what it took for me to finally let my wife, who thrives on paperwork, handle the family budget," photographer

Sam admits. "Or to hand over scheduling to an assistant. All my life, I thought I was the only one who knew how to do things right. That my way, in fact, was the only right way. And this in the face of constant screw-ups and mismanagement on my part. I know now that trying to master everything was a way to deny that I needed help and keep anyone from really knowing how out of control I was inside."

It may seem like a contradiction in terms for a person with ADD to be a control freak but, in fact, a strong need for authority and power is a common reaction to the disorder. "If I can't control what's going on inside my head," some adults with ADD say, "at least I can control what's going on around me." Although that's a healthy attitude when it comes to organizing paperwork or managing time, it can often backfire when it comes to relationships. In the end, a so-called control freak can end up either surrounded by people with no strong wills of their own—individuals most adults with ADD would quickly bore of—or within relationships filled with tension and resentment.

Three Ways to Loosen Control

- Accept imperfection in yourself and others.
- Relinquish one chore or activity every week to someone in your life. Let your spouse choose the restaurant; ask a colleague to deliver a report; have your kids wash the car.
- Learn to recognize and praise the efforts of others. By doing so, you'll remind yourself that you are not the only one with skills and talent and let them know their help and support is welcome.

The Helpless One

In many ways the opposite of the Controller, the Helpless One tends to find people to take over and manage life, often to the point of relinquishing all responsibility for both the problems and the accomplishments he or she encounters along the way. Ben, for instance, believes he has presented the image of being helpless much of his life, despite the fact that he feels quite ambitious and driven to succeed.

"I guess that by saying up front that I couldn't do something, I figured I wouldn't disappoint anybody," Ben explains. "But that kind of backfired, or rather was kind of a vicious cycle. The more successful I was in getting people to think I couldn't do things, the less they expected of me. I ended up believing that they were right, that I *couldn't* do anything. Most of the people in my life have been people who either felt sorry for me or were just as down on themselves."

Three Ways to Take Care of Yourself

- Make a list of all the tasks you know you do well—and be objective. Stop yourself from asking for help on any of the chores or activities on that list.
- Erase the negative self-talk tape that says "I can't" and replace it with one that says "I will."
- Find yourself a coach, someone who will encourage you to try new things and applaud your efforts no matter the outcome.

The Loner

"I've held myself back from every relationship I've ever been in, even with my family," says Amy. "I've always thought it was easier to be alone than to have to reveal myself, with all my flaws, to another person and face rejection, again."

Amy's instinct for self-protection is shared by many of her peers with ADD, sometimes because they've been disappointed and hurt so many times before, and sometimes simply because they feel inept and unwelcome even if others do not perceive them that way. Indeed, this attitude, like the others discussed here, may well become a self-fulfilling prophecy. Self-conscious, sometimes defensive, the adult with ADD who sees him or herself as a loner may shut down socially and emotionally until a pattern of true isolation exists, even within relationships.

"I know it sounds terrible," Amy says. "But I was most lonely within my second marriage. My husband was always there with me, but we were so far apart emotionally that I was terrified to let him see the real me. It took me three years after the divorce to start dating again."

Three Ways to Let Others In

- Continue to educate yourself about ADD, then let others know how it may have affected your relationships in the past.
- Don't assume that people will form a negative impression of you.
- Push yourself to participate in just one activity that will bring you into contact with new people.

PURSUING THE GOALS OF COMMUNICATION

In Chapters Six and Seven, we outlined three general goals—balance, structure, and satisfaction—that also apply very well to the subject of communication and relationships. Let's take them one by one:

Balance

When it comes to relationships, perhaps nothing is more important than learning to balance your needs and expectations with those of another person. What this requires is the ability to step out of yourself a little bit and see a situation through someone else's eyes. Many adults with ADD are so caught up in their own struggle with the disorder, however, that they lack both the energy and the perspective to consider the needs of the people around them.

What it takes to establish and maintain proper balance in relationships is the ability to listen and observe with care, as well as to express yourself clearly and with honesty. In addition, a more subtle but equally important quality is empathy—the ability to understand and share in another's emotions and feelings. In the second part of this chapter, we'll describe techniques that will help improve your skills in these important aspects of the communication process.

Structure

Every relationship is built upon an invisible emotional and physical framework, a structure that has very specific limits and boundaries. No matter how intimate or inconsequential a relationship is, the structure must be respected by everyone involved or the connection will fail to be made or end up broken, perhaps irreparably.

"I've never been very good at reading other people's motives or figuring out what they expected. I've always either gone way over the limit or missed the boat altogether," explains Ben. "This has happened with everybody—teachers, employers, my family—but especially with women. In high school, I'd pay all kinds of attention to some girl who wasn't interested in me at all but fail to see when another girl kind of liked me. So I'd spent all this time bugging somebody who thought I was a pest or worse, and hurting the feelings of someone I barely knew existed—all without knowing what I was doing wrong. Pretty soon, I learned not even to try anymore."

Unfortunately, this is an all-too-common scenario for many adults who grew up struggling with ADD. The same symptoms that frustrated their attempts to learn math or spelling—inattentiveness, restlessness, distractibility among others—also hindered their ability to pick up the social skills taught to children and adolescents in more indirect ways. These skills, which include reading body language and decoding vocal intonations, allow most people to readily recognize the boundaries of human relationships. Without them, however, the bonds that are created tend to be tenuous at best, and often filled with tension and confusion. As you'll see in the next section, it's never too late to learn or improve upon these skills and thus improve your ability to define and follow the rules of social interaction.

Satisfaction

Above all, the goals of communication are to learn, to progress, and to share the burdens and the joys of work, love, and everyday life with one another. For too many adults with ADD, however, the difficulties ADD symptoms present to the communication process undermine these goals. Instead, they often feel troubled and anxious about their relationships rather than buoyed and stimulated by them.

"Until I knew about my ADD, I used to get so frustrated at people and at myself," says Amy. "When I was younger, I'd fight against all the rules I thought were made up just to punish me for being different. Finally, though, I simply gave up and withdrew. Even in my marriages, I felt alone and lonely so much of the time. Now that I'm getting some therapy, and figuring out what I can do to change things, I'm starting to enjoy being around other people for the first time since I was a little kid."

Just like Amy, you too can begin to master some new communication skills that will help you raise the barrier that ADD may have placed between you and the rest of the world.

CLEARING A COMMUNICATION PATH

As a society, we share information in many different ways: through the mass media of television, radio, and movies, as well as through the written word in newspapers, magazines, and books. When we talk about communication here, however, we'll be discussing *interpersonal communication*: the private exchanges that take place between people in relatively small groups. It is through such interaction that we form nearly every relationship in our lives, from the most intimate associations to the most fleeting of acquaintanceships.

Understanding the Communication Process

The communication process is a complicated one. It consists of three main components: a sender, a receiver, and a message. The sender (or the speaker) imparts a message by using words, tone of voice, and other more subtle indicators of mood and meaning such as eye movements and body position. The receiver (or listener) derives the significance of the message by interpreting these verbal and nonverbal signals.

Successful communication takes place when the sender uses words and expressions that accurately represent the message he or she wants to pass on, and the receiver correctly decodes the message. Miscommunication occurs when the sender fails to express the true meaning of the message and/or the receiver incorrectly interprets it. This can happen for any number of reasons. Indeed, the communication process can break down at any point and when it does, the meaning of the message is lost and misunderstanding takes place.

As discussed earlier, the primary symptoms of ADD—hyperactivity, inattention, and impulsivity—often disrupt the communication process. They may have interfered with your ability to learn proper skills in the first place or prevented you from using these skills in an appropriate way. Fortunately, medication can alleviate these symptoms enough for many adults to gain some control over their social skills. Behavioral training, especially for those with ADD who are particularly impulsive, takes time, dedication, and hard work, but can help to promote healthier, more productive relationships.

In essence, you take on two roles—that of sender and receiver—every time you involve yourself in a conversation with another person. You send information by speaking, gesturing, and relaying your mood and intent with other nonverbal clues. We say these activities involve *expressive skills*, since they require you to take an active role in transmitting the message. You receive information by listening, observing, and sensing the mood and intent of others. These *receptive skills* demand just as much energy and concentration as the more active expressive skills. As an adult with ADD, you may need to improve both your expressive and your receptive skills in order to communicate more effectively. In this part of the chapter, we'll show you how to do just that.

DEVELOPING YOUR EXPRESSIVE SKILLS

I tend to talk too fast. _____

I'm often nervous because I'm afraid I'll use the wrong words. _____

People are always asking me to speak up (or quiet down). _____

I often lose my train of thought or go off on tangents. _____

My restlessness and fidgeting often belie or distort the meaning of what I'm trying to express. _____

I often feel that people don't see me as I truly am. _____

Self-expression—the accurate presentation of your opinions and personality to the outside world—is truly an art. With or without the additional challenge of ADD, getting your personal message across with grace and precision is no minor feat. As described above, it involves three interrelated activities: _speaking_, _gesturing_, and _relaying_.

Speaking

"I had no idea what I sounded like until a party I attended was videotaped," Bonnie says. "When I watched it, I saw for the first time what people had been telling me for years— sometimes kindly and sometimes not. That I talked too much, too fast, and sometimes about things that made no sense. The camera was on me for maybe three minutes, and I was just yammering away about some book I'd just read. The two people I was with looked a little dumbfounded, and they couldn't get a word in edgewise. Now that's something I want to work on."

Do you think that the way you speak has affected your ability to communicate effectively with others? Although not everyone with ADD has this problem, many find, as Bonnie has, that their symptoms do indeed have an impact on their vocal styles. Specifically, difficulties may exist in three areas: the rate of speech (*tempo*), the tone of voice (*intonation*), and the quality and rhythm of language (*fluency*).

Tempo: Although we tend to think that conversational styles differ widely from speaker to speaker and circumstance to circumstance, there is in fact a rather regular rhythm to casual discourse that, when significantly altered, rings untrue to the listener's ears. The average English-speaking person utters about 150 words per minute—about half the words on this page in 60 seconds—and speaks for only about 20 seconds at a time during his or her turn in the average conversation.

If you feel, or if you've been told, that you talk too fast or tend to dominate conversations, test yourself by tape-recording a few conversations (with your friends' permission!) and then timing the rate at which you speak. If it's much faster than 150 words per minute, your message may become distorted. Your listener may perceive a certain nervousness, insincerity, or even stubbornness when none is intended. If you talk for longer than approximately forty seconds at a time during a casual conversation, what you say may be considered by listeners to be a speech rather than a normal contribution. Over time, such a habit can become irritating to those around you.

Further, a pattern of interrupting others can be annoying as well. Many adults with ADD say that they find themselves interrupting because they fear they'll forget what they want to say when it comes time for them to speak, or because others speak too slowly. This habit is another one to look out for as you listen to yourself on tape.

Intonation: Tone of voice is another potential stumbling block along the conversational path for many adults with ADD. Too often, especially when nervous or overstressed, comments are snapped or shouted rather than spoken in a normal tone of voice by those with a tendency toward hyperactivity and restlessness. Inattention and impulsivity often cause a different set of problems. Because of these symptoms, some adults with ADD may fail to accurately read the mood and tenor of the conversation, and thus may speak too loudly, too sharply, or too flippantly than is appropriate at the time.

Fluency: A third component of vocal style is fluency: the ability to find the right words to express your meaning, pronounce them correctly, and utter them in a smooth and fluid manner. The truth is, everyone—with or without ADD—has fears about this aspect of speech. We're afraid that we stumble and stutter or fumble our pronunciation too often and, by doing so, sound uneducated or insecure.

The good news is that we should all relax a little; conversational speech is not meant to be perfect and, in fact, we usually consider someone who speaks without making any verbal errors to sound unnatural and rehearsed. Where some people with ADD could use some help, however, may be in improving their vocabulary. Because reading difficulties often coexist with ADD, the range of words they know and use on a regular basis may be limited. If you feel this could be a problem for you, there are several books written to help improve vocabulary skill.

Gesturing

Words are not the only method we have for relaying messages. In fact, our bodies do a great deal of the conversational work: The expression on our faces, the way we hold our bodies, and the gestures we make with our hands convey as much meaning as the words we use. Adults with ADD who suffer from the common symptoms of restlessness and inattention have particular difficulties with this aspect of the communication process for a number of reasons.

Eye contact: "I remember my wife almost screaming at me, 'Look at me, Rich, just look at me when you're talking to me,' because she judges so much of what I say on the way I look at her, and I always had trouble—usually because I was nervous or uncomfortable—looking directly at the person I was talking to," Rich explains. "Now I'm getting better at it, and it really helps. People seem to both understand me more quickly and somehow trust what I say a little better. And I feel less threatened by it."

Eye contact is one of the most important ways human beings connect with one another. If you avoid looking directly into someone's eyes when speaking, you may be perceived as being dishonest (hence the term "shifty-eyed") or distracted and, again, the true meaning of your message may get lost or become distorted. By making eye contact often, you'll not only encourage confidence in your listeners, you'll also be able to judge better how they are receiving your message by seeing the looks in their eyes and the expressions on their faces.

Facial expressions: Try this experiment: Look in the mirror and say the words "I was called into the boss's office today" with a smile on your face. Then say it again with a frown. Doesn't the statement appear to have two very different meanings depending on your expression? If you make the statement to your spouse with a smile, he or she is likely to assume that you were praised by your supervisor, or maybe even offered a raise. Speak it with a frown, and he or she will most likely conclude that you were reprimanded in some way.

The same words, then, may have completely different connotations depending on the way you look when you say them. This concept is important for adults with ADD to keep in mind, since many tend to think about something other than what they are speaking about. For instance, if you're chatting with a friend about the luncheon you just attended when the thought of an unpleasant project at work suddenly crosses your mind, your friend may assume you didn't enjoy the lunch at all because of the grimace that has just passed across your face. As you work at decreasing the number of distractions you allow yourself during a conversation, this may become less of a problem for you.

Body language: "When I saw a picture of myself with a group of people from work, I realized for the first time how I must appear to other people sometimes," Amy says. "I was standing a little bit further away from everyone else, my arms were folded, my head was bent, and I wasn't looking directly into the camera. I looked defensive and insecure, and alone."

"Stand up straight," our mothers frequently admonished us. And, as with so many of her words of wisdom, she was right about this one, too. The image we present to the world is based in large part upon how we carry ourselves. Standing tall denotes confidence; holding our arms at our sides signals accessibility; gently touching someone's arm or hand while speaking indicates intimacy and warmth.

For many adults with ADD, the symptoms of the disorder wreak havoc with body language. Or, rather, cause them all too accurately to reveal their internal chaos to the rest of the world.

"Even when I had everything under relative control," Marion says, "my staff would think that I was in a panic because of the way I moved. I'd rush around or fiddle with things on my desk while talking to them. I appeared to be so much less organized than in reality I was—and I was pretty disorganized. But I knew lots of people who at least had periods of confusion that they were able to hide because they seemed so calm and controlled. How I've envied people who could pull that off. I'm just learning to do that myself, and it feels great."

Relaying

A third level of expression is far more subtle and elusive to describe than either speaking or gesturing. *Relaying* pertains to the impression you convey by your external appearance, the way you approach people, and the surroundings in which you choose to converse.

Presentation: Although "clothes make the man" may be an outdated expression, it remains true that the way you dress and the state of your personal grooming communicate a great deal about you. Unfortunately, some adults with ADD do not pay close attention to this aspect of life and do not consider it very important.

"It's not as if I was a slob all the time," claims Mark. "But I felt that matching up outfits and getting the right haircut was truly the last thing on my list. What I looked like wasn't important, I thought, it was what I could do that mattered. Frankly, I liked feeling like a rebel and refusing to conform. I've found out since then that I can get a lot farther with people, that they trust me more, if I appear as if I respect myself and them by taking the time to look good."

We're hardly recommending that you go out and buy a designer wardrobe or undergo a complete make-over. Your style of dress and demeanor are quite personal to you. But if you think your image could use a little spiffing up, take the time to do so. Ask a trusted—and well-dressed—friend for advice.

Proximity: The distance you place between yourself and the person to whom you are speaking is a very subtle but crucial message in and of itself. Although every society and social circumstance has its own set of norms, in general, the closer you are to your conversation mate, the more familiar and confidential you intend your discussion—and hence your relationship—to be. A standard distance between casual conversation partners is about three to five feet; any distance closer than about twelve to twenty inches connotes confidentiality, if not intimacy.

Making a correct assumption about the appropriate level of involvement, however, requires a certain sensitivity to the situation and to other people's feelings—a sensitivity that the symptoms of ADD may inhibit. If you become so distracted or restless that you fail to interpret the situation correctly, you may find yourself crossing the very personal boundaries that people establish around themselves. When an individual's "personal space" is breached, he or she may be left feeling imposed upon, confused, or even angry.

If you find that people tend to back away from you, either physically or emotionally, take note of how you handle the personal space issue. Perhaps you are intruding in a subtle and completely unconscious way upon acquaintances, friends, and colleagues.

Context: "It's got something to do with 'not getting it,' as my wife puts it," says Sam. "I can't tell you how often she'd say, 'This isn't the time or place for this conversation.' I wouldn't read her mood right, or it'd be too noisy, or too quiet. I just had a real hard time picking up the spirit of the situation."

Another sometimes elusive but always crucial component of the communication process is the idea of context. Indeed, no conversation takes place in a vacuum and what is said may be received differently depending upon the environment in which it is uttered. A staff holiday party, for instance, is exactly the wrong place to tell a staff member that he is fired. Attempting to discuss problems with the family budget when your spouse isn't feeling well is likely to be futile, to say nothing of being potentially inflammatory and counterproductive. If you feel or have been warned that your timing is off, try to become more aware of the environment and mood before you launch into an important conversation.

Five Tips for Improving Your Expressive Skills

- Tape-record a conversation you have with someone. Take note of the following:
  - *How fast you speak* (aim for no more than 150 words per minute)
  - *How long you speak* (aim to speak no more than 30 to 45 seconds at a time in a casual conversation)

— *Your tone of voice* (in general, it should match the person's with whom you are speaking, and suit the context)

- Interrupt yourself occasionally to ask your conversation partner if he or she is following you, or if he or she has anything to add.
- Work on reducing or hiding restless movement as much as possible.
- Make a good impression with careful grooming and, over time, by establishing a style that truly expresses your personality.
- Monitor the distance you stand from the person to whom you are speaking (for casual conversation, a distance of about two or three feet is appropriate).

DEVELOPING YOUR RECEPTIVE SKILLS

- It often takes me several minutes to get the gist of a conversation.   _____

- I often get sidetracked from a conversation by extraneous noise or activity.   _____

- I frequently interrupt a speaker before he or she finishes a statement.   _____

- I'm not always sure what is meant by what is said.   _____

- I often feel out of place, as if I don't belong.   _____

- I feel threatened and uncomfortable when a conversation confuses me.   _____

Reception is the receiving of sound, sight, and information from the outside world. Usually when we think of reception, we think of our television sets receiving images and sounds sent from distant broadcast stations. If TV reception is bad, the images and sounds are distorted, and the message is unclear.

The same principle applies to conversation. If you are distracted, unprepared, or unobservant, it can be said that *your* reception is bad, and the messages you receive are likely to be unclear and misunderstood. Just as you do to your television set, you may need to fine-tune your internal reception in order to bring the picture into focus and the sound quality up to par.

Listening

"One of my biggest breakthroughs came when I figured out the difference between hearing and listening," claims Sam. "I used to think that as long as I was in the room and could locate the source of sound—like that of my client's voice—I was listening. But that wasn't true. I may have been hearing noise, but I wasn't always listening, which requires a whole other kind of concentration."

Sam is right. While hearing is a faculty most of us are born with, listening is a skill that must be developed and cultivated, especially if one also has a condition like ADD with its potential for distraction and confusion. Effective listening involves at least three components: preparing yourself to receive a message, concentrating on and interpreting the message, and then making an appropriate response to what you hear and understand.

Preparation: There probably isn't a person alive who has not been caught off guard by an unexpected verbal interruption at one time or another. You hear the words, but because you weren't expecting to receive a message, you aren't able to process the information the words contain. More often than not, you have to ask the speaker to repeat the message before you are able to respond.

Such an experience proves that hearing and listening are indeed two different activities: You must be prepared to listen or you may fail to isolate the sound and meaning of words from what you hear in the general environment. This principle is especially important for adults with ADD to keep in mind, since they tend to be lost in thought more often than their peers without the disorder.

In order to avoid being caught off guard, try to remain aware of your surroundings, the potential for conversation that exists, and even what kind of response from you is likely to be expected. If you stay focused on business matters while attending a staff meeting, for instance, you'll be more likely to pick up on messages having to do with work than if you're thinking about a basketball game you watched the night before.

Limiting distractions: Needless to say, the fewer visual and audible diversions present during a conversation, the easier it will be for the person with ADD to listen and to comprehend what is being said.

"I once went with a date to one of those Japanese restaurants where they cook your dinner right at the table," Bonnie recalls. "Do you think I heard a word he said? I was too busy watching the chef, playing with my chopsticks, talking to the people next to us about how cool everything was. There was just too much going on for me to pay attention to him. The next time we went out to eat, I chose a quiet booth in a tiny French bistro. We talked for hours."

Needless to say, it's not always possible to choose your surroundings. There will be times when the atmosphere is unavoidably noisy and chaotic and you must harness all of your powers of concentration and focus to really listen. Whenever possible, however, arrange to conduct important personal and business discussions in an environment that is conducive to paying attention.

Establishing empathy: Part of listening is responding— not just in words but in other, more subtle displays of acknowledgment. We let others know that we grasp, emotionally and intellectually, the meaning of their messages in a variety of different ways. We may nod our heads from time to time during conversation, smile when something amuses or delights us, or touch the speaker's hand or arm if we are moved by what is said. Such demonstrations show the speaker that we are listening to, and comprehending, what is being communicated to us.

Because many adults with ADD often have trouble staying focused on a conversation, they may not display the empathy that helps foster communication. As such, they may seem distant and cold to the people in their lives, even though their problem usually stems far more from the inability to concentrate than from any lack of caring. Reminding yourself that you can avoid making such an impression if you pay more careful attention and respond honestly to what you hear may help you stay more focused and alert during conversation.

Observing

When you think about it, your eyesight is almost as important as your hearing when it comes to interpreting what you hear. The expression on someone's face, the gestures he or she makes, and the look in his or her eyes add much meaning to the spoken form. Many adults with ADD, however, have difficulty picking up these nonverbal messages unless they remind themselves often to watch as well as listen. Even then, there is no guarantee that they'll be able to follow through. It's one of the many challenges for adults with ADD.

Making eye contact: As discussed above, one of the problems many adults with ADD have is remaining focused on the subject and the speaker during conversation. An appropriate way to reduce the tendency to become distracted is to make and sustain eye contact with your partner in conversation.

"My husband would get so angry with me because I would 'go off somewhere,' as he put it," explains Amy. "And he was right, because often when I wasn't looking directly at him, I wasn't really listening to him either. I would get distracted by the book I noticed on the coffee table or the bird flying by the window. Since we've been working on some of this, I've learned to kind of bring myself back into the conversation by making solid eye contact with whomever I'm talking to. It helps me not only pay closer attention, but also get the meaning of what's being said so much more quickly and accurately."

Reading facial expressions: Because so much about the meaning behind our words can be discerned from the expressions on our faces, it is essential for adults with ADD to look at their conversation partners often. Remembering to make eye contact often will help, but it is also important to identify and interpret facial expressions at the same time.

Noticing body movements: Body movements often reveal a great deal about a person's state of mind during conversation, particularly about how he or she perceives your relationship. Practice observing how your conversation mate stands and moves when he or she talks with you. Does he or she lean forward or touch you often, signaling that the discussion is an intimate or confidential one? Or are his or her arms folded and body turned away from you, denoting a more closed or cautious attitude? If you make the effort to notice such body language, you are more likely to perceive and relate to the meaning of the encounter more rapidly and accurately.

Sensing

Often far more subtle than either the words or the gestures used are the intangible elements that set the general tenor of the conversation. The relationship between you and your conversation mate, the setting in which the discussion takes place, and an even more elusive ingredient—mood—all need to be understood in order for you to perceive the true meaning of the message.

Understanding the relationship: There are two ways in which the nature of the relationship between you and the person to whom you are speaking is important. The first deals with differences in roles and status: Chances are, your boss will speak to you in a different manner than will a friend—and require from you a different level of listening skills. The second important aspect of the relationship concerns its history. A conversation between you and a stranger is often quite unlike that between you and an intimate. The more you know someone, the more familiar and personal your communication style will be.

Observing the setting: As discussed, communication does not occur in a vacuum. Just as it is important for you to choose a setting for a conversation with care, it is essential that you recognize the context in which your conversation mate has chosen to communicate with *you*.

Reading the mood: "The obvious ones I always got, like candlelight dinners for two or raucous nights at a dance club," claims Sam. "It was the more subtle times that I'd screw up, especially with my wife. Too often, I'd come home thinking about work, on a completely different track, and not notice that she was feeling sad or angry. Her tone of voice and everything else would seem normal and calm to me, so I just assumed that it was. If I'd paid attention a little more, though, I'd have seen that she was upset and listened with a whole other set of ears, so to speak."

Reading someone else's mood is never an easy chore for anyone, with or without ADD and, when it comes right down to it, no one should be expected to do so on a regular basis. However, like Sam, your relationships may improve if you can slow down a bit and try to pick up on the more subtle clues to the mood and intent of the person to whom you are speaking.

Five Tips for Developing Your Receptive Skills

- Keep an open mind about the speaker; you'll tend to listen with more attention.
- Try to reduce extraneous distractions by closing office doors, turning down radios and televisions, and forcing yourself to focus only on the conversation at hand.

- If you lose track of the conversation, cue yourself back in by reestablishing eye contact.
- Stop and think before you interrupt. Try to wait until a complete message has been sent, and you have taken the time to interpret it, before you make a contribution.
- Respect your relationship to the speaker and the context of the conversation.

APPLYING COMMUNICATION SKILLS TO RELATIONSHIPS

A review of basic communication skills like the one just provided should support your efforts to express and receive messages more clearly. As you are no doubt aware, however, forming and maintaining relationships requires applying these skills in different ways depending on the people and the setting involved. Here is a brief overview of some of the issues that may arise in various situations:

The Fine Art of Group Interaction

"I admit, I'm terrified to go to a party," Bonnie says. "All the conversation going on around me, the constantly changing topics, the different personalities and styles . . . I simply get overwhelmed. And the fact that I work alone all day, usually in a tiny, quiet room with a computer, only adds to my discomfort."

Bonnie is not alone. Many of her ADD peers find group interaction at parties and meetings among their biggest communication challenges, and for a number of different reasons. As Bonnie describes, large gatherings involve many people—each with his or her own unique style—usually speaking about several different topics at once, making conversation particularly challenging to follow for the adult with ADD.

Unfortunately, the nervousness many feel about being in large groups almost always exacerbates ADD symptoms, including the tendency to be impulsive in conversation. Some patients with ADD find that they interrupt more than usual at social gatherings or blurt out remarks that may seem inappropriate to others.

"I tend to be everywhere at once, especially at parties," says Rich. "I don't know if I have keener-than-usual hearing, but I'm often cluing into the conversation going on across the room as well as hearing the people I'm talking with. If I'm not careful—and I'm not always careful—I'll end up making a comment about a conversation taking place two groups away from the one I'm in."

If you have special trouble communicating at social gatherings, these tips may help you apply the skills discussed in this chapter to this situation:

Tips for Managing Well at Large Gatherings

- Prepare for a party or meeting by reading up on current events or the topic at hand.
- Try to stop yourself from thinking too far ahead about what you'll say next—focus instead on the speaker and his or her message.
- Get a coach who can help keep you on track and focused, as well as give you honest feedback on how you come across to others.
- Give yourself a break: Some people—with or without ADD—are simply not made for large groups. If you're one of them, give yourself permission to limit the number of parties or events you attend, and don't feel guilty about it.

Communicating on the Job

Rules and regulations—the bane of the existence of many an adult with ADD—are plentiful in most employment situations. In addition to the time management and organizational procedures involved, there are also many unwritten rules to learn and follow concerning relationships between employees.

These rules, together known as office protocol, are often even more difficult and stressful for adults with ADD to understand and comply with.

"Knowing who to speak with and how to present myself to him or her was always a big problem for me," explains Mark. "It seemed as if there was some kind of mysterious code that I wasn't in on that told people how to act and what to say to get ahead. I just never read the situation right. Then, when I didn't get what I wanted and didn't understand why, I'd get frustrated and angry. Now, I've learned a trick. I find someone I trust, someone who looks like he's in the know, and ask him to give me the inside scoop on who to talk to and how to get things done. Along with taking my medication and learning to curb my impulsiveness, this has really helped me get somewhere."

Another work-related challenge for many adults with ADD involves image: Looking relaxed, alert, and productive on the job is almost as important as *being* relaxed, alert, and productive on the job. Unfortunately, many of the symptoms of ADD function to undermine such an image: Hyperactive or restless employees tap their feet or pace instead of taking notes or perusing a report. Inattention causes many adults with ADD to appear to be daydreaming or otherwise wasting time. And impulsivity is often interpreted—sometimes correctly—as panic or disorganization by superiors, colleagues, and staff members.

Needless to say, managing your symptoms by taking medication and/or learning behavioral techniques is especially important at work. In addition to the strategies you've learned in this and past chapters, the following tips may help you gain further control in the workplace:

Tips for Fostering Productive Communication at Work

- Find a mentor to help you understand and follow office protocol.
- Limit job-related stress by following the time management and organizational techniques described in Chapter

Seven. This will help you reduce the amount of snapping at others and other emotional overreactions.

- If you intend to ask for assistance to help compensate for ADD symptoms, do so with care. Do not be demanding or overanxious.
- Make an agenda, and stick to it, for staff and other meetings. If you tend to get off track, practice what you'll say before the meeting. Write it down.
- Try to reduce restless body movements whenever possible. Nibble on the top of a pen or eraser (which may help you look as if you're deep in thought) rather than tap it on the table (which both annoys other people and makes you look bored).
- If telephone calls are part of your job, reduce distractions as much as possible before you pick up the phone. Outline your major points on a piece of paper ahead of time. Ask to call back if you are unprepared.

Establishing Intimacy

"Stepping over the line, that's what a few of the girls I dated in college said was my biggest problem. I guess I just never knew when to quit," says Ben. "Even with friends, I'd tend to get overinvolved. I'd think it was such a miracle that somebody understood me and liked me that I'd focus on them too much. And then they'd back away. After a while, I didn't try anymore, I just shut myself off."

As discussed earlier in the chapter, recognizing and respecting personal boundaries is often a challenge for many adults with ADD, especially when it comes to intimate friends and lovers. Because the symptoms of ADD may lessen the ability to read nonverbal messages correctly, those with ADD are often unable to translate the so-called unwritten language of love.

Like Ben, they may seem to be too needy or obsessive in their pursuit of romantic relationships. In other cases, a failure to read nonverbal signals may cause adults with ADD to remain too far back, too aloof, for the relationship to move forward.

Indeed, forming intimate relationships may be one of the biggest challenges for some adults with ADD: Although they may be smart, attractive, worthy people, something about their approach is often disturbing, which may lead others to misunderstand their true intentions and/or fail to explore other aspects of their personalities.

Furthermore, the same kind of impatience and inattention that hinders organizational or time management tasks also may interfere with adult ADD patients' ability to form lasting relationships.

"I never could 'take things slow,'" explains Bonnie, "because I knew how quickly I'd get bored and need to move on. Of course, I've since realized that I wasn't actually bored at all, I just couldn't focus on anything except my work for very long before I'd get restless and edgy. I also think I hurried through relationships because I was afraid that whatever man I was with would figure out how truly screwed up I was inside, how disorganized my brain was, how I felt like my life was held together by a thread. And who'd want to be around that, right? So I'd leave first, before he did."

Fear of rejection is a stumbling block for many adults—both with and without ADD—looking for love in today's world. It takes a certain confidence and sense of self to reveal oneself in an intimate way to another human being. Unfortunately, the level of self-awareness required is often inadequate and the fear of failure even greater for those who have struggled with ADD throughout their lives.

"Guilty. That's how I'd describe how I felt in most of my intimate relationships, including my marriages," Amy admits. "I felt guilty about not being there, really there, for the other person. And I felt guilty because I didn't know *why* I couldn't be there. And I really felt guilty because I never felt comfortable in a sexual way with men, even those whom I truly loved. Although I tried to hide it, sometimes I was just as unfocused and distracted during sex as I was trying to read a book or balance my checkbook. It was horrible."

Although a link between sexual dysfunction and ADD has

not yet been clinically investigated, enough anecdotal evidence exists to know that Amy is not alone in her problem. Some adults with ADD feel unable to quiet their thoughts enough to focus on sexual intimacy; others find that their restlessness and general edginess makes being touched and caressed by another person uncomfortable, even unpleasant.

"I finally got the courage to talk to my doctor about it," Amy says. "It was such a relief to know that it wasn't all in my head. My husband and I are really working together on this problem now, and I feel so much better and more satisfied."

Tips for Establishing and Maintaining Intimate Relationships

- Communication is the key: Hone your expressive and receptive skills, and use them with care and consideration with your partner.
- Guard against negative self-talk when meeting new people. Keep an open mind about yourself and about others.
- Try to match the level of your intensity with that of your partner. Study the strategies for sensing the mood and level of involvement of others described earlier.
- When you are comfortable, inform new friends and lovers about your ADD. Be specific as to how it may affect your behavior.
- Be patient, both with yourself and your partner.
- Keep a sense of humor about all aspects of your relationship, including your sex life.

MOVING FORWARD

It is crucial to recognize an important fact: The symptoms of ADD have been present in your life for many years and thus may have affected both the quality of past relationships and your expectations about relationships today and in the future. To help you move forward, you may have to amend some of the patterns of communication that have been established over the years.

Start with a Clean Slate

You may remember this goal from Chapter Seven in connection with clearing away physical clutter in order to establish some organization and structure in your environment. The same principle applies to the management of relationships in the context of a recent ADD diagnosis. Now that you know how the symptoms of ADD may affect your ability to communicate, and have become aware of ways to alleviate or compensate for these symptoms, you should attempt to banish thoughts of past failures and regrets from your mind. Practicing the skills discussed in this chapter and experiencing some success will, over time, help you to do this.

In large measure, this involves releasing yourself from the unhealthy relationship patterns you may have set up in the past. As discussed, your image of yourself—as a victim, as a perfectionist, or as someone unworthy of being loved or helpless to change your situation—may have had a negative impact on your capacity to form satisfying relationships. If that is the case, you'll have to work hard both to see yourself in a different light and to repattern your relationships—at home, at work, and in your social life—to reflect your newfound understanding and abilities.

Be Honest

Hiding your true feelings and expectations may have become second nature to you as you've attempted to conceal your struggle with ADD from the people around you. As difficult as it may be to break that habit, it is essential that you do so in order to establish solid, sincere relationships with colleagues, friends, and family.

That's not to say you should simply blurt out whatever is on your mind or in your heart without regard to someone else's feelings; in fact, such impulsivity may have been what contributed to your difficulties in the first place. Instead, follow the rules described earlier for choosing the appropriate time and place—and using the right words and tone of voice—to clear up sensitive matters or to explain your feelings to the people you care about.

Make a Commitment to Follow Through

So far, we've talked a great deal about learning to say what you mean, but very little about the flip side of that coin: meaning what you say. For a variety of reasons related to symptoms of ADD, many adults find it difficult to follow through on agreements and keeping promises. You may have let people down in the past because of a tendency to overcommit your time and energy, or because you were so distracted and over-stimulated that you lost track of your obligations amid all the chaos.

Whatever the reason, it is likely that your behavior has caused some people in your life to doubt your word, and it's up to you to show them that you can change. If they feel you aren't trying to learn new patterns of behavior now that you have the means and the knowledge, you run the risk that they will give up on the relationship altogether.

"For a while after I got the diagnosis, I really did nothing about my relationships, especially at home," Mark admits. "I used ADD as the excuse I never had to justify all of my screwups, if you know what I mean. I figured I couldn't be expected to remember my wife's birthday because 'I have ADD.' It wasn't my fault if I missed my daughter's dance recital because 'I have ADD.' My wife finally snapped and said that I had been letting my family down for too long. If knowing about ADD and taking medication for it could help me to organize my finances and get through school, I could certainly start paying attention to my family's needs, too. And she was right."

Like Mark, many adults with ADD have deep-seated family

issues that may need to be resolved as they come to grips with the effects the disorder has had on their relationships. In fact, family life itself, which involves structuring a daily routine, delegating responsibilities, and disciplining children among other priorities, poses special challenges to those with ADD. In addition, because ADD has a strong genetic component, many adults with ADD discover that one or more of their children also suffer with the disorder. Chapter Nine will help you and your family come to terms with these and other family issues.

IMPORTANT QUESTIONS AND ANSWERS ABOUT CHAPTER EIGHT

Q My husband is amused by my tendency to "go off on my own" during our conversations. I've tried to explain the leaps in logic and weird connections I make, but he just doesn't get it. My best friend, though, loves this part of my personality and we have a blast together. How can I get my husband to get into the act?

A The ways you think and express yourself are unique parts of your personality and—with or without ADD in the picture—you and your husband might never have followed the same patterns of communication. That's why Opposites Attract remains true. You may decide it's worth trying to explain the way you think to your husband, or you may choose to simply appreciate the different wavelengths you two are on. In the meantime, make the most of the relationship you have with your best friend.

Q Even though my sister says she understands that the symptoms of ADD were responsible for some of the problems I had growing up, she still seems to resent me so much. And every time we get together, we end up fighting. We're both in our thirties now, both our parents have passed away, and I really want a relationship with her. What can I do?

A First of all, try to be patient, with yourself and with your sister. Remember, the pattern of your relationship is now at least three decades old and it will take some time to heal past wounds and understand them in a different context. It is also important to encourage your sister to express her feelings about how your disorder affected her childhood and how it affects her now. Use the listening skills described in this chapter to establish some true empathy with your sister. Let her know you understand her problems and work with her to resolve them.

Q My boss has a son with ADD, so it was pretty easy for me to talk to her about the problems the disorder caused me at work. She lets me go to the library when I need to work on my sales reports, and I got a special divider to screen off my office so I'm not distracted when I make phone calls. My work has been great, but my co-workers really resent me, saying I get special treatment and that I'm just using ADD as an excuse. What can I do?

A Two things come to mind. First, educate your colleagues about ADD. Make sure they know how the disorder affects you and others who have it, and outline the reasons that your boss has made special arrangements for you. Get your boss to help you, since she is familiar with ADD. Second, check your attitude. Consciously or unconsciously, you may be taking on one of the roles discussed in this chapter—victim, controller, loner, or helpless one—and thus perceived as difficult by your co-workers. Ask a trusted friend at work for his or her opinion about the way you project yourself.

Chapter Nine

ADD:
THE FAMILY
CONNECTION

Efficient organization and open communication. How can a family function in a healthy, loving way without these two essentials? As many adults with ADD can attest, the answer to that question is "not very well." Indeed, the organizational, time management, and communication challenges posed by ADD often affect family relationships in rather negative and disruptive ways. In this chapter, we'll outline those challenges as well as explore some of the most effective ways you and your family can work to meet them.

"It's sad to say, but for me, family life has too often been just another source of frustration and tension," Rich admits. "As hard as I've tried to be there for my wife and two kids, I know that my general ADD craziness has really gotten in the way. And not just because of all the birthday parties and piano recitals I missed when I lost track of time at work. I think it's my mood swings and erratic way of dealing with everybody that have been most upsetting. It's ironic, too, because I swore I wouldn't make the same mistakes that my father made with me. I wouldn't break promises. I wouldn't snap at my kids. I wouldn't be inconsistent with rules and discipline. But that's the way it turned out, and it's going to take a lot of work on my part to make it up to my family."

Rich, a forty-eight-year-old father of two and husband for twelve years, is just now coming to terms with the impact ADD has had on his marriage and family life. Like many of his peers with ADD, Rich realizes that his wife and children have suffered almost as much as he has from the effects of the disorder. Although he looks back with some guilt and regret, he is now able to face the future with optimism and resolve. He is finding that the better he's able to manage his symptoms and adapt his behavior, the more satisfying his family relationships become.

"It hasn't been easy," Rich remarks. "It's like we've had to get to know each other all over again and set up whole new systems. But it's worth it. My wife and I are having fun together for the first time in I don't know how many years, and my kids are starting to trust me. The whole household runs more soothly and without so much tension."

THE IMPACT OF ADD ON THE FAMILY

The roadblocks to successful living that are exacerbated by the symptoms of ADD—including a variety of potential organizational and communication problems—have already been covered in some depth in previous chapters. Suffice it to say, these roadblocks often pose particularly difficult challenges to family relationships and issues of daily family life. Let's take a look at some of the effects ADD may be having on your family.

Organizational and time management confusion: Getting a household to run smoothly is an enormous challenge for any family, with or without the presence of ADD. It involves establishing and maintaining physical order, coordinating schedules and activities, and accepting and meeting responsibilities—all trouble spots for many adults with ADD.

Financial pressure: Chronic employment problems, impulsive spending, and erratic bookkeeping and bill paying are just a few of the financial challenges that may face adults with ADD. As difficult as such problems may seem to you as an individual, they become even more imposing when the needs of other people depend upon your ability to manage money responsibly.

Child-rearing obstacles: Raising healthy, well-adjusted children requires patience, sound judgment, good humor, and, above all, loving guidance and discipline. As we'll discuss later in this chapter, a parent with ADD often has difficulty in providing such guidance to their children on a consistent basis.

Marital tension: As discussed in Chapter Eight, the presence of ADD often hinders the development of intimate relationships for a variety of reasons. Although many adults with ADD enjoy successful, satisfying marriages, the disorder almost always adds a certain amount of extra tension and pressure to the union. More often than not, the non-ADD spouse bears an additional burden of responsibility for keeping the household running smoothly and meeting the needs of the children, the spouse with ADD, and, if he or she has time, his or her own priorities.

Emotional chaos: You want to provide support, affection, comfort, and inspiration to those with whom you've pledged to spend your life. In return, you expect the same emotional blessings to come to you from them. With ADD in the picture, however, this give-and-take process often short-circuits. Too often, love, admiration, and trust are replaced with a variety of negative feelings.

Not knowing what to expect, or when to expect it, from a spouse or parent with ADD creates an air of uncertainty and *anxiety* within the family. Over time, even a low level of tension can eventually fray the fabric of caring and commitment.

Resentment is another negative emotion that often erupts among various family members when ADD is present. The spouse without ADD may resent the additional responsibilities he or she must take on to compensate for a mate's shortcomings. Children often subconsciously resent the fact that their parent with ADD is "different" and cannot always be counted upon to meet their expectations.

A related emotion frequently present in a family coping with ADD is *defensiveness*. Spouses, children, and ADD patients alike may become extremely guarded when anything is amiss in the household. Afraid of being accused of doing something wrong—either for failing to perform the expected task or failing to compensate for difficulties presented by ADD symptoms—family members may withdraw behind a self-protective, defensive screen, a screen that prevents them from communicating in an open and honest way about anything negative or positive that occurs.

Finally, *loneliness* is often cited by family members as one of ADD's most upsetting side effects. The non-ADD spouse often feels left out and rejected by the spouse with ADD, children are often confused by their parents' behavior and the general disorganization that so often exists, and the person with ADD sometimes imagines that he or she inhabits a separate, confusing universe that even family cannot understand.

"When my five-year-old son said that he missed me even when I was home, I was struck by the sad truth of his innocent comment," Rich remembers. "Although we all love each other very much, and certainly have had some very good times together, I know I haven't paid as much attention as I should have to my kids or my wife. And I know that my wife has had to work extra hard to take up my slack at home, and that's created some tension between us. But no one feels comfortable talking about any of it. Instead of coming together, too often we go to separate corners when things get crazy. And what's strange, or maybe not so strange, is that I'm living my childhood all over again. The loneliness my son feels is exactly the same way I felt about my relationship with my dad."

Rich brings up two important points in his portrayal of his family relationships. First, ADD does not prevent men and women from falling in love, marrying, and raising healthy, well-adjusted children. In fact, although problems in communication and organization may arise, many adults with the disorder are able to enjoy full and satisfying family lives. Second, it is not uncommon for family difficulties related to ADD to pass down from generation to generation. Although it is impossible to know for sure if Rich's father suffered from ADD (he passed away about ten years ago), Rich's childhood memories point to that possibility. He remembers his father as having a quick temper, being distant, and seeming preoccupied. He wonders now what might have frustrated his father's relationship with his family.

"It could be that his moods were just an aspect of his personality," Rich says about his father. "But when I asked my mother about him, she told me about the trouble he had holding a job and following other people's rules, about how frustrated he'd get trying to read or balance a checkbook. She might have been describing me before I was diagnosed and treated for ADD."

As Rich's experience reveals, the presence of ADD does not doom a family to a lifetime of struggle and frustration, even if the disorder affects both parent and child. Later in the chapter, we'll provide you with more information about helping a child with ADD flourish. In the meantime, here are some strategies to help your family form and maintain a healthier relationship.

Moving Toward a Healthier Family

- I find it difficult to talk about ADD with my family.   _____

- When my spouse and I argue, we spend a lot of time blaming each other for past mistakes and problems.   _____

- There tends to be more fault-finding than praising going on among members of my family.   _____

- The time we spend really talking together as a family is minimal. _____

- Sometimes it seems like we concentrate on the tiniest problems and fail to see the big picture. _____

- Our lives appear to be so haphazard; we seem to go from crisis to crisis. _____

- Although we're often emotionally distant, it seems like we're always getting in each other's business. _____

- I can't remember when we all took the time to truly relax—either individually or as a family. _____

- No one we know really understands what a family goes through when coping with ADD. _____

Do any of the above statements depict problems that you and your family are experiencing today? If so, it is likely ADD and its symptoms are affecting your family's ability to communicate and cooperate in healthy, productive ways. Fortunately, like all other challenges posed by ADD, family conflicts can be alleviated by accepting the presence of the disorder, learning and practicing new skills, and by harboring patience, empathy, and compassion for one another. Following are specific suggestions for improving family relationships.

TEN TIPS FOR HEALTHIER FAMILY LIVING

1. Educate Everyone in the Family

As discussed earlier, knowledge is power. The more you, your spouse, your children, and principal members of your extended family know about ADD and its potential effects, the more you will be able to work together to minimize the problems it may create within the family.

• Keep explanations of ADD as simple as possible. Generally speaking, the younger your children are, the less detail you need to provide about the disorder.

• Be sure to explain any and all symptoms and side effects that you experience, even if you think other people may not notice them. This is particularly true in relation to mood swings or temper flare-ups; many family members may be blaming themselves for your difficulties.

• Do not neglect to inform your parents, siblings, and other members of the extended family about your condition, especially if they interact often with your spouse and children. Bear in mind that not all family members will greet the news of your or your child's condition with immediate and unconditional support. Some will be skeptical that ADD is really at the root of your family's problems. Try to educate them as much as possible and reassure your child that they mean well even if they are not aware of all of the facts.

• Have pamphlets and this book available to family members.

• Arrange a family meeting with your doctor to answer any additional questions about the disorder and its potential effects.

2. Wipe the Slate Clean

"A lot has happened in the twelve years my wife and I have been married," says Mark, "and our two kids—a five-year-old son and a fourteen-year-old daughter from my wife's first marriage—have seen too much of it. They've seen the fights and felt the tension. They've been on the wrong end of my temper way too often. Now that we know that ADD has caused at least some of these problems, we've made a pact not to bring up the past unless we can really learn from it."

Mark and his family are following a wise course in their decision to stop blaming each other for past mistakes and problems. Far too often, families are so burdened by lingering resentment and low-level anger—directed not only at the person with ADD, but frequently at each other as well—that they are unable to move forward, even when new solutions and strategies are available to help them. However, now that the source of at least some of your familial distress has been identified, you and your family should make a commitment to let go of these destructive emotions and embrace the future with optimism.

• Agree with your family that today marks the beginning of a new way of life for all of you.
• Foster the belief that you each have the power to change your own attitude and behavior.
• Encourage a "we're all in this together" approach to family life.

3. Accentuate the Positive

Instead of concentrating on faults and shortcomings, learn to recognize and reinforce one another's talents, skills, and aspirations. Indeed, each member of the family has a unique personality that, if allowed to grow and flourish, will contribute an essential spirit to your home life.

• Ask each member of the family (infants and toddlers are excused, of course) to make a list of what he or she considers his or her best qualities. Then each person should make another list of what he or she likes best about his or her siblings, parents, and/or spouse. Share the lists with one another.
• Have everyone make it a point to bestow at least one compliment a day upon every other member of the family.

4. Keep Communication Lines Open

As discussed in depth in Chapter Eight, nothing is more important to the creation and maintenance of healthy relationships than clear communication.

• Set up regular family meetings. If possible, everyone should try to eat at least one meal together every day. Take it as an opportunity to voice concerns and keep one another up-to-date on activities and priorities.

• Create a "Family Bulletin Board" where reminders and messages can be placed. Encourage members of the family to review it on a regular basis.

5. Prioritize Problems and Goals

"The history of my family's struggle with this disorder is very long," Ben admits. Although single, he lives with his parents and thus has his own set of family challenges to conquer. "There are a lot of unmet expectations and festering problems between me and my parents, and me and my brothers, too. When I was first diagnosed with ADD, I wanted to solve everything at once: I wanted to organize my living situation better so that there would be less tension in the house; I wanted to get a better job so that my parents would be proud of me; I wanted to heal some of the wounds my brothers and I have inflicted on each other over the years. For a while, I was too overwhelmed with all my goals to get anything done. Finally, we all sat down together and came up with a plan."

As discussed in Chapter Seven, establishing priorities is the first step on the road to a more satisfying future for adults diagnosed with ADD—and that's especially true within the family setting.

• Have each member of the family make a list of his or her most pressing concerns and goals for the future. Work together to establish an action plan to resolve conflicts and accomplish tasks.

• Meet on a regular basis to reevaluate priorities and celebrate the fulfillment of goals.

6. Clarify Expectations

Rules can help a household run more smoothly and with less tension—as long as they are clearly spelled out and agreed upon (or at least understood) by all family members.

Each member of the family should be expected to contribute to the management of the household in his or her own special way. In fact, chores are much more likely to be accomplished without complaint if responsibilities are delegated based on personal talents and proclivities. If your spouse is particularly adept at handling family finances, for instance, he or she may want to take over that duty. If your eight-year-old daughter loves the outdoors, perhaps she could be responsible for weeding the garden during the spring and summer.

• Make a roster of chores and responsibilities family members can refer to on a regular basis.

• Have a system of rewards in place for accomplishing goals and finishing tasks. (See Chapter Seven under "Celebrate Success" for more suggestions.)

7. Aim for Consistency

Many families with ADD report feeling as if they were simply lunging from one crisis to another, with no two days the same and no routines to follow. Although a certain amount of flexibility is necessary in order to adapt to the ever-changing needs of family life, applying some structure and form to daily living usually allows people to feel more comfortable and productive.

• Set up a regular schedule for mealtimes, study times, and leisure activities, and stick to it as much as possible. A change in routine should be the exception, not the rule.

• Anticipate problem spots and make plans to deal with them ahead of time. If you know that you always get tense and irritable when you do the family budget, for instance, plan for the children to go to the movies with a babysitter or with your spouse on that afternoon.

8. Respect Boundaries

Control is an issue for many families coping with ADD. In some cases, it is the ADD patient who insists on attempting to manage every aspect of family life; in other cases, family members try so hard to compensate for the ADD patient's shortcomings that they intrude more than is necessary. In either case, the boundaries and limits we use to define ourselves and our personal space—boundaries that even young children deserve to have maintained—are often crossed in the process.

• Create zones of privacy for each individual. Everyone should have a private space (a bedroom or a den) or a block of time spent away from the home that they can use for rest and recovery from the day's stresses and strains. Other family members should respect these private spaces as much as possible.

• Accept one another's emotional boundaries. Everyone has a limit as to how much emotional information he or she wants to share.

9. Relieve Stress

Nothing undermines a family more than unresolved, pent-up frustration and tension. We've already described how important it is for the ADD patient to learn to release excess energy by exercising on a regular basis, taking frequent breaks from routine to blow off steam, and getting plenty of rest. The same holds true for other family members as well, especially children who also suffer from the disorder.

• Encourage every family member to pursue a hobby or activity that provides him or her with special pleasure and excitement.

• Plan family get-aways, preferably ones that involve plenty of physical activity.

10. Find and Accept Support

"I cannot tell you what it meant to my wife to talk with another woman who had to deal with both a husband and child with ADD," Sam says. "She thought she was completely nuts until she realized that the feelings she had, and the things she had to do to keep the household running smoothly, were perfectly normal considering what she was up against when it came to my ADD. And my son, well, it sure helped him to know that he wasn't the only kid who had trouble sitting still and behaving. To say nothing of how much I was helped by talking with other men and women with the disorder."

It cannot be stressed enough: You and your family are not alone in your struggle to cope with ADD and its effects. There are literally millions of other families—like those of the eight men and women you've met in this book—who are attempting to cope with the effects of ADD.

• Show your spouse and children the statistics that prove you are not alone: It is conservatively estimated that 4 to 10 million adults and many more children have been diagnosed with the disorder.

• If possible, join a local support group that serves both families and children and have everyone go together to at least one meeting.

WHEN YOUR CHILD HAS ADD

"My son Andy was diagnosed a year ago, when he was nine years old," Sam says. "Although Andy was always a pretty hyper kid, we brought him in for an evaluation because his grades really started to slip in fourth grade. His teachers complained that he wouldn't pay attention, that he disrupted the class, and that he didn't seem to care about any of his subjects. I knew he wasn't just a 'problem child' like his teacher said, so we took him to a psychologist who diagnosed him with ADD. In fact, it was while the psychologist was explaining ADD to us that it occurred to me how many symptoms I experienced, too. On the spot, I arranged to be evaluated myself. It was a day that really changed all of our lives."

Sam's experience is far from unique. In fact, although no one knows exactly how often ADD affects more than one member of a family, enough anecdotal and scientific evidence exists to indicate that there may be a genetic component to the disorder. If you have ADD, it is possible—though by no means certain—that your child may also suffer from the disorder. If so, you will want to provide him or her with the professional help needed to manage the disorder as soon as possible to prevent the escalation of difficulties.

It should be noted that raising a healthy, well-adjusted child with ADD often involves a great deal of special care and attention, and it goes beyond the scope of this book to provide you with all the information that will help you do so. The following section highlights some of the more important concerns. It is up to you to seek support and guidance from your child's doctor, teacher, and guidance counselor, as well as from local support groups dedicated to helping children and families with ADD.

Recognize Signs and Symptoms

In chapters One and Two, we provided a thorough description of ADD and how it affects both adults and children. As your child matures, stay alert for signs that he or she suffers from any of these symptoms and related behaviors. At the same time, it is extremely important not to overreact to every potential symptom your child displays. Many children have high energy levels, for instance, that are completely unrelated to hyperactivity. Others enjoy lively imaginations that could be mistaken for inattention, or assertive personalities that might look like impulsivity to an overanxious parent. It may take a couple of years of school before it can be determined that the behaviors you see in your child are actually due to ADD.

If you suspect that your child may indeed have ADD, discuss the possibility first with his or her teacher and guidance counselor. If you are still concerned, seek advice from a psychologist or health professional trained to evaluate ADD.

Obtain a Proper Diagnosis

Fortunately, ADD in children is one of the most thoroughly researched and well-documented psychological conditions. Hence, you and your family may face far fewer obstacles in obtaining an accurate diagnosis for your child than you yourself may have encountered. Nevertheless, it is important to find a health professional experienced in childhood ADD to evaluate your child. To do so, ask advice from your child's teacher and guidance counselor and follow the tips provided in Chapter Three.

Explain ADD in Reassuring Terms

How you tell your child about ADD, and how you answer his or her questions about the disorder today and in the future, may have a lasting effect on your child's ability to manage the condition, thrive at school and in social situations, and develop a healthy sense of self-esteem.

From the outset, it is important to be honest with your child about all aspects of ADD. Without being overly dramatic, let your child know that ADD may well be at the root of his or her difficulties in keeping still, minding teachers, performing schoolwork, and/or getting along with friends. Keep in mind, too, that your child's experience with the disorder may be quite different from yours, especially since more is known about it today than when you were growing up. Although learning that he or she has to visit a doctor and perhaps take medication may be initially disturbing, chances are that your child will ultimately feel quite relieved that there is a way to manage troublesome symptoms and succeed in his or her own environment.

One thing to keep in mind as you explain ADD to your child is how language can influence our perceptions of any situation. If you refer to ADD as a raging psychiatric disorder, your child is likely to think of him or herself as severely handicapped or defective. If ADD is described as a disability that presents a set of challenges that is highly treatable, on the other hand, your child may look at the disorder in a more positive light, recognizing it as requiring special care and treatment, but not necessarily preventing him or her from fulfilling goals and living out dreams. Keep in mind that some children and adolescents will not readily accept the diagnosis and may actually resist any attempts to get them to understand the disorder or begin treatment. Later, sometimes after experiencing further failures and disappointments, many young people will eventually accept the need to better manage ADD symptoms and be more open to treatment.

Begin Treatment Immediately

As you may well have discovered yourself already, education and medication and behavioral therapy in combination, are often extremely effective in alleviating ADD symptoms. Once you have obtained an accurate diagnosis for your child, follow the doctor's recommendations for therapy. The sooner your child gets help, the sooner he or she can begin to realize and express his or her own true gifts.

Monitor Your Child's Attitude

Make sure to explain to your child why he or she needs to undergo tests, take medication, and/or receive special help at school. Ask him or her on a regular basis if there are any questions about ADD or its treatment, and encourage your child to speak openly with his or her doctor. In addition, because your child may have fears and concerns that are hard to express directly, it's important for you to watch for any changes in behavior, such as unexplained crankiness, crying, or withdrawal that may indicate that your child is afraid or upset.

"After improving for a while after he started on Ritalin, Andy began acting out and throwing temper tantrums like he was two years old again," Sam recalls. "We even talked to his doctor about changing his dosage of medication. Finally, he and I had a real heart-to-heart talk, and he confessed he'd been teased at school because kids found out he was taking medication. I felt so bad for him. Kids can be so cruel. But we spoke to his teacher, who managed to talk to the class about ADD without embarrassing Andy. And I helped him realize that there would always be people who, out of ignorance, would make fun or give him a hard time, but he was strong enough and smart enough to stand up for himself."

Accept Your Child

In Chapter One, we discussed the sometimes painful process many adults go through as they come to terms with a diagnosis of ADD. You may very well pass through the same stages of the coping process after learning about your child's ADD. Although it is likely that your son or daughter will learn to manage symptoms and thus develop appropriate intellectual and social skills, the truth of the matter is that he or she does face special challenges, challenges that you and your spouse did not anticipate or desire. You may try to deny that your child has a problem, or become angry and frustrated at how unfair life seems to be to your child and your family. You may even grieve for the challenges your child must face because of the difficulties ADD places before him or her.

If you yourself have ADD, however, you may be able to put some of these feelings into a healthy perspective more quickly than most parents. In addition, you can offer your child a sense of the positive aspects of the disorder—such as a quick imagination and lots of energy—as well as provide him or her with some of the skills you wish you had learned as you were growing up.

In the end, it is essential that you learn to accept your child for the person he or she is today, complete with the challenges ahead and the potential for success that is inherent in all of us. Appreciate your child's special qualities and directly acknowledge his or her talents and capabilities as often as possible.

Build Self-esteem

The development of self-esteem is a lifelong process that begins the moment we are born. As adults, we are able to measure our worth based on objective criteria. At least to some extent, we can evaluate our accomplishments, values, and the quality of our personal relationships by comparing them to those achieved by others as well as to those set forth by the belief systems—religious and/or academic—to which we choose to adhere. Although much of our self-concept is derived from our experiences in childhood, adults do have the ability to make relatively impartial judgments about their own self-worth and past experiences.

Children, on the other hand, largely depend on cues they receive from the outside world—from parents and other family members, teachers and other authority figures, and their own peers—to establish and value their sense of self. Children who receive positive feedback from the people around them are generally able to develop a sound self-image and a strong inner confidence that allows them to mature into well-adjusted adults. With an excess of negative input, such as constant criticism and punishment, children run the risk of developing a poor self-image and a lack of self-confidence that may last a lifetime.

As an adult with ADD, you probably know better than most people the barriers ADD can place between a child and a healthy sense of self-esteem. No matter how hard you tried, you never managed to live up to your own or other people's expectations. You were constantly reprimanded for behaving badly or failing to perform well at school. Perhaps other children made fun of you because you didn't fit in with your peer group. Even your siblings showed signs that they resented you and the challenges you posed to the family.

As painful as your experience may have been, some good may come of it yet. With your special knowledge of the impact ADD often has on childhood development, you can intervene with your child to make sure that the positive input outweighs the negative. Not only can you encourage your child yourself, but you can establish a constructive atmosphere within the home environment.

In addition, as we'll discuss later in this chapter, you can advocate for your child at school, helping to ensure that his or her special needs are considered and that every effort is made by teachers and school officials to provide your child with the best education possible. As we've stressed throughout this book, the key is to accentuate the positive aspects of your child's personality, acknowledge his or her talents, and encourage his or her dreams.

Allaying Sibling Rivalry

Friends, competitors, sometimes even self-declared ene-mies, siblings have uniquely intimate relationships. Indeed, rela-tionships between siblings form some of the strongest, most enduring bonds in a person's life. Brothers and sisters help shape one another's personalities, contribute to one another's self-esteem, and prepare each other for experiences with peers and as adults.

Nevertheless, sibling rivalry remains an issue for almost every family with more than one child, even if one sibling doesn't suffer with a chronic condition like ADD. Feelings of resent-ment, jealousy, anxiety, and anger are all common between siblings at one time or another during their childhood—even their adulthood—and when one child has special challenges, those feelings tend to be more intense and come to the fore much more quickly than in families in which all children are equally healthy.

Despite the often pressing needs of your child with ADD, as well as your own, it is important to keep in mind that your other children face their own set of challenges—challenges that stem as much from who they are as individuals as those that arise from having a brother or sister and a parent with a condition like ADD. Growing up healthy and strong in today's complex world is no easy task for any child, and it is important to recognize and respect the effort that all of your children must make in order to survive and thrive.

If you have other children, tell them the truth about ADD and how it affects your family as soon as possible. Again, the language you use and the attitude you take will make a difference in how the children take the news. If you're upbeat and optimistic about the effects of ADD, they will probably feel the same way. Nevertheless, it is likely that your children will pass through many of the same stages of acceptance you and your child with ADD probably have experienced. Denial, anger, and depression are common reactions to the news that a sibling has a special problem.

Without question, however, resentment is the emotion most often mentioned. Siblings often feel that their brother or sister with ADD gets more attention from everyone, is let off the hook when he or she misbehaves, and is able to change the household routine at the drop of a hat. Many siblings feel resentful because they think they always come second after the child with ADD and that there is no way to fairly compete for parental approval (a normal part of sibling rivalry) against someone with the "odds" so stacked in his or her favor. This may make it harder to ask for what they need, as well as to sincerely offer their love and support to either their parent or their brother or sister with ADD.

To help compensate for some of the impediments to satisfying and nurturing sibling relationships, you and your spouse may want to follow these tips:

• *Listen and watch for signs that your other children are upset and concerned.* Keep in mind that children may not be able to put a finger on their fears about the disorder and its effects on the family. In fact, many may not realize that what they are feeling *is* fear. If you notice your other children acting in an unfamiliar way, take the time to talk to them and help them sort out their feelings.

• *Spend special time with your other children.* Balancing attention and support between a child without ADD and one with the disorder is a difficult task for many parents. The very real needs of the children without ADD often take second place to the ongoing imperative of caring for a child suffering from the disorder. It is essential that you make a sincere effort to spend time with each of your other children, preferably one at a time, in order to discuss their concerns or to simply have fun away from the rest of the family.

• *Put ADD into perspective.* Very gently remind your other children that while it may be true that their brother or sister gets more attention, it is attention that he or she would much rather forego. Indeed, let them know that resentment works both ways: Their brother or sister probably resents them some-times, too, for all the freedom, time, and success their relative health provides them.

• *Encourage your children to explore their own interests.* Stress how important it is for the sibling to lead his or her own life, while at the same time conveying how much you appreciate any help and support he or she can offer to you and the rest of the family.

• *Foster communication between all of your children.* Per-haps the most important thing you can do to help your children get along is to open the lines of communication between them. The more they can talk matters over between themselves, with-out you or your spouse acting as a mediator, the better off the whole family atmosphere is likely to be. Be aware, however, that there will always be tension and arguments among siblings, even in the calmest of environments and happiest of families.

The Fine Art of Discipline

Without doubt, every family needs to have rules and regulations in place in order to function as a workable, cooperative unit. And the truth is, most children are secretly grateful for the limits that parents put on their behavior and for the expectations they are encouraged to live up to. Even more than most, children with ADD appreciate having some sense of structure, control, and order in their lives, even though they may resist it.

Dispensing measured, thoughtful discipline may not come naturally to a parent with ADD, however. Because they are so distracted and disorganized, some parents with ADD tend to be more lax than is appropriate and fail to follow through consistently with rewards and punishment. They either fail to recognize when rules have been broken or disregard the penalties they've put in place for breaking them.

"I didn't realize that my kids thought of me as the 'softie,'" Sam admits. "They'd always come to me first if they'd done something wrong, like staying out past curfew or getting a bad grade on a test. They figured out early on that I was so much into my own scattered world that I didn't have much time or energy to be really hard-nosed with them. My wife, on the other hand, was known to be pretty strict, which meant she was forced to play the bad guy all the time. In fact, the kids learned to play us against one another pretty well, until we were angrier with each other than we were with them."

Other parents with ADD may react in the opposite way: They tend to be extremely strict when it comes to enforcing rules and meting out punishment. Mark, for instance, found himself being particularly tough on Angela, his wife's fourteen-year-old daughter from another marriage.

"I was rough on everybody in the family," Mark confesses. "I laid down the law and everyone was expected to follow it to the letter. The fact that I was all over the place with my moods and my behavior didn't matter; with my wife and kids I was a tyrant. And Angela got the worst of it. Maybe it was because she reminded me of the way I was when I was her age, and I hated living through all the frustration and pain again. Since we found out that both of us happen to have ADD, we've begun to heal some of the rough spots in our relationship."

Like Sam and Mark, you and your family may face special challenges when it comes to creating and maintaining structure and discipline if one of your children also has ADD. The following tips may help you establish a healthy and productive atmosphere of mutual respect and caring:

- *Make it clear that all of your children—and even you and your spouse—are expected to live by certain rules.* Create some rules by which all members of the family must live. Telephoning ahead if you're going to be late is one rule that works across the board; so is performing certain chores every day and keeping a civil tongue when communicating with one another, no matter how angry you are. Other rules will depend on the age and level of maturity of each child and include curfews, television privileges, and health-related proscriptions such as medication schedules and other therapeutic interventions.

- *Come to an agreement about the rules with your children.* Children—especially those with ADD—are much more apt to follow rules they've helped to create than those that have been sent down from above. Discuss the reasons why a particular rule is necessary, work to find a compromise if your children feel a rule is unfair, and make sure they understand and accept what the consequences will be for breaking the rule. Be very concrete about this, even if that means writing rules and regulations down and posting them in each child's room.

- *Make sure that the punishment fits the crime.* At the same time that you and your family create a coherent set of rules, outline a set of fair and equitable sanctions to be enforced if they are broken. If punishment is too severe for minor infractions, children will lose respect for the whole process. If no consequences exist for breaking the rules, on the other hand, children will have no reason to curb their impulses and change their behavior. What is too strict or too lax in your family is a matter of personal judgment and can often be determined only through trial and error.

• *Offer praise and affection.* It's crucial to remember that for discipline to be effective, it must include more than just punishment and criticism. Indeed, the reinforcement of good behavior with rewards and compliments should be an equal partner, especially when it comes to creating a healthy, supportive environment for a child with ADD.

Try this experiment: For one week, keep track of how often you scold your children. Then, the next week, try to praise their behavior twice as often. Even a child with a behavior problem related to ADD has many positive aspects in his or her personality to commend. By doing so, however, you will not only reinforce whatever good behavior he or she does manage, you'll also bolster what may well be a flagging sense of self-esteem.

• *Be consistent.* As hard as it may be for a parent with ADD to be steady and dependable, those are among the essential qualities necessary for successful parenting. You and your spouse should let your children know that the rules you make today are the same ones you will enforce tomorrow, and that the repercussions of ignoring or disobeying the rules will remain the same as well.

Be consistent, too, with how you mete out punishment between siblings. Although it is tempting to give the child with ADD more leeway or, conversely, ease up on siblings because they usually provoke far less anxiety in you and your spouse, differences in punishment are sure to create more behavior problems down the line.

• *Don't confuse consistency with inflexibility.* There are always exceptions to rules, and there will be times when you should let an infraction pass without enforcing punishment. But those exceptions should be relatively few and far between, or the rules themselves should be amended. Otherwise, your children will lose respect for the discipline process altogether. Choose your battles carefully, concentrating on reinforcing the most positive and beneficial behaviors in your child.

In this regard, it's important to listen to children's explanations for their actions. "There's no excuse for such behavior" is a common expression voiced by millions of parents every day. And often it's quite true. However, if you make a sincere effort to listen to your children as they attempt to explain behavior, you may learn a lot, not only about the action itself, but about the way your children think and feel about the world around them. In addition, you'll be sending a very important message, one that your child with ADD especially needs to hear. By listening, you're telling your children that what they have to say is important and that you respect their right to say it.

• *Don't lose control.* Anger is the least productive emotion when it comes to disciplining your children. No matter how infuriated you become—and a hyperactive child can certainly push your own ADD mood swing buttons—you should never strike or verbally demean your children. If you try to deal with your children when you're angry, you'll only engender fear and fail to earn respect.

If you sense that your emotions are getting the better of you in front of your children, count to ten, leave the room, or do anything else that will help you gain some perspective on the situation. Many families choose to enforce "time-outs"—periods of several minutes or longer in which both parents and children retreat to their own private spaces to cool off. Only when you've all calmed down will you be able to get at the root of the problem.

• *Trust your children.* Expect the best from your children. The more faith you have that your children will do the right thing, the more likely they are to live up to your expectations—and that's particularly true for the child with ADD.

Making Your Child's Education Count

In the United States today, all children are entitled to an education, free of cost, from the age of five to eighteen and, in most states, they are required to attend until they are about sixteen years old. School is an important force in all our children's lives, providing as it does an intellectual, physical, and social framework upon which to build their lives.

The degree to which American schools are succcessful at educating our children remains a subject of considerable debate. Nevertheless, parents continue to send their children to school with certain expectations. For those expectations to be fulfilled for any child, extraordinary tenacity and hard work on the part of parents, students, and teachers is necessary. When a child faces special challenges such as those imposed by ADD and its symptoms, the effort required is even greater. Here are a few tips to help you through the education maze:

• *Monitor your child's treatment plan.* Needless to say, the medication and behavioral therapy prescribed by your child's doctor has the best chance of working if you pay close attention to your child's progress or lack of progress and report your findings to the doctor. Among the data you supply are your child's grades, teacher reports, and his or her own feelings about school.

• *Establish an environment of learning and success at home.* As in all things, your children take their cues from you. If your son or daughter with ADD sees that you have an honest respect for education—and are not nagging about grades simply for the sake of nagging—he or she is more likely to pick up a book to read for pleasure or delve into a science project with energy and curiosity. If you, as a man or woman who may have struggled with the same difficulties in concentration and focus, can show your child ways to compensate and thrive, you will be doing an immeasurable service.

• *Create a School Planning Notebook with your child.* Remember the Planning Notebook we suggested you create in Chapter Seven? It may help your child feel in more control of his or her academic life if you develop a "School Planning Notebook" together. The first section might be devoted to keeping track of homework assignments and other daily details, the second section to "Things to Do" the next day, and the third section to long-range planning for the month, semester, or school year.

"Angela's freshman year in high school has been a remarkable one," Mark says. "It really started as soon as eighth grade ended. During the summer, she volunteered part-time at a veterinarian's office and decided that she wanted to become a vet more than anything else. But for that, she knew she'd have to bring up her grades in science and math and really start concentrating. We wrote down her goals in a notebook and brought it with us to a meeting with her principal and guidance counselor. Throughout the year, she's been keeping track of her progress and looks ahead with so much more optimism and energy."

• *Form a partnership with school officials.* Because ADD is often an invisible condition that can be mistaken for obstinacy, aggression, willful inattention, or even mental slowness, your child's teacher may have no reason to suspect that the pretty girl or handsome boy sitting in class has a neurobiological problem that requires special attention. Although your child would probably like to keep it that way, it is essential that the teacher and school nurse be informed about the condition, especially if your child is currently taking medication. Try to speak with teacher and nurse together and, if possible, with your child present.

The greater the teacher's understanding of your child's personality and severity of ADD symptoms, the more likely the teacher will be willing to work to more effectively meet your child's needs. Written information, in the form of pamphlets or brochures, is very helpful to the teacher who may not have an accurate understanding of ADD, its effects and treatment.

During the discussion with your child's teacher, bring up the need both you and your child have for frequent progress reports. Ask the teacher to make note of how your child is doing academically, socially, and in managing his or her ADD-related symptoms. Frequent communication gives all of you a chance to assess if your child's needs are being met with success.

Other tips for teachers include:

- posting lists of rules and procedures in the classroom so that children can remind themselves.
- using positive reinforcement for good behavior more than punishment for bad behavior.
- providing frequently scheduled breaks during the school day.

- *Understand the law.* Generally speaking, most children with ADD are able to learn within a traditional classroom situation, particularly if their teachers are aware of their condition and are willing to provide some of the supportive measures discussed above. However, it is important for parents of children with ADD or learning disabilities to know that there are laws that protect their children's right to an education. Specifically, Public Law 94-142, also known as the Individuals with Disabilities Education Act, or IDEA, was passed by the United States Congress in 1975. This law is designed to give all children equal access to educational opportunities, and states must comply with it in order to get federal funding for education. In addition, each state has its own regulations that must meet federal standards.

Under this law, schools are required to evaluate children whose school performance indicates that they may need special education. All areas of development must be tested, including health, vision, hearing, social and emotional status, general intelligence, academic performance, communication ability, and motor skills. In addition, the opinions of the people who know the child best—the parents—are taken into consideration.

Based on the child's evaluation, a program can be designed to address his or her needs in the most effective way possible. If your child also has a learning disability such as dyslexia, for instance, he or she may require remedial reading classes in order to learn new skills.

In addition, Section 504 of the Rehabilitation Act—another

federal law passed by Congress in the 1970s—may provide help and relief to children who are not eligible under IDEA.

If the school does not have the resources necessary, the school system is required to provide them in another setting without cost to the family. The details of Public Law 94-142 and other related legislation are complex, and the standards of review and quality of services available to students with ADD vary considerably from school district to school district across the country. If you think your child may have special needs, you should meet with the special education director of your school district (if one exists) or the superintendent of schools. If you find that you're having trouble finding your way through the maze of public service agencies, consider meeting with a hospital social worker or parent advocacy organization for help and support.

FOSTERING A HEALTHY MARRIAGE

As discussed in the last chapter, establishing intimacy with a spouse is often a difficult challenge for men and women with ADD. When children are added to the mix, the increase in pressure can be enough to challenge any marriage. And when the child of a parent with ADD is also diagnosed with the disorder, the tension and stress escalate even more.

By now, you may have started to take medication to alleviate your symptoms and learn new skills to compensate for those difficulties that remain. With any luck, you and your spouse will continue to give each other love, support, and understanding and can now look toward the future with the extra hope and strength that comes from pulling together and consolidating your emotional and physical resources.

However, before you can move forward, it may be necessary for you both to come to terms with the past. Although no statistics have been compiled about the kinds of problems faced by couples in which one partner has ADD, enough anecdotal evidence exists to suggest some common themes. Indeed, the

symptoms of ADD pose very special challenges to the establish-
ment and preservation of intimacy. Some of those challenges,
such as those that derive from poor communication skills and
the physical discomfort some ADD patients experience in intimate settings, were discussed in Chapter Eight. But there are
other common marital problems that may be related to ADD
as well, and some of them can be quite damaging.

"It's not something I like to talk about very much, because
I truly love my wife and kids," Rich admits. "But I've had a
few affairs over the years. Talk about impulsive. That's just
what they were: impulsive, selfish acts. Was it because I had
ADD? Who can ever be sure? But now that I feel better able
to think—really think—about the consequences of my acts
before I commit them, I truly can't imagine risking what I have
for something so fleeting and hurtful to other people."

In addition to the impulsiveness involved, some adults with
ADD enjoy the high-risk quality—the "living on the edge"
feelings that come with the surreptitious nature of extramarital
or extra-relationship affairs.

"I've always 'cheated' on the man I was with," says Bonnie,
"because it made me feel really alive and excited in a way that
a monogamous relationship never could. In fact, although I'm
deeply ashamed to admit it now, I've also indulged in some
pretty risky sex, too. Really irresponsible stuff that could have
destroyed my life. I'm lucky I survived intact, but I know I hurt
a lot of people in the process."

In order to move on, Rich, Bonnie, and other adults with
ADD have had to face their past, forgive themselves, and mend
some fences. "I can't say that all has been forgiven," Rich relates.
"But with some help from a therapist, my wife is beginning to
learn to trust me again. And I know I can trust myself."

Patience, understanding, and commitment will go a long
way in helping couples with ADD stay together and grow even
closer.

Nevertheless, there will likely be some rough spots along
the way. The good news is that the solution to most marital
problems, including those that stem from the symptoms of

ADD, lies in open, honest communication. By talking out your frustrations and fears, you may be able to find a way to work together to make things better for you and your family. In order to develop and enhance your communication skills, both you and your spouse should take the time to reread the strategies outlined in Chapter Eight.

In addition to those suggestions and the ones outlined at the beginning of this chapter, you and your spouse should make every effort to:

• **Stop playing the "blame game."** "My wife and I spent so much time arguing with each other about who did what and when and why everything went wrong that we never got around to making any positive changes," Sam remarks. "She'd blame me for staying at the studio and missing dinner, I'd blame her for not calling to remind me, etc., etc. The worst arguments we had were over our son Andy. Before he was diagnosed with ADD, I blamed my wife for his bad behavior. If she only disciplined him better, I thought, he'd be okay. After he was diagnosed, though, she blamed me—but never out loud—for passing the disorder on to him. And I blamed myself, too. It was awful. And Andy was the one who really suffered."

Sam's twelve-year-old marriage was on the verge of crumbling when he himself was diagnosed with ADD. With help from a marriage counselor, Sam and his wife worked at resolving past difficulties and creating new goals for themselves as a couple as well as for their family. In fact, Sam found that the challenges he and his wife faced were even more formidable than some of his professional goals or personal frustrations.

"The marriage counselor explained to my wife, Sandy, and me that we had to go back and kind of rewrite our marriage contract to take into account all of the broken promises and unmet expectations we both have experienced in the last decade or so, recognizing that at least some of them have been due to ADD," Sam explains. "We talked a lot about what expectations we had about the marriage from the beginning, and how they had changed. We worked out what we needed from each other today, and what we could realistically expect to be able to give each other now that we knew about ADD. It's been an amazing adventure, and it's really helped us to grow closer together and work together as a team."

In seeking help from a marriage counselor, Sam and his wife joined many other adults with ADD and their spouses. Indeed, because of the long-standing and exceedingly intimate nature of marriage, the problems presented by the disorder may be particularly entrenched and painful within that relationship. Issues of trust, commitment, and sexual intimacy are particularly pressing for many couples in which one partner has ADD. If you feel that you and your spouse might be facing some similar problems, you should talk to your therapist about getting additional support. For Sam and Sandy, joining a support group of adults with ADD in addition to couples therapy proved very helpful.

"I'm not saying it's easy, but we've learned to try to stop and think before we speak in anger," Sam says. "And 'It's all your fault' has been eliminated from our vocabulary."

• *Reevaluate former roles.* Now that you know some of the challenges you face as individuals and as a couple, you and your spouse owe it to yourselves to examine how you typically behave with one another. Reread the section on role-playing in Chapter Eight and if you find that you or your spouse fall into any of those categories, agree to start fresh. Try to look at each other with new eyes and new hope. Recognize that you each have a responsibility to work at achieving a successful outcome.

• *Make time just for each other.* Nothing is more vital to a healthy marriage than spending private, intimate moments together whenever possible. Although that may be a tall order in today's pressure-filled world, it is well worth the trouble that may be involved. Budget funds for an occasional babysitter to care for your kids while you and your spouse take in a movie or have a picnic in the park. Ask your parents or in-laws to take the kids for a weekend once a year so that you and your wife can enjoy some time together, even if you just stay at home alone. Above all, use whatever time you manage to carve out to express your understanding and respect for one another and to keep your love alive.

If your marriage is showing signs of serious dysfunction, find a marriage counselor to help you cope with your challenges in a healthier way. In addition, talk with the spouses you encounter at support group meetings and listen to what they have to say. They have firsthand knowledge of the struggles you face.

The Often Silent Partner: The Spouse without ADD

Often there is a "power behind the family," so to speak, a person whose love, support, and management skills are largely responsible for keeping the family up and running. Because you have been struggling with the symptoms of ADD, it is very likely that your spouse is that person—and he or she deserves a special mention in this book. After you finish reading these pages, hand the book over to your partner to read, too. You may both benefit from the advice we offer here.

• *Recognize your partner's frustration.* The role that your husband or wife has taken on—that of a loving partner to someone with ADD—is not an easy one. He or she probably often feels shut out and ignored, overwhelmed and underappreciated. Let your partner know that he or she has every right to express those feelings to you, to other adult family members, and especially to a therapist or a support group specializing in helping families cope with ADD. Warn your partner that keeping emotions bottled up in order to "spare" you or your children may end up only backfiring: He or she is apt to become more stressed, irritable, and unhappy.

• *Encourage your partner to be assertive.* As difficult as it may be to balance your needs with the needs of your partner, you must try to do so if you want your marriage to continue to grow and flourish. Make sure that your partner feels free to voice his or her opinions and needs, and make every effort to hear them, understand them, and respect them, even if you don't agree with them.

• *Help your partner to better manage stress.* In Chapter Six, we outlined some important guidelines for living a healthy, balanced life, including eating a nutritious diet, exercising on a regular basis, and learning relaxation strategies. By all means, your spouse should take the time to peruse that chapter and apply some of that advice to his or her own life. Indeed, he or she probably carries an extraordinary burden of stress and pressure that may end up damaging his or her physical and mental health if not released in healthy, constructive ways.

Encourage your husband or wife to spend an hour or two each week away from you and your concerns, away from your child with ADD and his or her challenges, away from as much of the nitty-gritty details of life as possible. You'll be surprised at how much better your partner will feel afterward, and how much your marriage and family life will benefit from the love and commitment the two of you show each other.

In the next and final chapter, we'll show you how to take all that you've learned about ADD and its impact on your family, career, and social life and make that knowledge work for you today and in the future.

IMPORTANT QUESTIONS AND ANSWERS ABOUT CHAPTER NINE

Q My thirteen-year-old son has been struggling with a severe case of Attention Deficit Disorder since he was about four or five years old. For several years, he was pretty out of control, very aggressive and hyperactive. His behavior disrupted the whole house and his two older brothers deeply resented the trouble he caused in the household. Now, even though he's much better and doing well at school and at home, the older boys—and even my husband and I—tend to blame him for everything that goes wrong. Everything seems to be his fault. What can I do to smooth things out?

A What's happening to your son is not all that uncommon. Your older kids are using him as a scapegoat—an easy person to blame when something goes wrong—especially something for which they might otherwise be blamed. As you say, for many years he was indeed at the root of many of your family's difficulties, so perhaps you remain a little too quick to point the finger at him. The important thing to do now is to sit down together and wipe the family slate clean of blame and recriminations. Make it a point that *everyone* gets to start fresh, not only the child with ADD, but your other kids and you and your spouse as well.

Q I have three children, two dogs, a husband, and ADD. Keeping the household running smoothly is getting a little bit easier since I started treatment, especially since my husband and I initiated the "family meeting." Every week, we all sit down and sort out the chores that need doing, the arguments that need settling, and the schedules that need to be devised. I find that we all work together really well for about two or three days, but then it all falls apart. I lose track first, but the rest of the family isn't very far behind. Pretty soon, we're right back where we started from. Is there a way we can keep the momentum going?

A It sounds as if you might need to have a couple of "mini family meetings" during the week in order to keep everybody on track. Does your family eat breakfast or dinner together on a fairly regular basis? If so, take ten minutes or so during the meal to update the To Do list or revise your schedule. Create a family bulletin board where messages and reminders can be posted on a daily basis. Above all, don't give up. It takes time and practice to make any new system work.

PLANNING FOR
A FULLER
LIFE

"Potential. From the time I first heard that word when I was seven years old, I hated it," Rich says. "To me, it was everything I wasn't 'living up to.' But the truth is, the word itself is really quite positive. It comes from the Latin *potentia*, meaning 'possessing potency or power.' Power, think of that! And now that I know about ADD and am learning how to manage it better, I think of the power I finally have to live the way I want to live, to pursue my dreams and feel that I have as good a chance as anyone of fulfilling them."

Rich speaks for hundreds of thousands of men and women— and hopefully you're among them—who acquire a new sense of "potential" along with a diagnosis of ADD. For some, the relief that comes from putting a name to a set of mysterious and disturbing symptoms is enough all by itself to jump start their attitudes. Others find that the practical and psychological improvement that often comes from medication and/or therapy is what unleashes a renewed sense of optimism and confidence.

In this brief closing chapter, we'll help you tap into your own power and potential, recognize your dreams, and create a realistic plan to realize your goals to the best of your newfound abilities. To employ a well-worn but very apt expression, "Today is the first day of the rest of your life." With the knowledge you've acquired from your doctor, from reading this book, and (hopefully) from talking with other adults with ADD, you are in a perfect position to make the rest of your life really count.

ACCEPTING THE PROCESS OF CHANGE

"My life didn't suddenly change overnight," Marion remarks. "I wasn't made a vice president in the ad agency the week after I was diagnosed or anything. But now, a year later, I see that treatment has allowed me to make a lot of little changes which, taken together, add up to a much more satisfying life. And yes, I have had some real successes at work that probably wouldn't have been possible before I knew about my ADD."

Like Marion, Rich can look back on the eighteen months since he was diagnosed and trace a series of small but significant steps forward, building momentum as he went along. Although he always enjoyed his work as a journalist, he never really believed he was—or ever could be—truly successful at work or in his family life. Slowly but surely, Rich's confidence has grown and now he feels able to handle a few more assignments at the newspaper, looks forward to (instead of dreading) quiet times alone with his wife and kids, and most impressive of all to Rich, he has finally been able to work steadily on a novel which has been sitting half-written in a drawer for years.

For most adults with ADD, progress is made in much the same way—slowly, steadily, and with occasional setbacks along the way. Amy, for instance, decided to go off Ritalin for a time after gaining some control over her symptoms, but decided to take it again when she felt herself slipping back just when new challenges in her life were emerging. Mark felt a tremendous surge of confidence and energy after he first started treatment, but became frustrated when his employment problems and home life didn't improve immediately.

The fact is, as we've discussed before, the problems caused by ADD are usually too complicated and deep-rooted to be resolved with any quick fix. Patience and perseverance are essential requirements, and ones that often exist in short supply among the adult ADD population. And even when symptoms are better managed with treatment, the condition may well impose some frustrating limits on certain aspects of your life.

In fact, with or without ADD, we all arrive at a certain point in our lives when we come face to face with the stark reality that not everything *is* possible. Not every little boy (or little girl) who dreams of playing center field for the Red Sox has the talent or the luck to end up at Fenway Park. Only a relatively few of us have the intellectual or financial resources to make it through the eight or more years of higher education it takes to become a medical doctor, no matter how much we would like to. And ADD and its symptoms, though by no means an impenetrable barrier, will certainly have an impact on those realizations.

At the same time, however, you, like so many of your peers with ADD, probably have put all of your dreams—even the more practical ones—on hold for too long. Having met with so few real successes, at least in your own mind, you may well have assumed long ago that what you want for yourself is and always will be out of reach and beyond your capabilities to achieve.

Once you've had a little time to see how well you respond to treatment, make time to reexamine your true aspirations and desires to determine just how possible it might be to live up to them.

ON THE ROAD TO REALIZING YOUR DREAMS

After you read the next few sentences, close your eyes and think about your future. Answer the following questions as honestly as you can. Really let yourself imagine what it would be like to live out your dreams.

- If I could live anywhere in the world, I would choose _____.
- If I had free time and extra money, I would choose to _____.
- If I could be in the perfect intimate relationship, it would be one of _____.
- If I had the job of my dreams, it would be doing _____.

Now take a look at the dream life you've imagined for yourself. How far away is it from reality? How possible is it for you to make some changes to bring you at least a little closer to your ideal? Knowing what you know now about ADD and its effects on your life, how has the disorder held you back from even attempting to achieve your inner desires? Are you starting to manage those symptoms better and thus clear away some of the roadblocks you've met with in the past?

It would be futile to try to answer all of these questions right now. But as you read the rest of this chapter, and reflect upon what you've come to understand about yourself since learning about ADD, keep your dreams in mind and work, slowly but steadily, to fulfill them to the best of your abilities.

FORGING A SATISFYING CAREER

What did you come up with as an ideal career for yourself? Is it completely different from the one you are in now? Is it one that might truly suit your talents and work habits?

In his book *Focus Your Energy: Hunting for Success in Business with Attention Deficit Disorder*, author Thom Hartmann makes an interesting distinction between people without ADD, whom he calls "farmers" and adults with ADD, referred to as "hunters." According to Hartmann's somewhat controversial theory, the symptoms of ADD can be likened to the qualities most necessary to survive in a primitive hunting society—the ability to act quickly and impulsively, to scan the environment rapidly without becoming too focused on one thing, and to take risks that other, more taciturn people would not. Farmers, on the other hand, require quite different characteristics, such as patience, follow-through, and—in order to pass the time while crops grow or fields lie fallow—highly developed communication skills.

Hartmann's theory provides some insight into the kinds of jobs and careers that might be better suited to a "hunter." High-risk, fast-paced industries such as sales, advertising, and the creative arts, in fact, do seem to attract a high percentage of men and women with ADD, and these people appear to succeed better than their ADD peers who have jobs requiring more structure and administration. Rich, a journalist, and Marion, an advertising executive, are two prime examples of this theory in action. In addition, entrepreneurship—owning one's own business—appeals to many adults with ADD who chafe against other people's rules and regulations.

There are exceptions to these general observations, however. Bonnie, for example, thrives in her career as an engineer even though it involves strict supervision, paying close attention to detail, and the ability to work as part of a team. For Bonnie, the structure imposed upon her "from above" motivates her and keeps her from becoming too distracted.

"I have no desire to change my job, even though I feel like there are other things I'd be able to do now that I have a handle on my ADD," Bonnie says. "But there are a number of people in my ADD support group who decided to really change their lives. A couple of them went back to school, a few went after new jobs. I know one guy who had wanted to open his own beauty salon for years, but could never get it together. Nine months after starting treatment, he signed a lease on a shop and was ready to roll. It's very exciting."

Deciding to Make a Change

When Ruben looks back on the last several years, he gets frustrated. An aspiring actor, he worked as a waiter to pay his bills and tried to convince himself, month after month, that it was just bad luck that had held him back from succeeding on the stage.

"But it wasn't just luck. And it wasn't a lack of talent, either. It was a lack of organization and focus—classic for somebody with ADD, no?" Ruben says. "I finally took a hard look at where I was, where I wanted to be, and the steps I needed to take to get there."

Working with his therapist and a counselor with Actors Equity, Ruben made some changes in his life. First, he talked with his restaurant manager to arrange to work more evenings, leaving him free to attend auditions during the day. Second, he signed up to take an acting class to hone his skills. And third, he set up a system to track upcoming auditions and casting calls so he'd be better prepared ahead of time.

"Acting is high-risk enough without leaving everything to chance," Ruben admits. "I finally decided to stop blaming ADD, the fates, or my agent, and take the bull by the horns myself."

Although Rich, Marion, Bonnie, and Ruben decided to remain in their chosen professions, many of their peers with ADD choose to make significant career changes once they reassess their "potential." Ben, for instance, had always harbored a secret desire to own and operate an auto shop, but never believed he had the resources to do so.

"And more than that, I never could sit down and think long enough to see clearly what was really involved," he says. "But with therapy, and the help of a career counselor, I started to explore the possibility more seriously."

Ben's career counselor had him perform a simple exercise. He was asked to imagine his ideal job, consider his current position, envision an acceptable compromise, and figure out some of the prerequisites required to meet his goal. Here's what Ben came up with:

The Dream: To own his own automobile/motorcycle repair shop.

The Reality: Although Ben is a terrific mechanic, he has very little cash and a bad credit history (mostly due to impulsive spending related to ADD). He has been working as a night clerk selling tickets at a bus station for four years, earning the respect of his boss and his co-workers, but feels both trapped by the job and scared to leave it. He knows he'd need to hire a book-keeper and receptionist in order to make his dream of a repair shop work.

The Accommodation: Although Ben would like to own the business himself, he could go into partnership with his brother Ron, whom he knows is looking for a new opportunity. However, he would have to first convince his brother that he is capable of handling the business, no easy task after years of having difficulty even holding down a steady job.

The Requirements: Ben has several things he should do before approaching his brother: (1) research the need for another garage in his town; (2) find out the start-up costs for the kind of shop he has in mind; (3) scout out a few potential locations and find out their cost; (4) obtain a copy of his employee evaluations—all superior—from his boss at the bus company; (5) make a list of friends and family for whom he has worked as a mechanic.

Once Ben outlined the steps, he found the prospect of confronting his brother and asking for help much less daunting. In a way, this process mirrors the one described in Chapter Seven concerning breaking down big projects into smaller, more manageable parts. In fact, Ben used his Planning Notebook to strategize about opening his new business.

Let's explore one more example. Amy, a thirty-five-year-old woman diagnosed a year ago with ADD, has been a housewife since receiving her college degree after a long, seven-year struggle to graduate. Her dream—to be a criminal defense attorney—has seemed so far out of her reach that she's never told a soul about this very real but secret ambition. Now that she feels more secure about herself and her abilities, she's thinking about applying to law school. Here's what Amy's plan of action looked like:

The Dream: To become a criminal defense attorney.

The Reality: Amy is thirty-five, with no experience in the law. She could not afford to go to law school full-time and is concerned that her ADD-related problems with concentration and focus would undermine her.

The Accommodation: After much consideration, Amy decided to work at becoming a paralegal instead of an attorney, at least to start. That way, she would see what life in a law firm would be like without investing at least three years and thousands of dollars in law school. At the same time, Amy could study to take the LSATs, the scores of which are required for entrance to law school, and get some hands-on experience.

The Requirements: Amy first located a paralegal training course and enrolled. She then called a lawyer acquaintance and asked for advice about which law firms to approach after she completed the six-month course. She learned when the LSATs would be given next, bought a study guide, and found an adult-ed review course available should she decide to take the test. Finally, Amy sent away for applications to local law schools for possible future use.

If you've been considering making a career change, try thinking through the steps you'd have to take in order to do so. Are they manageable? Realistic? Appealing? If not, you may need to reconsider your choice of a dream job. Remember, the satisfaction you derive from your career should come from the actual work that is involved in getting there and doing it, not in the prestige it carries or the money it earns you. If you are unhappy in your current situation, but are unsure of where to go next, contact a career counselor or job-training center for guidance.

Going Back to School

Too often, adults with ADD are prevented from getting ahead in the workplace by the lack of a high school, college, or advanced degree. Ironically, the kinds of jobs that are available to people without advanced skills tend to be those requiring speed, organization, and repetition—just the skills most adults with ADD may often lack. Conversely, the jobs most attractive to adults with ADD—those that involve creativity and flexibility—are usually the ones that require more education.

Unfortunately, the memory of past failures and frustrations makes the prospect of returning to the school environment complete anathema to many people with ADD, even those who feel in more control of their symptoms. Ken, for instance, resisted enrolling in community college for two years after receiving treatment and starting a job in his desired field.

"I fell in love with computers and seem to have a natural talent for working with them. Even programming came easy to me," Ken says. "My boss offered to promote me, but said I needed to get at least an Associate's Degree before I could take the job. The company even said they'd pay part of my tuition. But when I thought about high school—which I quit in my junior year; I got my GED when I was twenty-two—I couldn't even bring myself to fill out the application. Finally, I sat down with a counselor at the college and worked it through. I'm about halfway to my degree now and it hasn't been nearly as hard as I thought it would be. It's even been fun at times."

If you believe that furthering your education would help you fulfill one or more of your dreams—or if getting a degree *is* one of your dreams—don't hold back any longer, at least not out of fear. The advice below should help you get started on the road back to school:

• *Talk to your doctor.* Many adults with ADD are afraid that they are destined to fail in an academic setting. If that's what bothers you about returning to school, discuss with your doctor exactly how your symptoms might interfere with your studies, and ask for suggestions on how to alleviate those potential problems.

• *Take it easy.* If you've been out of school for a while, you may want to take things slowly at first. Enroll in one or two classes instead of a full load to avoid setting yourself up to fail by taking on too much work.

• *Take advantage of the help available.* Armed with a letter from your doctor explaining your condition, visit the college's Office of Students with Disabilities or its equivalent. Often, there is an array of special services, including tutors and counselors, who will be able to help you through the system and stay on track. It won't be easy, but with proper accommodations and treatment, it will likely be far less frustrating and more successful than in the past.

ENHANCE YOUR SOCIAL LIFE

"So much of my time had been spent immersed in my own struggle with ADD, with getting by at work, with just trying to live, that I never looked beyond my own front door," Ken confesses. "Don't get me wrong. I'm not beating myself up about it. It's been hard. But now that I'm starting to handle things better, I want to give something back and to really feel a part of the world that I live in."

Many adults with ADD have shared Ken's sense of personal and social isolation. Overwhelmed by day-to-day details and a lack of self-esteem, they have withdrawn behind a seemingly impenetrable curtain. Some are lonely, some are bored, but most people with ADD—even those with families—claim to feel unconnected to the world around them in a fundamental way.

When we talk about our social lives, we usually mean the time we spend with friends, family, or at social gatherings. In fact, however, a social system also may involve extending oneself into the community at large. For many people, church provides a focal point for interacting with others in a meaningful way. Others have hobbies, such as bird-watching, bowling, or, like Mark, white-water rafting, that brings them into contact with people with similar interests but often from diverse backgrounds. Still others choose to donate their time and energy to a cause that is particularly important to their political or social ideals. Getting involved in a hobby or cause can be beneficial to both your own sense of self and to others with whom you come in contact.

No matter what kind of activity you choose, the important thing is to stay connected and involved in the world outside of your family and your work if at all possible.

"I became a Big Sister last year," Marion says. "And it's been terrific. The experience has really helped me to put my own problems and challenges, including ADD, into a much more realistic perspective. Plainly speaking, when I'm with my Little Sister, I'm not thinking about myself, which is a big relief."

Perhaps your work and your family are more than enough for you to manage at this time. If so, we certainly don't want to make you feel inadequate or selfish, especially if you feel that your life is a full and satisfying one. Indeed, now is hardly the time to take on too much responsibility. However, if and when you feel ready, consider extending yourself in a way that will enrich your life and contribute to a spirit of community.

CULTIVATE A SATISFYING FAMILY LIFE

For more and more men and women, creating a family doesn't necessarily mean getting married and having children. Today, perhaps more than ever before, families come in all shapes and sizes: Unmarried partners of same and different sexes, extended families of in-laws and ex-in-laws, and single people who surround themselves with dear friends and siblings each form their own special units of love and respect known as family.

What all members of loving families have in common are feelings of commitment and responsibility toward one another. In the practical world, these feelings usually translate into the need for thoughtful, long-range planning—often of a financial nature—so that we can help each other survive, thrive, and live out our dreams.

Long-range planning, however, does not come naturally to most adults with ADD. Often, they have all they can do to get through the day or the month with their egos and their checking accounts intact. But if their treatment helps them to better think and plan ahead, their day-to-day priorities often become much more clear and they seem to have more energy to complete them.

"I woke up when I realized my daughter would be old enough to attend college in four years and that I really wanted her to be able to go," Mark admits. "Until then, I was kind of floundering, doing better at work since taking medication, but still without a real goal in mind. Now I'm really motivated. I even consulted a financial planner to help me create a budget."

Where do you see yourself and your family in ten years? Do you have children in need of college funds? Would you like to own your own home? Have you started a retirement plan? As you consider these questions, it may be time to take a closer look at your financial situation as it stands today.

Budgeting for the Future

Inattention = losing track of money, checks, and bills.
Impulsivity = careless spending, overloaded credit cards, impulsive buying.
Hyperactivity = too little time spent planning, too much time spending.

As you can see, the three cardinal symptoms of ADD have the potential to undermine your attempts at achieving financial stability or to make realistic plans for the future. If you've been having trouble keeping track of your finances or saving money to meet future goals, you may want to consider consulting with a financial adviser.

"I really found it helpful, and it didn't cost much," Mark says. "The financial planner charged me a tiny percentage—I think it was two percent—of what I make in a year to help me work out a monthly family budget that allowed us to save for my daughter's college, and even put some money away for a family vacation. He also showed me where I was wasting money stupidly—like not buying a bus pass for my daughter, which saved me about thirty-five dollars a month, or buying magazines off the rack instead of subscribing. And he also gave me the excuse I'd been looking for finally to stop smoking. When I figured out I was spending some two thousand dollars a year on the stuff, I was finally able to quit!"

In addition to seeking advice from a financial adviser, try following some of the tips below to get you started down the road to creating some financial security for you and your family:

• *Prioritize.* The first step is for you to determine your day-to-day expenses, your income, and the difference between them. If you're currently running a deficit and are constantly in debt, you clearly have to cut your spending or try to earn a higher wage. The same is true if you don't make enough to save to meet future goals. If you're able to meet your bills every month, on the other hand, and are able to save enough money on a semi-regular basis, you're definitely on the right track.

• *Figure out how much you make and how much you spend.* How many times do you say, "I just don't know where the money goes"? Chances are, the answer is "quite often." If so, try writing down everything you spend and what you spend it on. See how many unnecessary items you can eliminate. You may be surprised at how much money you can save.

• *Think twice before you buy.* Impulse buying can be a real problem for adults with ADD. Train yourself to stop and think before you pull out a checkbook, credit card, or cold, hard cash.

SUSTAINING BALANCE, STRUCTURE, AND SATISFACTION

Balance: a state of harmony. *Structure:* the interrelationship of all the parts of a whole. *Satisfaction:* something that brings gratification, pleasure or contentment. In Chapter Six and elsewhere in this book, these three qualities of life were advanced as worthy goals for all of you who have struggled for so long against the unseen influence of ADD.

As you begin to come to terms with the effects that ADD has had on your life, and learn to manage your symptoms better, you will hopefully find your life becoming more balanced and structured. Satisfaction may come a little more slowly, but with patience, perseverance, and commitment, you will continue to move closer and closer to it.

In the pages that follow, you'll find a list of resources that will help you to continue learning and growing. Use them well, and good luck.

IMPORTANT QUESTIONS AND ANSWERS ABOUT CHAPTER TEN

Q Since I started treatment for my ADD, I've been able to do things I never thought I could do. I read a novel from cover to cover for the first time in my life and enjoyed it thoroughly. I've even thought about going back to school. The problem is, ever since I took over from my husband the job of paying the bills, I keep screwing up the family budget. It's never right, and I get so frustrated. What can I do to correct this?

A The most important thing for you to do is accept the fact that, despite your remarkable progress, you'll never be able to do everything there is to do in the world perfectly—nor should you expect that of yourself. With or without ADD, we all have talents, proclivities, and limitations that determine the paths we choose in life. Talk to your husband and admit your frustration. Chances are, he'd be happy to take over the family finances once again. If you insist on improving that aspect of your life, you could seek the help of a financial planner. Above all, be patient with yourself.

Q My wife and friends seem to think that now that I'm getting treatment, I should be this dynamic go-getter. The truth is, I don't feel that much different—a little more organized and focused, maybe, but I'm still the same person I always was. I'm not sure I'll ever live up to their expectations.

A You are indeed the same person you were before you were diagnosed, with the same interests and spirit. You do have, however, more information about yourself than ever before, information that may make you more confident and sure of your goals and the actions you must take to meet them.

People will always have expectations of you, some of which you'll both want and be able to live up to. But now is the time for you to clarify your own ideas about your capabilities and aspirations. Once you're more sure of what you want, and can outline a realistic plan to achieve it, impress upon your friends and family that you know what will give your life meaning and you'd appreciate their support as you pursue it.

APPENDIX:
RESOURCES

FOR INFORMATION ABOUT ATTENTION DEFICIT DISORDER

Adult ADHD Clinic
Department of Psychiatry
University of Massachusetts Medical Center
55 Lake Avenue North
Worcester, MA 01655
TEL: (508) 856-2552
FAX: (508) 856-3595

CH.A.D.D.
Children and Adults with Attention Deficit Disorder
499 NW 70th Avenue, Suite 109
Plantation, FL 33317
TEL: (305) 587-3700
FAX: (305) 587-4599

The CH.A.D.D.ER Box, a quarterly 16-page newsletter, and a quarterly full-color magazine called *ATTENTION!* are available from this organization. CH.A.D.D. chapters sponsor a number of adult support groups, in addition to the 670 established chapters currently serving parents.

Adult ADD Association
1225 East Sunset Drive, Suite 640
Bellingham, WA 98226

You can find out about the ADD support groups located in your state by writing to the above address.

Suggested Reading

Two quarterly publications for adults with ADD are:

ADDendum (for adults with ADD)
c/o C.P.S.
5041-A Backlick Road
Annandale, VA 22003
Paul Jaffe, editor

ADDult News
c/o Mary Jane Johnson
ADDult Support Network
2620 Ivy Place
Toledo, OH 43613

Barkley, Russell A., Ph.D. *Attention Deficit Hyperactivity Disorder.* New York: Guilford Press, 1991.

Fowler, Mary. *Maybe You Know My Kid: A Parent's Guide to Identifying, Understanding, and Helping Your Child with Attention-deficit Hyperactivity Disorder.* New York: Birch Lane Press, 1994.

Hallowell, Edward M., M.D., and John J. Ratey, M.D. *Driven to Distraction.* New York: Pantheon, 1994.

Kelly, Kate, and Peggy Ramundo. *You Mean I'm Not Lazy, Stupid, or Crazy?* New York: Scribner, 1995.

Latham, Peter S., J.D., and Patricia H. Latham, J.D. *Attention Deficit Disorder and the Law.* Washington, D.C.: JKL Communications, 1992.

Latham, Peter S., J.D., and Patricia H. Latham, J.D. *Succeeding in the Workplace—Attention Deficit Disorder and Learning Disabilities in the Workplace: A Guide for Success.* Washington, D.C.: JKL Communications, 1994.

Levinson, Harold N., M.D. *Total Concentration.* New York: M. Evans and Company, Inc., 1992.

Nadeau, Kathleen, Ed. A *Comprehensive Guide to Attention Deficit Hyperactivity Disorder in Adults.* New York: Brunner/Mazel, 1995.

Silver, Larry B., M.D. *Attention Deficit Hyperactivity Disorder. A Clinical Guide to Diagnosis and Treatment.* Washington, D.C.: American Psychiatric Press, 1994.

Weiss, G., and Hechtman, L. *Hyperactive Children Grown Up.* New York: Guilford Press, 1993.

Weiss, Lynn. *Attention Deficit Disorder in Adults.* Dallas, TX: Taylor Publishing, 1992.

Weiss, Lynn. *The Attention Deficit Disorder in Adults Workbook.* Dallas, TX: Taylor Publishing, 1994.

Wender, Paul. *The Hyperactive Child, Adolescent, and Adult.* New York: Oxford University Press, 1987.

FOR INFORMATION ABOUT LEARNING DISABILITIES

Orton Dyslexia Society
8600 LaSalle Road
Baltimore, MD 21204-6020
TEL: (410) 296-0232

National Center for Learning Disabilities
381 Park Avenue South
New York, New York 10016
TEL: (212) 545-7510

Learning Disabilities Association of America
4156 Library Road
Pittsburgh, PA 15234
TEL: (412) 341-8077

HEATH Resource Center
National Clearinghouse on Postsecondary Education for
    Individuals with Disabilities
American Council on Education
One Dupont Circle NW, Suite 800
Washington, DC 20036
TEL: (202) 939-9320
TEL: (800) 544-3284

Suggested Reading

Goldfarb, Lori A., et al. *Meeting the Challenge of Disability or Chronic Illness—A Family Guide.* Baltimore, MD: PH Brooks Publishing Co., 1986.

FOR INFORMATION ABOUT NUTRITION AND EXERCISE

American Alliance for Health, Physical Education, and Recreation
1201 Sixteenth Street, NW
Washington, D.C. 20036
(Write for information.)

The President's Council on Physical Fitness and Sports
400 Sixth Street, NW
Washington, D.C. 20201
TEL: (202) 272-3430

The American Heart Association
7320 Greenville Avenue
Dallas, TX 75321
TEL: (214) 373-6300

Suggested Reading

Bailey, Covert. *Fit or Fat.* New York: Houghton Mifflin, 1978.
Editors of the University of California Wellness Letter. *The Wellness Encyclopedia.* Boston: Houghton Mifflin Company, 1991.
Gershoff, Stanley W., with Catherine Whitney and the editorial advisory board of the Tufts University Diet and Nutrition Letter. *The Tufts University Guide to Total Nutrition.* New York: Harper and Row, 1990.

FOR INFORMATION ABOUT MEDITATION AND RELAXATION

Stress Reduction Clinic
University of Massachusetts Medical Center
55 Lake Avenue North
Worcester, MA 01655
TEL: (508) 856-2656

Mind/Body Health Sciences, Inc.
393 Dixon Road
Boulder, CO 80302
TEL: (303) 440-8460

Suggested Reading

Benson, Herbert. *The Relaxation Response*. New York: Outlet Books, 1993.

Benson, Herbert, and William Procter. *Beyond the Relaxation Response*. New York: Putnam/Berkley, 1984.

Borysenko, Joan. *Mending the Body, Mending the Mind*. New York: Bantam Books, 1988.

Goleman, Daniel. *The Meditative Mind*. Los Angeles: Jeremy P. Tarcher, Inc., 1988.

Kabat-Zinn, Jon. *Full Catastrophe Living*. New York: Delta, 1990.

Kabat-Zinn, Jon. *Wherever You Go, There You Are*. New York: Hyperion, 1994.

Roth, Robert. *Transcendental Meditation*. New York: Donald I. Fine, Inc., 1988.

ADDITIONAL SUGGESTED READING

Bolles, Richard Nelson. *What Color Is Your Parachute?* Berkeley, CA: Ten Speed Press, 1994.

Dominguez, Joe, and Vicki Robin. *Your Money or Your Life*. New York: Penguin, 1992.

Hedrick, Lucy H. *Five Days to an Organized Life*. New York: Dell, 1990.

Lakein, Alan. *How to Get Control of Your Time and Your Life*. New York: Signet, 1989.

Mundis, Jerrold. *How to Get Out of Debt*. New York: Bantam, 1988.

St. James, Elaine. *Simplify Your Life*. New York: Hyperion, 1994.

Winston, Stephanie. *Getting Organized*. New York: Warner Books, 1991.

GLOSSARY

Antidepressant: Medication designed to alleviate depression. Some patients with ADD may benefit from treatment with an antidepressant, either by itself or in combination with a stimulant. Among the most commonly prescribed antidepressants are Prozac, Norpramin, and Tofranil.

Anxiety: A feeling of worry, upset, or fear that may or may not arise in response to a real threat. Many adults with ADD suffer from anxiety due to their long history of perceived underachievement, poor communication skills, and low self-esteem.

Attention Deficit Disorder (ADD or ADHD): A treatable neurobiological disorder characterized by symptoms of inattention, impulsivity, and oftentimes hyperactivity, with an onset in childhood that causes significant impairment in school, work, or social adjustment. Officially known by the American Psychiatric Association as Attention Deficit Hyperactivity Disorder, or ADHD.

Avoidance: A psychological term used to describe the tendency many people have to stay away from situations that have made them uncomfortable or feel like failures in the past.

Behavior therapy: A type of psychological counseling that focuses on changing behavior and actions in order to solve problems and improve the quality of life.

Catecholamines: A group of neurotransmitters. Certain catecholamines (specifically dopamine, serotonin, and norepinephrine) are believed to be involved in helping an individual to concentrate and focus, and hence may be implicated in Attention Deficit Disorder.

Chronic: Pertaining to a symptom or condition that generally develops slowly and persists for a long period of time, often for an individual's entire lifetime. Chronic conditions, including ADD, often have no known cure.

Cognitive therapy: A type of psychological counseling that focuses on changing the way one thinks about oneself and the world in order to affect one's behavior and circumstances.

Cognition: The mental/intellectual process of knowing, thinking, learning, and judging.

Compensatory skills: Habits and skills learned in order to make up (or compensate) for neurological or other deficiencies. People with ADD may develop both positive and negative compensatory skills in order to make up for the difficulties they have concentrating or controlling their impulses.

Conduct Disorder: A psychological problem largely affecting adolescents and marked by aggressive, sometimes delinquent and criminal, behavior.

Cylert: One of the commonly prescribed stimulant medications used to treat ADD.

Depression: An emotional state in which there are extreme feelings of sadness, low self-esteem, and emptiness; there is a loss of interest or pleasure in all or almost all activities and may involve poor appetite or overeating, sleep difficulties, low energy, and feelings of hopelessness. Depression may be mild (a state called *dysthymia*) or severe. Many patients with ADD may also suffer from depression due to their perceived lack of self-worth and their lifelong difficulties in achieving their goals.

Dexedrine: A stimulant medication frequently used to alleviate symptoms of ADD.

Diagnostic procedure: The process by which a physician or psychologist evaluates a patient's symptoms in order to identify a disease or condition. Physical signs, history, and laboratory tests are tools used in this procedure.

Dopamine: A chemical substance known as a *neurotransmitter* that is thought to play a role in concentration and control of motor and cognitive impulses. Some medication used to treat ADD works to increase the amount of dopamine available in the brain.

Dyslexia: A developmental disorder affecting one's ability to read and write. Dyslexia or other learning disabilities may be present in approximately 25 percent of those with ADD.

Endorphins: Brain chemicals produced in the brain as a response to pain and known to produce feelings of euphoria.

Frontal lobes: The portion of the brain located behind the forehead suspected to be the site of working memory, concentration, and focus.

Glucose: The most common simple sugar and the body's essential source of energy.

Hyperactivity: Excessive motor activity in children and/or feelings of excessive restlessness and agitation commonly associated with Attention Deficit Disorder in adults.

Hyperthyroidism: A condition in which the thyroid gland, which is responsible for the production of several important hormones including those that control metabolism, is hyperactive. The symptoms of ADD and hyperthyroidism are similar and may be confused.

Impulsivity: Acting or speaking too quickly before considering the consequences of one's behavior. A common symptom of ADD.

Inattentiveness: The inability to focus one's attention on a particular task or activity over a sustained period of time. A common symptom of ADD.

Learning disability: An abnormal condition in which children have difficulty learning such fundamental procedures as reading, writing, and arithmetic. There are several different types of learning disabilities.

Limbic system: A complex system of nerve pathways believed to be involved in the expression of instinct and emotions.

MAO inhibitors: Medication commonly used to treat depression and sometimes used to treat patients with ADD when other, more standard medications have not been successful.

Minimal brain dysfunction: Another name for Attention Deficit Disorder that was used in the past.

Multimodal treatment: An approach to treatment that utilizes the resources of counseling, education, and medication to address a patient's needs.

Neurobiological: Related to the function and chemical makeup of the brain and central nervous system. ADD is considered a neurobiological disorder because it is thought to occur when certain brain chemicals become unbalanced.

Neurotransmitter: A chemical substance that carries impulses from one nerve cell to another.

Norepinephrine: A powerful neurotransmitter known to affect several body functions, including heart rate, blood pressure, and respiration. It also appears to be involved in transmitting messages in the frontal lobes of the brain where concentration and focus are believed to reside.

Oppositional Defiant Disorder (ODD): A psychological disorder seen primarily in children and adolescents and characterized by aggressive, contrary behavior toward authority figures. Approximately 30 to 40 percent of adults with ADD are thought to have had ODD as well during their adolescence.

PET scan (positron emission tomography): A sophisticated nuclear X-ray technique used to evaluate brain activity.

Prozac: An antidepressant medication used to treat a number of psychological conditions including depression in adults. Some adults with ADD find that Prozac also helps to alleviate symptoms of ADD.

Rebound effect: An apparent intensifying of symptoms including agitation and low frustration tolerance experienced by a patient when one dose of medication begins to wear off and the next dose has yet to take effect.

Ritalin: The most common stimulant medication used to treat ADD.

Serotonin: A neurotransmitter believed to be involved in concentration and motor and cognitive control. Some of the medications used to treat ADD work to increase the amount of serotonin available to the frontal lobes of the brain.

Socialization: The process by which children learn to associate with others in acceptable ways. Social skills are often stunted in children and adults with ADD who have had difficulties in communicating effectively and/or curbing impulsive behavior.

Stimulant: A medication used to increase brain activity. Commonly prescribed stimulants include Cylert, Dexedrine, and Ritalin.

Tourette's Syndrome: A chronic condition involving multiple tics, including vocal tics such as involuntarily obscene speech. The condition usually begins in childhood. Some Tourette's Syndrome patients may also have ADD.

INDEX

Hartmann, Thom, 266–67
health insurance, 60
heart conditions, 91
  Ritalin and, 100
  stress and, 131
helpless one, role of, 200–1, 225, 228
high blood pressure (hypertension), 80,
    88, 91, 92
  medications for, 64
  stress and, 131, 132
honesty, in relationships, 225–26
humor, 137
hyperactivity, xii, xiii, 4, 8–9, 10, 11,
    13–14, 15, 19, 27, 31, 33, 49, 50,
    65, 283, 285
  in children, 5, 6, 37, 38, 40, 41, 42,
    241
  communication and, 10, 13, 191–92,
    205, 208
  financial situation and, 274
  in infants, 36
  restlessness, see restlessness
  Self-Exploration Exercise for evaluat-
    ing, 56
  signs of, 13–14
  speech habits and, 10, 13, 208
  stimulants and, 88
  work and, 221
  see also Attention Deficit Disorder
hyperkinesis, 8
hypertension, see high blood pressure
hyperthyroidism, 63, 285

imipramine (Tofranil), 79, 87, 89, 91–92,
    283
impatience, 16
impulsivity, 7, 9, 10, 11, 14, 15, 18, 19,
    27, 31, 33, 49, 65, 283, 285
  affairs and, 257
  career choices and, 267
  in children, 41, 42, 242
  communication and, 14, 190, 193–94,
    205, 208, 219–20
  diet and, 125

financial situation and, 14, 231, 274,
    276
  relationships and, 225–26
  Self-Exploration Exercise for evaluat-
    ing, 56
  signs of, 14
  speech habits and, 14, 208
  stimulants and, 88
  in teenagers, 46
  work and, 194, 221
inattentiveness, xi, xv, 4, 9–10, 11, 12–13,
    15, 27, 28, 29, 30, 31, 33, 49, 50,
    51, 65, 283, 285
  career choices and, 267
  in children, 38, 40, 42, 241
  communication and, 192–93, 205, 208
  distractibility, 7, 26, 51, 118, 215, 216,
    218
  financial situation and, 274
  gesturing and, 208–9
  in infants, 36
  planning and, 154
  relationships and, 223
  Self-Exploration Exercise for evaluat-
    ing, 55
  signs of, 12–13
  speech intonation and, 208
  stimulants and, 88
  work and, 192–93, 221
Individuals with Disabilities Education
    Act (IDEA), 255
infancy, 35–39
  ADD in, 16, 32, 36
  difficult, 35–37
insurance, health, 60
intimacy, 222–24
  ADD as hindrance to, 188–98
  see also communication; marriage; rela-
    tionships

Kübler-Ross, Elisabeth, 69

laughter, 137
lead, 23

ABOUT THE AUTHORS

Kevin R. Murphy, Ph.D., is Chief of the Adult Attention Deficit Hyperactivity Disorder Clinic at the University of Massachusetts Medical Center in Worcester, Massachusetts. He is a member of the advisory board of Children and Adults with Attention Deficit Disorders (CH.A.D.D.), which is the leading ADD organization in America, with over 25,000 members. Dr. Murphy has written extensively on the subject for professional publications and regularly speaks to and conducts workshops for professionals and lay audiences across the country. He lives in Shrewsbury, Massachusetts.

Suzanne LeVert is a health and medical writer with seven health care titles to her credit. She lives in Boston.